Media Law

A Legal Handbook for
the Working Journalist

by Katherine M. Galvin

Legal Editor: Stephen Elias

NOLO PRESS • 950 Parker Street, Berkeley, CA 94710

Printing History

Nolo Press is committed to keeping its books up-to-date. Each new printing, whether or not it is called a new edition, has been completely revised to reflect the latest law changes. If you are using this book any considerable time after the last date listed below, be particularly careful not to rely on information without checking it.

First Edition: May 1984

Please read this: We have done our best to give you useful and accurate information on the law as it affects journalists. But please be aware that laws and procedures are constantly changing and are subject to differing interpretations. You have the responsibility to check all material you read here before relying on it. Of necessity, neither Nolo Press nor the author makes any guarantees concerning the information in this book or the use to which it is put.

Book Design & Layout	*Keija Kimura*
Illustrations	*Mari Stein*
Production	*Stephanie Harolde*
	Sue Imperial
	Anna Weidman
Typesetting	*Accent & Alphabet*
Printing	*Delta Lithograph*

■

ISBN 0-917316-75-4
Library of Congress Catalog Card No.: 84-060496
© copyright 1984 by Katherine Galvin

Dedication

This book is dedicated to Marco Antonio Cacao Muñoz, a thirty-year-old Guatemalan radio news director, who was murdered by government security forces in 1980 for reporting the news as he saw it. He is representative of many brave Salvadoran and Guatemalan journalists who, despite government repression, continue to do their job of informing the public.

Acknowledgments

This book has been three years in the making. It would not be before you now but for the patience, criticisms, and solid contributions of my two editors, Ralph "Jake" Warner and Steve Elias. My sincere and deepest thanks to them both. The Nolo Press family also deserves my appreciation, including Barbara Hodovan, Toni Ihara, Carol Pladsen, John O'Donnell, Glenn Voloshin, Amy Ihara, Charlotte Johnson, Kate Miller, and Elizabeth Ryan. In particular, I would like to thank Stephanie Harolde, both for her endless keyboarding and helpful comments, and Keija Kimura for her excellent book design, Mari Stein for the witty illustrations, and Gloria Frymm for her copy editing. Thanks guys.

Special thanks also go to the many lawyers and media workers who offered helpful suggestions, including Arthur Berney (who first taught me the Constitution), Abby Goldman, Sally Harmes, Doron Weinberg, and Michael Helm.

Most of all, I want to thank my friends for their economic and emotional support, especially Nancy and Patty who have been there for me from Boston to Berkeley.

About the Author

   Kathy Galvin graduated from Boston College Law School in 1974 and practiced in Massachusetts for five years. Since her arrival in Berkeley, California in 1980, she has been an editor for Nolo Press, National Director of the Lawyers' Committee Against U.S. Intervention in Central America, and an instructor of Mass Communications Law at California State University at Sacramento. She is currently with a law office in Oakland, California, which represents plaintiffs in asbestos lawsuits.

About the Illustrator

   Mari Stein is a free lance illustrator and writer. Her published work has been eclectic, covering a wide range of subjects: humor, whimsy, health education, juvenile, fables and Yoga. Among the books she has written and illustrated are "Some Thoughts for My Friends," and "VD The Love Epidemic." She has also illustrated childrens' books, textbooks, magazine articles, and a book of poetry. This is her third collaboration with Nolo Press; she illustrated "29 Reasons Not to Go to Law School" by Ralph Warner and Toni Ihara and "Author Law & Strategies" by Brad Bunnin and Peter Beren. She works out of a studio in her Pacific Palisades home, where she lives with her dogs and rabbits, cultivates roses, and teaches Yoga.

Table of Contents

Introduction

Here is a practical legal guide for the working journalist and those who desire a better understanding of how the law and journalism intersect. Our goal is to arm you, the journalist, with both the legal information and practical techniques necessary to cope with the legal complexities and uncertainties you will inevitably face in your efforts to inform the public.

A journalist's job has never been an easy one in this country. Ever since the famous trial of Peter Zenger in the eighteenth century, journalists have been locking horns with the law. It's not an exaggeration to say that the legal complexities and dangers threatening journalistic freedom are almost daily becoming more threatening. For example, multi-million-dollar verdicts in libel suits are increasingly common, and several newspapers are on the brink of bankruptcy as a result. The entire U.S. journalist corps was recently barred from Grenada while the U.S. invaded that island. Journalists were convicted of trespass and their convictions upheld by the Supreme Court for their attempts to view and report on the arrests of nuclear power plant protestors. Many journalists have been threatened with imprisonment or contempt of court for refusing to disclose the identity of their sources.

In the last three years, the government has attempted to institute a policy of censorship and control of information that is rivaled only by that in operation during the McCarthy era. The foundations of this policy are directly contrary, even hostile, to the premise that a democratic society depends for its continued existence on the wide dissemination of information. Since January 1981, the government has limited the effectiveness of the Freedom of Information Act (FOIA); taken steps to classify vast amounts of information; sought to subject government officials to an unprecedented system of lifetime censorship on their speech and writings. Although these measures are not directly aimed at the press, denial of access to information fundamentally erodes the media's role as watchdog of the government.

What exactly is media law? On the most abstract level, media law is the way our legal system resolves conflicts between all kinds of personal and governmental "rights" on the one hand, and the freedom of expression on the other. Thus, in a particular situation, the public's right to know may conflict with the right of the government to keep military information secret, or that of an individual to a fair trial, or to privacy, or to the maintenance of a good reputation. These conflicts are commonly manifested in the courts in such proceedings as libel suits, closed preliminary hearings and jury questioning, and even occasional jail sentences for those journalists who refuse to disclose their sources when ordered to do so.

More concretely, media law consists of a variety of legal doctrines, each concerned with a different aspect of journalistic enterprise. The chapters of this book could give you an overview of the most important of these, such as libel, and the right of access to criminal trials. Lawyers and journalists alike have written separate volumes on these and many other topics presented here, such as censorship and invasion of privacy. We don't attempt to compete with these. The task we have set ourselves is to distill the overabundance of information on how law and the media interact into one convenient reference manual which deals with the primary issues you are sure to face from one day to the next.

Media Law is not designed to be read from cover to cover. Feel free to focus your attention on the subjects of your primary interest. We do recommend, however, that you first review the material in Appendix A on the structure and function of the U.S. legal system. Unless you have been to law school, it should prove a valuable review of how and why our federal and state legal systems work and interact. We also think all readers will benefit from a close reading of Chapter 1, which puts our present battles over freedom of expression in historical context. The one other part of the book we consider to be almost mandatory reading is Appendix B, which outlines the fundamentals of legal research.

Throughout this book we have included important portions of the decisions of the U.S. Supreme Court as well as other federal courts and several state supreme courts. This is fine as far as it goes, but whenever you have to understand and report on a court decision or legislation, there is really no substitute for direct access to the entire thing. Appendix B, outlining the fundamentals of legal research, will facilitate your use of a law library and your understanding of the materials contained there.

Please be aware as you read what follows that the legal areas covered in this book can and will change with bewildering speed. We present the information to give you a sense of how law and legal relationships are important to your work, but also to alert you to when you might need legal assistance. Before relying on anything we say here, you should check to see both that it is current and that your understanding of the particular law or court decision is accurate. In other words, this book is not and does not pretend to be a substitute for the advice of a competent media lawyer.

A matter of style: We both understand and disapprove of the symbolic and political meaning of always using "he" when referring to a human being in general. We also dislike the awkwardness of "he/she" or "he or she." So we've compromised by using "he" in some chapters and "she" in others, more or less chapter by chapter, and we hope that it all evens out in the wash.

Finally, a personal note. Over the last decade, hundreds of reporters have been subpoenaed, threatened, even arrested and jailed, for trying to inform the public of the events that shape all of our lives. Others, because of outside pressure or editorial caution, have become less aggressive in disseminating unpopular information or material critical of the powers that be. If the material and advice in this book encourages even a few journalists to aggressively further and protect the public's right to know, it will have achieved its purpose.

Freedom of Expression

A.   A Brief History

The "state" — that is, the entity in control of a particular society — has always recognized the unsettling force of free speech, an opposition press, and public assemblies. Whether in the Judea of Jesus, the England of Henry VII, Iran, Argentina, El Salvador, or South Africa, individuals want and demand civil liberties, whereas government all too often adopts violent and repressive techniques to suppress opinion it finds disagreeable.

Before we deal with the nitty gritty of the First Amendment rights and privileges of today's media, it's important to understand there is nothing new about the issues of free speech and free press. While it is arguable whether "our forefathers" really "brought forth a new nation upon this continent, conceived in liberty and dedicated to the proposition that all men are created equal," it is clear the framers of the First Amendment were by no means the first to deal with the right of men and women to express themselves freely. Indeed, a concern for freedom of expression (which is commonly claimed to be necessary to advance knowledge) and the suppression of that freedom (usually asserted to be necessary to preserve the status quo) are as old as recorded history.

Perhaps the most familiar story about freedom of expression involves the Greek stonemason, Socrates, a most disputatious man. He argued in the Assembly, in public places, in the homes of his friends in Athens, and in any other place where there was an audience. His method was to question everything, including popular assumptions about religion, politics, and social behavior, while always claiming he was a loyal Athenian working for a better society. Eventually, when the disintegrating Athenian community was surrounded by the Spartan armies, Socrates was tried and found guilty of "corrupting the youth." In a fashion repeated often throughout the next few thousand years, Socrates' dissenting ideas were deemed a danger to the maintenance of the "legitimate" government and the mobilization of the populace against the enemy.

At his trial, Socrates rejected help from the legal profession of the day and represented himself. This was the occasion of his famous "Gadfly" remarks, an argument near and dear to the hearts of all people who work in the media:

> And now, Athenians, I am not going to argue for my own sake, as you may think, but for yours, that you may not sin against the God by condemning me, who am his gift to you. For, if you kill me, you will not easily find a successor to me, who, if I may use such a ludicrous figure of speech, am a sort of gadfly, given to the state by God; and the state is a great and noble steed who is tardy in his motions owing to his very size, and requires to be stirred into life. I am that gadfly which God has attached to the state, and all day long and in all places am always fastening upon you, arousing and persuading and reproaching you. You will not easily find another like me, and therefore I would advise you to spare me. [1]

Unfortunately, this argument failed, as it has many times since. Years passed and the Roman republic replaced Greece as the pre-eminent power in the Mediterranean world. When it came to civil liberties, however, little had changed. People who voiced demands not to the liking of the rulers commonly ended up behind bars or underground. Take the case of the two brothers, Tiberius and Gavis Gracchus, who championed the cause of the dispossessed during the years when the gap between rich and poor in Roman society was widening. The brothers wanted to limit the size of estates that could be owned by one family, to resettle landless farmers either abroad or on state-owned lands in Italy that had been leased to farmers, and to give the poor of Rome relief by allowing them to buy grain from the state at cost. Tiberius was assassinated in 133 B.C. by outraged Roman senators and Gavis killed himself in 121 B.C. to avoid a similar fate.

Perhaps the most ironic of the many examples of speech suppression are those associated with religion. The history of Christianity is typical. Jesus of Nazareth preached a message of reform — some have said revolution — which threatened both the Jewish religious leadership of Judea and the political order of Rome. The fact that his fate was crucifixion, and that the inscription on the cross to which he was nailed stated, "Jesus, King of the Jews," written in Latin, Greek, and Hebrew, indicated that the Romans treated him as a political agitator.

Sadly, once Jesus' followers grew from a small, obscure sect persecuted on all sides, to an established religion, they adopted a similar attitude towards the new dissenters. As far as freedom of expression went, little changed as centuries passed. Wars between Christians and non-Christians, and later between Catholics and Protestants, raged across Europe in the late middle ages and in many places the intolerance and hatred that fueled them continue unabated.

You doubtless remember Martin Luther, who bravely tacked the Ninety-Five Theses to the church house door when the established church refused to give ear to his reform proposals. After he was excommunicated and outlawed by the Church, he gained a political following, including social reformers who were connected to the peasant revolts of that time. Luther, the religious revolutionary, was horrified at the peasants' opposition to civil authority. When informed they were staging revolts in his name, Luther is reported to have said, "Kill them. The princes of the world are gods, the common people are Satan."

After Lutheranism was — not surprisingly — adopted as the state religion by the princes in a number of countries, governmental power was used to prevent public worship in any other

---

1. Plato, The *Apology*.

form, and members of other Protestant sects, as well as Catholics, were banished, imprisoned or killed.

The success of the Reformation eventually led to the response of the counter-Reformation, which has also been called the Catholic Reformation. Rather than side with the inquiring minds of the early Renaissance, however, Catholic leaders opted for more of the same. In Spain, the Inquisition was employed through a special court which severely persecuted Jews, Moors, Protestants, and even Catholics with unacceptable views. In Italy, Bruno was burned and Galileo humiliated because their representations concerning the solar system were contrary to the official Church views.

A final example of how people in power tend to repress free expression occurred during the early days of our own country. Most of us were taught about how the Puritans fled to the New World colonies to escape persecution for daring to worship in a manner not approved by the Church of England. Certainly, the story of the brave little band of men and women setting out from Europe to find a home in the new World is an inspirational one.

What happened once these pioneers survived their first few winters in the Massachusetts Bay Colony and became themselves, for all practical purposes, the government, is emphasized less often. The Puritans established a theocratic government that was far more intolerant to dissent than anything they had experienced in England. For example, the right to vote was based on church membership, which meant that by the 1700s, only about one in five colonists could legally mark a ballot.

Roger Williams was banished and fled to Providence from Massachusetts Bay Colony in 1636 because he "broached and divulged divers new and dangerous opinions." Williams was guilty of arguing for the separation of church and state, and went so far as to advocate democracy and equality for all — even for Native Americans.

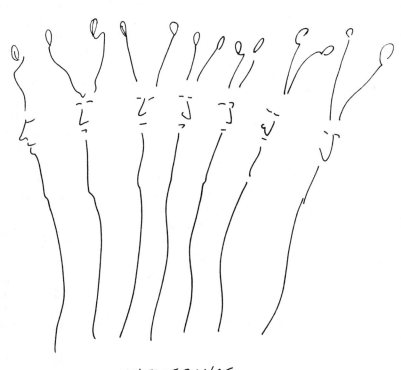

INTOLERANCE

Anne Hutchinson met with similar treatment. Hutchinson preached a doctrine that claimed an individual's direct intuition of God's love to be superior to obedience to the laws of the theocratic Massachusetts Bay. Perhaps even more threatening, she held meetings at her Boston home "for women only." In 1638, Hutchinson was tried for heretical and seditious teachings. Forced to incriminate herself, she was excommunicated and banished. With her fourteen children, she fled to New York where she and many of the children were killed in an Indian raid.

The suppression of unpopular views has obviously been a common practice of all sorts of governments down through the ages. Most often repression is against the groups which espouse the unpopular views, but commonly it is also directed at those who report them. For example, anti-Nazi editors of German newspapers in the 1930's were carted off to concentration camps; the writers and editors of the *Washington Post* during the Watergate investigation were told by H.R. Haldeman, "We will get you"; and even as you read these words, brave journalists in dozens of countries around the world face daily persecution. They know firsthand that when the state moves to crush unpopular views, the intellectual freedom and sometimes even physical safety of those who work in media are quickly threatened.[2]

B.   State Control vs. a Free Press

The concept of media was born, in the sense we know it, with the introduction of the printing press in 1476. Censorship laws followed almost immediately. With the wide dissemination of information now possible, people with odd and different ideas had the capacity to influence peasants, kings, and even governments. Accordingly, those in power feared that the rapid exchange of opinions would be used to encourage opposition to them.

For example, in England under Henry VIII, material intended for publication had to first be submitted to crown officials. These men were empowered to censor objectionable passages and determine if the publisher would receive a license to print the work. Publication without this official imprimatur was a crime. Since there were those who believed that writers, editors and printers, not kings, should decide what would be published, a few published clandestinely. Thus, the printing press created a new class of criminal.

Between 1585 and 1641, under the rubric of licensing, a complex system of prior restraints upon the press was established in England. It included the infamous Court of Star Chamber which defined what constituted criminal activity and passed judgment on offenders. Fines, press seizures, the cutting off of ears and the splitting of noses, and imprisonment were penalties which the court meted out to those who ignored or protested press licensing laws. In 1643, Parliament issued yet another censorship law requiring the pre-licensing of publications. This statute was enacted to prevent the "defamation of religion and goverment."

In reaction to these parliamentary decrees, John Milton published his essay, *The Aeropagitica*, eloquently protesting government press licensing and censorship. Milton's view that truth can only emerge through free discussion is the foundation of what today is termed the "marketplace of ideas" theory in constitutional discourse.

> And though all the winds of doctrine were let loose to play upon the earth, so truth be in the field, we do injuriously by licensing and prohibiting to misdoubt her strength. Let her and Falsehood grapple; who ever knew truth put to the worse, in a free and open encounter?[3]

---

2. Physical harm is not confined to media within a country but has also been extended to foreign journalists in certain situations (e.g. El Salvador and Chile). See Anne Nelson, "One Way to Kill the Story," *The Nation*, July 24–31, 1982, p. 75.

3. Milton, *Aeropagitica*, ed. Jebb, Cambridge University, 1918, p. 58, Also see Justice Holmes' famous dissent in *Abrams v. United States*, 250 U.S. 616, 40 S.Ct. 17, 63 L.Ed. 1173 (1919).

Despite Milton's passionate advocacy of free discussion, even he did not believe in letting every "falsehood" participate in the great cosmic grappling for truth. Roman Catholics, it seems, were beyond even Milton's intellectual protection. In fact, he served as a censor in the years after the Protestant Oliver Cromwell seized both the crown and head of the Catholic King Charles.

Press licensing ceased in England in 1695, although it continued in the American colonies for several decades thereafter. In its place arose an even more insidious form of censorship—the crime of "seditious libel." This doctrine was applied *after* publication and thus was not technically a "prior restraint" on publication, like licensing. However, penalties were so severe that the chilling—and in many cases deep freezing—effect on all sorts of publishing activities was comparable to prior restraint, because printers often were frightened into self-censorship.

Seditious libel has always been a rather vague concept. As it developed in England, however, stripped of its fancy rhetoric, the crime of seditious libel constituted any remark which could be construed as lowering the government in the public esteem. In the eighteenth century, this law was vigorously enforced both in England and America as the major way to control the press. The most famous colonial prosecution was that of New York printer and editor of the *New York Weekly Journal*, John Peter Zenger.

Zenger was arrested in 1734 and jailed for eight months before trial. The official charge was publishing seditious libel. The real reason for Zenger's arrest was primarily because his paper was a vehicle for criticizing the colonial governor of New York. Under the seditious libel law of the time, the only issue for the jury to decide was whether the defendant had in fact published the critical statements. The judge was to decide whether the publications in issue had been maliciously intended and of a bad tendency. Truth was not allowed as a defense. If a "libel" were true, it was argued, it was even worse than if it were clearly false, since true criticism would increase the tendency of the people to breach the peace and therefore result in a diminishment of the rulers' authority.

Against this legal background, it was a stunning accomplishment for Zenger's lawyer, Andrew Hamilton, to win the case. He did so by persuading the jurors to recognize truth as a defense, notwithstanding the judge's instructions to the contrary. Deciding that Zenger's criticisms were in fact true, the jury acquitted him. It was this new right of the press to criticize the government that made the Zenger case the most celebrated victory for freedom of expression in the pre-revolutionary period.

C. The First Amendment

We come now to the First Amendment. Demanded by several states as a condition for their ratifying the Constitution, these brave words were enshrined in that document in 1792 as the First Amendment of the ten contained in the Bill of Rights:

> Congress shall make no law respecting an establishment of religion, or prohibiting the free exercise thereof; or abridging the freedom of speech, or of the press; or the right of the people peaceably to assemble, and to petition the government for a redress of grievances.

This guarantee of freedom of expression did not arise in a vacuum. The struggle to gain political and economic freedom from England had generated a predictable number of demands for free speech and a free press. In particular, newspaper editors, printers, and pamphleteers bore the brunt of many forms of repression and were extremely vocal in their concern that such repression never be repeated.

SELF EXPRESSION CIRCA 1700

In high school most of us learned a good deal about the history of free speech. In addition, we were taught that by and large the First Amendment has over the years effectively shielded the rights of Americans from the tyranny of the state. The truth, unfortunately, is somewhat different. Undoubtedly, the First Amendment has protected many forms of freedom of expression in all sorts of circumstances. However, in times of national crisis, when it has been needed most, it more often has functioned like a sieve than a shield.

Although we will spare you a definitive history of freedom of expression in the United States, it is essential to an understanding of media law that we look at how the First Amendment protections have fared in the slightly less than two centuries since their adoption.

1. The Sedition Act of 1798

The first real test of whether the First Amendment would provide meaningful protection for those with unpopular views came in the first decade of the new American republic. France and England were again at war and our new nation was being pressured to take sides. John Adams and the Federalists leaned toward England while Thomas Jefferson and the Republicans were sympathetic to revolutionary France. The pro-England stance of the Adams administration increasingly drew criticism from the Republicans, who were the majority party in many areas of the country. Republican newspapers regularly depicted President Adams as the lackey of the English throne.

In response to this criticism, the Federalist administration enacted the Alien and Sedition Acts in 1798. These laws made it a crime to publish or print "any false, scandalous, or malicious writings to bring the Government, Congress, or the President into contempt, or disrepute, excite popular hostility to them, incite resistance to the law of the United States, or

6

encourage hostile designs against the United States."

The Republicans contended with considerable factual support (prosecutions were brought against the editors of the four leading Republican newspapers and against three of the more outspoken Republican officeholders) that this act was designed and used to silence Republican critics of the Adams Administration.

The Alien and Sedition Acts expired in 1801. Jefferson, who had defeated Adams in the election of 1800, promptly pardoned all those who had been convicted. For this reason, the question of whether these repressive enactments were constitutional did not reach the Supreme Court for decision. Even so, the fact that such laws were passed and enforced was an affront to the spirit and letter of the recently enacted First Amendment. Newspaper editors, politicians, and ordinary citizens learned that notwithstanding the words of the First Amendment, speech alone could still land a person behind bars in a new nation which had just fought a bloody war for freedom.

2. The Civil War

Fifty or so years after the Alien and Sedition Acts expired, the refusal of our Southern states to join the international movement against slavery created another period of intense national strain, culminating in the Civil War. Again, free expression in America suffered.

In the pre-war South, state governments tried to completely suppress anti-slavery dissent. With the exception of Kentucky, every Southern state eventually passed laws controlling and limiting adverse discussion of the slavery "question." For example, Louisiana's penalty for conversation "having a tendency to promote discontent among free colored people, or insubordination among slaves" ranged from 21 years at hard labor to death. Abolitionist literature was banned from the mails and academic freedom was heavily suppressed. The passage of such laws was justified as a means of preventing slave revolts.

Many southern judges, perhaps aware that the laws were constitutionally overbroad and vague, meted out fairly mild punishments. This caused at least some slave owners, who were dissatisfied with such leniency, to turn to the law of the long rope and high branch. As there was little opportunity to appeal from this sort of judgment and sentence, the legal issues involved in the southern repression of the abolitionist movement never reached the Supreme Court.

While civil liberties enjoyed somewhat better protection in the North in the years before the war, constitutional safeguards disintegrated quickly once the gunfire began. President Lincoln, for one, claimed extraordinary executive power because of the military emergency. He closed the post office to treasonable correspondence, subjected passengers to and from foreign countries to passport controls, and suspended the *writ of habeas corpus*, which meant the citizens were denied their right to contest an illegal imprisonment. As many as 38,000 men suspected of disloyalty, some of them journalists, were arrested and confined without being charged with any crime or given the right to defend themselves. They were simply informed that their incarceration would last as long as the federal government and the military saw fit.

The constitutional problems inherent in these executive orders were not reviewed by the Supreme Court during the war. The issue of whether the government had authority to summarily arrest and incarcerate its citizens came before the Supreme Court years after the guns had been stacked at Appomattox Court House.[4]

With the crisis safely over, and all the prisoners released, the Supreme Court finally ruled a military commission had no authority to lock people up and that the *writ of habeas corpus* could not be suspended so long as the courts were open and functioning. Although these decisions

---

4. See *Ex parte Mulligan*, 71 U.S. (4 Wall.) 2 (1866).

came too late to help those whose right to free expression was violated during the war, optimists felt they provided a guarantee against similar repression in the future.

3. World War I

Unfortunately, the American entry into World War I in 1917 and the strains that war produced, proved once again that government repression of unpopular speech was alive and well in "the land of the free." Indeed, during the First World War, the right of free expression was subjected to its most extreme restriction in U.S. history. Some of this repression had to do with the pressures of the war itself. Much can also be traced to a fear of socialism, anarchism, and syndicalism. Since 1900, these movements had taken firm hold in the U.S., nourished in the poverty and sweat-shop conditions of industrial cities and in the lumber and mining camps of the West. Many saw them to be a more fundamental threat to the established order than the armies of the Kaiser.

World War I gave the various state governments the excuse they needed to crack down on radicals. They did so with a vengeance. Two-thirds of the states passed laws making it a crime to advocate fundamental changes in the economic and political system through the violent overthrow of the government. Congress, not to be left behind, passed the Federal Espionage Act of 1917, and in 1918 added an amendment to outlaw sedition.

During this wartime period, seditious statements were defined as those which caused insubordination or disloyalty in the armed forces, or obstructed enlistment. This legislation was the federal government's direct response to hostility to the draft and American participation in the war voiced by various dissenting groups. About 1900 individuals and over 100 newspapers and pamphlets were prosecuted under the act. Eugene Debs, the Socialist Party leader, aged 63, was jailed from April 1919 to December 1921 for making anti-war statements. While in prison, Debs received 919,799 votes in the presidential election of 1920.

The repression of speech and press during World War I was true to the American pattern of clamping down during periods of severe national stress. Instead of the normal post-war period of relaxation, however, the years after World War I saw the continued and expanded use of federal power to control expression. What went on in these years is doubly significant to us. Not only were the peace-time restrictions on the freedom of expression unique, but the court battles resulting from this repression began the modern era of constitutional theory. The American law of freedom of speech and press is, in the main, a post-World War I phenomenon.

D.   Freedom of Speech and Press in the Supreme Court

Despite the clarity of the First Amendment — "Congress *shall make no law* . . . abridging the freedom of speech, or of the press . . . ," — no Supreme Court Justice has ever proposed that *all* speech is protected under *all* circumstances against *any* regulation or punishment by government. The positions they have taken and continue to adopt are as many and varied as they are inconsistent and confusing. Thomas Emerson, a leading First Amendment scholar, summed it up as follows:

"(T)he outstanding fact about the First Amendment today is that the Supreme Court has never developed any comprehensive theory of what that constitutional guarantee means and how it should be applied in concrete cases. At various times, the

Court has employed the bad tendency test, the clear and present danger test, an incitement test, and different forms of the ad hoc balancing test. Sometimes it has not clearly enunciated the theory upon which it proceeds. Frequently, it has avoided decision on basic First Amendment issues by involving doctrines of vagueness, overbreadth, or the use of less drastic alternatives. Justice Black, at times supported by Justice Douglas, arrived at an "absolute" test, but subsequently reverted to the balancing test in certain types of cases. The Supreme Court has also utilized other doctrines, such as the preferred position of the First Amendment and prior restraint. Recently, it has begun to address itself to problems of "symbolic speech" and the place in which First Amendment activities can be carried on. But it has totally failed to settle on any coherent approach or to bring together its various doctrines into a consistent whole. Moreover, it has done little to deal with some of the newer problems, where the issue is not pure restraint on government interference, but rather the use of governmental power to encourage freedom of expression or the actual participation by government itself in the system of expression.

It is not surprising that this chaotic state of First Amendment theory has produced some unhappy results. The major doctrines applied by the Supreme Court have proved inadequate, particularly in periods of tension, to support a vigorous system of freedom of expression . . . All in all, doctrinal support for the system of freedom of expression is in a sad state of disarray. And this has had a most unfortunate effect upon the work of the lower Federal and State courts, upon the performance of government officials, and upon the understanding of the public.[5]

Although many are fascinated with the complex development of First Amendment theory over the past 75 years, we plan to focus more on what has actually happened under the First Amendment in our courts and legislatures than on the rhetoric of the judicial opinions as such.[6]

Using this approach, we can see the Supreme Court rulings in freedom of expression cases are broadly consistent with the cyclical pattern of repression and relaxation discussed above. The more a particular form of expression is perceived to threaten American institutions or national safety, the more likely a justification will be found to repress it. However, if expression appears merely trivial, obnoxious, or annoying, and not fundamentally frightening given the political climate, it will very likely be protected.

In addition, individual court decisions on First Amendment cases are at least as strongly influenced by the political attitudes of the individual judges as by fundamental principles. This means that sometimes the First Amendment has been bravely employed to guarantee the effective expression of unpopular views despite their real or perceived threat to the State, while at other times it has been read to allow the repression of trivial dissent.

All in all, the most prominent First Amendment decisions form a legal mirror of our nation's attitudes toward freedom of expression. It is almost impossible to discuss or understand contemporary media law without referring to them. A brief review of these cases is therefore in order.

---

5. Thomas I. Emerson, *The System of Freedom of Expression*, New York, Random House 1970, pp. 15–16.
6. If you wish to further explore the labyrinth of Supreme Court legal interpretations in this area, see *Political and Civil Rights in the United States*, Vol. 1, by Norman Dorsen, Paul Bender and Burt Neuborne. 4th Ed. Boston; Little Brown, 1976. The book does not deal with freedom of the press *per se* but rather with the development of First Amendment doctrines. It also specifically discusses how the First Amendment applies to the journalist's work.

1. Wartime

a. Clear and Present Danger

During World War I, the Federal Espionage Acts provided the legal basis for the repression of a widespread and vociferous antiwar movement. The acts were vigorously enforced in almost 2000 prosecutions. Many more people were prosecuted under similar state laws.

Holding that the Constitution did not protect speech which could lead to a "clear and present danger" of violence or physical harm, the U.S. Supreme Court rejected the First Amendment-based claims of the dissenters. In every decision the Supreme Court affirmed the government's right to stifle dissent.

One of these cases involved the general secretary of the Socialist Party (Schenck by name). The party printed a leaflet espousing opposition to the war and draft, stating that anyone violated the Constitution when he refused to recognize "your right to assert your opposition to the draft . . . ." Schenck was convicted of violating the Espionage Act. The Supreme Court affirmed. Justice Holmes, who wrote the Court's opinion, made it clear the First Amendment did not protect all speech: "The most stringent protection of free speech would not protect a man falsely shouting fire in a theatre and causing a panic . . .," he claimed before going on to say:

> The question in every case is whether the words used are used in such circum-
> stances and are of such a nature as to create a clear and present danger that they will
> bring about the substantive evils that Congress has a right to prevent. [7]

Other court decisions went even further in sanctioning the curtailment of free expression. For example, in 1918 Eugene V. Debs, head of the Socialist Party, was prosecuted on the basis of a speech in which he admonished his audience that "you need to know that you are fit for something better than slavery and cannon fodder." Debs was given a ten-year sentence and the Supreme Court unanimously upheld the conviction, further sanctioning curtailment of wartime expression. [8]

As dramatic evidence of how punishment can result in one case and exoneration in another, depending on the judges and the times, we need only remember that speech opposing the Vietnam War was held by the Supreme Court to be protected under the First Amendment. This was so even though the same laws which had caused the imprisonment of the WWI protesters were still on the books. Julian Bond provides a case in point. In 1966, Bond was refused his elected seat by the Georgia House of Representatives because of statements made by the Student Nonviolent Coordinating Committee (SNCC), of which he was Communications Director:

> We are in sympathy with, and support, the men in this country who are
> unwilling to respond to a military draft which would compel them to contribute their
> lives to United States aggression in Vietnam in the name of the "freedom" we find so
> false in this country. We recoil with horror at the inconsistency of a supposedly "free"
> society where responsibility to freedom is equated with the responsibility to lend
> oneself to military aggression. We take note of the fact that sixteen percent of the
> draftees from this country are Negroes called on to stifle the liberation of Vietnam, to
> preserve a "democracy" which does not exist for them at home.

---

7. *Schenck v. United States*, 249 U.S. 47, 39 S.Ct. 247, 63 L.Ed. 470 (1919).
8. *Debs v. United States*, 249 U.S. 211 (1919).

We ask, where is the draft for the freedom fight in the United States?

We therefore encourage those Americans who prefer to use their energy in building democratic forums within this country. We believe that work in the civil rights movement and with other human relations organizations is a valid alternative to the draft. We urge all Americans to seek this alternative, knowing full well that it may cost their lives — as painfully as in Vietnam.[9]

In comparison to the statements denied protection in the *Schenck* and *Debs* cases, Bond's speech was clearly the more vociferous. Nevertheless, in 1966 the Supreme Court unanimously held that the refusal to seat Bond violated his First Amendment rights: "Certainly there can be no question but that the First Amendment protects expressions in opposition to national foreign policy in Vietnam and to the Selective Service System. The state does not contend otherwise."[10]

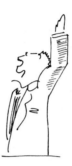

b. Symbolic Speech

By the mid-1960's, the general right to express strong dissent to war and defense policies had been broadly accepted at least as far as print media was concerned. Optimists saw this as a step forward in the battle for free expression. Cynics, however, noted that the electronic media revolution had made the written word obsolete as far as provoking direct political action was concerned. Certainly the day when Tom Paine or Karl Marx could threaten the establishment with the written word had given way to an age when the average person spent five hours a day in front of a TV set and barely read the newspaper.

As the Vietnam War progressed, protesters adopted techniques never before ruled on by the courts to call attention to their views. Most were designed for the TV camera, a journalistic tool as revolutionary as moveable type. Political protestors quickly learned that burning draft cards, physically obstructing draft boards, lying down in front of troop trains, and pouring blood over draft board files produced more seconds on the evening news than conventional speech making, no matter how flamboyant the speech. TV producers, they realized, were bored by "talking heads."

These new protest methods were categorized by the courts as "symbolic speech" to differentiate them from the ways people used to communicate in the pre-electronic age. The issue for the court, therefore, was whether symbolic action should be treated as "speech" for First Amendment purposes. Should such action enjoy the traditional free speech protections, or should it be considered as beyond speech and therefore subject to regulation?

One of the first decisions involving symbolic speech involved a draft card burning.[11] On the morning of March 3, 1966, David Paul O'Brien and three friends burned their Selective Service certificates on the steps of the South Boston courthouse. After the burning, O'Brien was

9. *Bond v. Floyd*, 385 U.S. 116, 87 S.Ct. 339, 17 L.Ed.2d 235 (1966).

10. 385 U.S. at 132.

11. *United States v. O'Brien*, 391 U.S. 367, 88 S.Ct. 1673, 20 L.Ed.2d 672 (1968).

attacked by the crowd, arrested by the FBI, and charged with violating a 1965 amendment to the Selective Service Act making it a crime for anyone to "knowingly destroy" or "knowingly mutilate" his draft card. In 1968, the Supreme Court, by a vote of seven to one, upheld the statute as constitutional and rejected O'Brien's argument that burning his draft card was speech protected by the First Amendment.

Refusing to acknowledge the legislation was specifically intended to punish expression (even though destroying a small piece of paper is not usually punishable by five years in prison), the court reached its decision by invoking a judicial device called the "balancing test." This measures the value of First Amendment protections against other conflicting rights and interests — e.g., privacy, property, or national security. Many critics claim that this type of test provides no protection since it depends heavily on the personal views of judges doing the testing. Others, however, claim that all the First Amendment decisions involve some sort of "balancing." In any event, the symbolic speech of draft card burning was not accorded the same protections as pure speech at that time.

In the following years, however, as opposition to the war escalated, the Court upheld the right of a man to wear a jacket bearing the words, "Fuck the Draft," [12] and treated the slogan as pure speech. The Court also upheld the right of public school children to engage in symbolic speech by wearing black armbands to school to protest the Vietnam War. [13]

As expression, it is difficult to distinguish between burning a draft card and wearing a slogan or armband, except that the symbolic protests in the latter cases were not obstacles to the normal activities of a courthouse or school, whereas destroying draft cards theoretically threw a monkey wrench into the draft machinery.

12. *Cohen v. California*, 403 U.S. 15, 91 S.Ct. 1780, 29 L.Ed.2d 284 (1971).
13. *Tinker v. Des Moines Independent School District* 393 U.S. 503, 89 S. Ct. 733, 21 L.Ed.2d 731 (1969).

2. Advocating the Overthrow of the Government by Force and Violence

The advocacy of political doctrines that call for revolution or for the use of violence and lawlessness as political tactics has been the central issue of political speech in the American experience. It has elicited some of the most profound judicial reflections on the meaning of freedom of speech, and it has produced a series of cases from World War I to the present that provide rich material for understanding the dynamics of dissent in a free society.

a. Early Twentieth Century

The first case to involve a state law prohibiting speech calling for the violent overthrow of the government[14] reached the Supreme Court in 1925 — *Gitlow v. New York*.[15] The New York state criminal statute provided a person was guilty of a felony who "by word of mouth or writing advocates, advises or teaches the duty, necessity, or propriety of overthrowing or overturning organized government by force or violence, or by assassination of the executive head or of any of the executive officials or by any unlawful means."

Benjamin Gitlow and three comrades were convicted under the Anarchy Statute of New York for publishing a radical manifesto in their newspaper, *The Revolutionary Age*. They urged mass strikes and repudiated the policy of centrist socialists aimed at "introducing socialism by means of legislative measures on the basis of a bourgeois state." About 16,000 copies of the manifesto were distributed. According to the Supreme Court, there was "no evidence of any effect resulting from the publication and circulation of the manifesto." Nevertheless, the convictions were upheld.

In its written opinion, the Supreme Court rejected the clear and present danger test for a given case and ruled instead that a statute could constitutionally prohibit specific types of speech so long as it was reasonable to do so. In other words, the Court established the "legislative reasonableness" of a statute as the criteria for deciding its constitutionality in a particular context. Using this approach, the question of whether Gitlow's words were protected under the Constitution became irrelevant so long as the statute itself could be justified as reasonable.

Ironically, the lasting significance of the *Gitlow* case has been positive. Almost off-handedly, the Court opinion contained language making the protections of the First Amendment applicable to the state governments. Until this decision, the guarantees of freedom of press, religion, speech, and assembly had only been thought applicable to the federal government. At first this language was not of much significance, due to a generally restrictive view of these protections taken by the Supreme Court during the 1920's and early 1930's. Later, however, when the Court gave fuller expression to the First Amendment, this expansion applied to the states as well as the federal government.

The next major case after *Gitlow*[16] that considered whether people could advocate changing their government by violent means was *Whitney v. California*.[17] Here the Supreme Court upheld the conviction of Anita Whitney for violation of the California Criminal Syndicalism Acts. That law defined criminal syndicalism as "any doctrine or precept advocating,

---

14. The main provisions of the New York Criminal Anarchy Statute declared that any person was guilty of a felony who "[b]y word of mouth or writing advocates, advises or teaches the duty, necessity or propriety of overthrowing or overturning organized government by force or violence, or by assassination of the executive head or of any of the executive officials of government, or by any unlawful means."

15. 268 U.S. 652, 45 S.Ct. 625, 69 L.Ed. 1138 (1925).

16. Benjamin Gitlow and his associates were pardoned by Governor Alfred E. Smith of New York after three years in prison.

17. 274 U.S. 357, 47 S.Ct. 641, 71 L.Ed. 1095 (1927).

teaching or abiding and abetting the commission of crime, sabotage . . . or unlawful methods of terrorism as a means of accomplishing a change in industrial ownership or control, or effecting any political change."

Anita Whitney, a Socialist (and a niece of then Supreme Court Justice Stephen J. Field) attended a convention in Chicago which resulted in the formation of the Communist Labor Party. Among the provisions in the new party's platform was one that rejected social change through parliamentary methods. Along the lines of Gitlow's *Revolutionary Age*, the Communist Labor Party urged support for the revolutionary class struggle. As it happened, Whitney actively opposed this portion of the platform and voted against it, but she remained a member of the party and was charged with a violation of the statute.

At her trial, Whitney asserted she had not foreseen the development of this position before she attended the convention and contended that her mere presence at a place where others made allegedly illegal statements could not possibly be construed as a crime. Nevertheless, she was convicted of criminal syndicalism and the Supreme Court affirmed. Justice Sanford, writing for the majority, treated the case as similar to *Gitlow*, an ordinary matter of conspiracy unrelated to free speech as such.

Today, however, the *Whitney* case is remembered principally because of the concurring opinion of Justice Louis Brandeis. In this opinion, which was more like a dissent, Brandeis clarified and refined the "clear and present danger" doctrine and sought to analyze the rationale of constitutional protection for freedom of expression:

> Fear of serious injury cannot alone justify suppression of free speech and assembly. Men feared witches and burnt women. It is the function of speech to free men from the bondage of irrational fears. To justify suppression of free speech there must be reasonable ground to fear that serious evil will result if free speech is practiced. There must be reasonable ground to believe that the evil to be prevented is a serious one . . . To self-reliant men, with confidence in the power of free and fearless reasoning applied through the process of popular government, no danger flowing from speech can be deemed clear and present, unless the incidence of the evil apprehended is so imminent that it may befall before there is opportunity for full discussion. If there be time to expose through discussion the falsehood and fallacies, to avert the evil by the processes of education, the remedy to be applied is more speech, not enforced silence. [18]

b. The New Deal Era

After First Amendment freedoms had been so severely repressed in the years directly following the First World War, the pendulum swung toward a more open attitude during the New Deal. From 1930, when Charles Evans Hughes was appointed Chief Justice, until the end of World War II, the Supreme Court consistently expanded the constitutional guarantees of First Amendment rights.

c. World War II

World War II did not produce the same number of First Amendment cases as have earlier wars, probably because of the relative lack of organized dissent to the war against Hitler and Japan. However, the willingness of the government to dispossess an entire racial group of their citizenship rights, and the upholding of this massive deprivation of civil liberties by the Supreme

---

18. Despite these brave words, Brandeis concurred in upholding Whitney's conviction and sentence to jail. In fact, Whitney was pardoned by the California governor before serving any time.

Court,[19] illustrates the firm connection between national crises and the willingness of the government to engage in, and the courts to sanction, massive repression.

d. McCarthyism and the Smith Act

In the years after WWII, the political climate in the U.S. again turned nasty. The "cold war" began and before long the destructive hysteria known as "McCarthyism" gripped much of the country. At the federal level, efforts to deal with political dissent during this era center around the Smith Act.

Sections 2 and 3 of the Smith Act, 18 U.S.C.A. Sections 10, 11 (see present 18 U.S.C.A., Section 2385), provide as follows:

> Sec. 2.
> (a) It shall be unlawful for any person —
> (1) to knowingly or willfully advocate, abet, advise, or teach the duty, necessity, desirability, or propriety of overthrowing or destroying the government in the United States by force or violence, or by the assassination of any officer of any such government;
> (3) to organize or help to organize any society, group, or assembly of persons who teach, advocate, or encourage the overthrow or destruction of any government in the United States by force or violence; or to be or become a member of, or affiliate with, any such society, group, or assembly of persons, knowing the purposes thereof.
>
> * * *
>
> Sec. 3. It shall be unlawful for any person to attempt to commit, or to conspire to commit, any of the acts prohibited by the provisions of this title.

In July 1948, the government indicted twelve members of the Central Committee of the Communist Party of the United States, for conspiracy under this act. The defendants in this case, known as *Dennis v. U.S.*,[20] were convicted. The Supreme Court upheld their convictions, even though the justices could reach no agreement on what legal theory justified the convictions.

Chief Justice Vinson, who wrote the majority opinion, suggested the clear and present danger test as a means to assess the constitutionality of the Smith Act. In doing so, however, he changed the test so it would provide less protection than previously. In Vinson's view, the danger [of the speech] must be grave [serious], but it was no longer necessary that it be immediate [present]. By removing the "present" from the "clear and present danger" equation, Vinson removed the most significant protection the doctrine provided for freedom of expression.

After the *Dennis* decision, the government prosecuted many minor Communist Party leaders under the Smith Act. Convictions were secured in every case taken to trial and the decisions were all upheld by the courts of appeal. The Supreme Court refused to review any of these cases until 1956, when it finally granted "certiorari" in *Yates v. U.S.*[21]

Yates involved the conviction of fourteen defendants in California on charges of conspiracy to advocate overthrow of the government by force and violence. Unlike the result in the *Dennis* case, the Supreme Court ordered the acquittal of five of the defendants. Charges against the

---

19. Nevertheless, the incarceration of Japanese-Americans in prison camps made from converted animal stalls indicates that the ephemeral concept of civil liberties takes a back seat to other considerations when our society perceives itself to be in danger.
20. 341 U.S. 494, 71 S.Ct. 857, 95 L.Ed. 1137 (1951).
21. 354 U.S. 298, 77 S.Ct. 1064, 1 L.Ed.2d 1356 (1957).

other nine defendants were dismissed by the trial judge on the basis of the *Yates* opinion. *Yates* caused existing prosecutions under the Smith Act to collapse and no new ones were instituted. [22]

Dennis was decided in 1951 during the height of the McCarthy era. By 1957, when *Yates* was decided, the reaction against McCarthyism had set in and with it a receding of the almost hysterical fear of communism that had characterized the Korean War years. These political facts are probably more important in understanding why the court upheld convictions in *Dennis* and overturned them in *Yates* than the consitutional theories put forth by the various justices deciding these cases. *Dennis* and *Yates* once again confirm the general rule that the First Amendment functions reasonably well in times of calm, but has not worked particularly well to protect unpopular speech when society perceives itself to be in danger.

It's interesting to note that with a few exceptions, such as Edward R. Murrow, most established media people did not see the Smith Act cases as fundamentally affecting their right of free expression. Even today, some people believe these dangerous limitations on the right to communicate were legitimate since they primarily affected Communists.

e. Post-McCarthyism

From the late 1950's into the 1970's there was an extraordinary group of Supreme Court Justices collectively known as the "Warren Court," after Chief Justice Earl Warren. Made up of men like Hugo Black, William Douglas, William Brennan, Jr., Thurgood Marshall, and Chief Justice Warren himself, this court was more sensitive to individual rights than any other in our history. By 1969, the Warren Court had completely recanted many of the earlier "anti-Communist" decisions and moved towards a trend of civil libertarianism.

In *Brandenburg v. Ohio*, [23] for example, the Court dealt with a state criminal syndicalist statute which had been upheld in *Whitney v. California* and successfully enforced in the early 1900's against socialists, anarchists, and members of the International Workers of the World (Wobblies). In the 1960's, this law was brought out of moth balls and used to prosecute and convict Brandenburg, a Ku Klux Klan organizer.

Brandenburg's crime had been preaching hatred of Jews and blacks at a Klan rally. In addition, the state presented evidence at his trial that a pistol, a rifle, a shotgun, ammunition and a Bible were present at the rally. The Supreme court reversed the conviction, struck down the Ohio criminal syndicalist statute, and reversed *Whitney* in the process, ruling that the state may not forbid advocacy of the use of force "except where such advocacy is directed to inciting or producing imminent lawless action and is likely to incite or produce such action." This is the current standard by which subversive advocacy cases are measured. Only if speech actually merges with criminal action will it be considered as outside the protection of the First Amendment.

3. Fighting Words and Hostile Audiences: The "Heckler's Veto"

One final First Amendment-related doctrine that deserves mention is the "fighting words" theory. This says that speech can be outlawed if, in the understanding of ordinary people, it is

---

22. Of the 141 persons indicted for violation of the Smith Act, 29 served prison terms. Two of the original *Dennis* defendants were still serving their sentences at the time of the *Yates* decision and petitioned the Supreme Court for a rehearing upon the basis of the *Yates* case. The petition was denied.
23. 395 U.S. 444, 89 S.Ct. 1827, 23 L.Ed.2d 430 (1969).

likely to cause a fight. The doctrine was first stated by the Supreme Court in the case of *Chaplinsky v. New Hampshire*[24]:

> There are certain well-defined and narrowly limited classes of speech, the prevention of which has never been thought to raise any constitutional problem. These include the lewd and obscene, the profane, the libelous, and the insulting or "fighting words"—those which by very utterance inflict injury or tend to incite an immediate breach of the peace. It has been well-observed that such utterances are no essential part of the exposition of ideas, and are of such slight social value as a step to truth that any benefit derived from them is clearly outweighed by the social interest in order and morality.

Although the "fighting words" doctrine would seem to directly inhibit a speaker from engaging in speech likely to cause a fight, the courts recognized the First Amendment problems with the concept and have characteristically left a confused trail of judicial pronouncements attempting to reconcile the two.

In post-war Chicago, a Catholic priest named Terminello delivered a flamboyant speech attacking the "Communistic Zionist Jews," blacks, and others, before a crowd of 800 Christian Veterans of America. Outside an angry, largely black, crowd gathered. Terminello was arrested, tried, and found guilty of disorderly conduct because of the "fighting nature" of his words. The Supreme Court, in a 5-4 decision, reversed. Justice Douglas wrote:

> [A] function of free speech under our system of government is to invite dispute. It may indeed best serve its high purpose when it induces a condition of unrest, creates dissatisfaction with conditions as they are, or even stirs people to anger . . . That is why freedom of speech, though not absolute, is nevertheless protected against censorship or punishment, unless shown likely to produce a clear and present danger of a serious substantive evil that rises far above public inconvenience, annoyance or unrest.[25]

A more recent (1978) incident involving the "fighting words" doctrine resulted from a planned march of the American Nazi Party through Skokie, Illinois, a predominantly Jewish suburb of Chicago. Attorneys for Skokie contended the prospect of marching Nazis carrying swastikas was the equivalent of "fighting" words, bound to provoke a hostile reaction in a community where many survivors of the World War II holocaust resided.

Nevertheless, in three cases brought by the Nazis, the courts upheld their right to assemble and speak, ruling that displaying the swastika did not constitute the use of "fighting words," and was instead a form of symbolic speech entitled to constitutional protection. The courts observed that the anticipated hostile audience problem could be avoided by the audience simply avoiding the march.[26]

4. The First Amendment and the Media

Most of the important First Amendment cases have involved the use of state power against individuals rather than direct assaults on the media. The Pentagon Papers case, in which the U.S. Government tried to directly limit the rights of several major newspapers to publish, is a major exception.

---

24. 315 U.S. 568, 62 S.Ct. 766, 86 L.Ed. 1031 (1942).
25. *Terminello v. Chicago*, 337 U.S. 1, 69 S.Ct. 894, 93 L.Ed. 431 (1949).
26. See *Village of Skokie v. National Socialist Party*, 373 N.E.2d 21 (Ill., 1978) and *Collin v. Smith*, 578 F.2d 1197 (7th Cir. 1978).

There are probably several reasons why the government restricts the rights of individuals more than the media. Media people are usually more aware of their rights. They have the power to publicize any attack upon them and often have the economic clout to get good legal help fast.

Additionally, it may be argued that since much of the U.S. media establishment is supportive of dominant societal attitudes and groups, there is little occasion to repress their views. In an age where big business, big labor, and big government have learned to co-exist to the profit of all, gigantic, and often hugely profitable, media organizations often seem content to go along.

The alternative press, while often politically feisty and anxious to print unpopular views, is relatively weak. Thus, for the most part, the powers that be have learned that ignoring it makes more sense than fighting it. However, when a particular crisis occasionally brings an anti-establishment publication to a position of influence, the government has not hesitated to sabotage its operations.[27]

The violations and intrusions on freedom of expression of individuals are directly relevant to attacks on freedom of the press. In Chapters 6 and 7, we discuss several types of cases in which journalists or news organizations have been searched, subpoenaed, or prosecuted by the police and judges. In Chapter 2 we cover government censorship of the media. While these topics don't always involve issues of national security, it is clear the constitutional protection for newsgathering is always under serious attack when anyone, media person or not, is prosecuted for dissenting from established views.

To conclude, we stress again that the way the courts perceive the social, economic and political pressures of the time affect First Amendment decisions as much as any other factor. While court opinions will be heralded at various times as defeats or victories for individuals or the media, it's often a mistake to get too involved in the various theoretical legal arguments of any particular decision. Viewed over time, most of these seem to be so contradictory and confusing as to have little real intellectual consistency of honesty, despite their undoubted importance for the individuals involved at the time. The central concern of the press is and must continue to be that those who wish to speak on matters of political and social controversy are free to do so.

---

27. Angus Mackenzie, "Sabotaging the Dissident Press," *Columbia Journalism Review*, March/April 1981.

Censorship

A. Introduction

Censorship takes as many forms as there are ways to communicate. At an overt level, books can be burned, movies suppressed, and newspaper editors imprisoned. More subtly, a climate of fear can be fostered which discourages dissenters from expressing themselves. Here we will look at how censorship has been, and continues to be, used in the U.S. to inhibit certain types of communication.

   SELF-CENSORSHIP NOTE: Of course, there are a multitude of ways you may be prevented from publishing or airing a story that has nothing to do with the First Amendment. Your editor or producer may refuse to run a particular piece, or may change it so that it becomes unrecognizable. In some situations, you may even censor yourself, fearing that if you don't, you will never be able to sell your story or keep your job. These sorts of limitations on freedom of the press must be viewed with real alarm at a time when a dozen or two large corporations control the majority of American media. Nevertheless, they are outside the scope of a book which speaks to legal rights and responsibilities.

B. Prior Restraint: An Historical Perspective

Governmental restrictions imposed upon speech or other kinds of expression in advance of publication are commonly called "prior restraint." As we discussed very briefly in Chapter 1, from the time of the first English printing press until well into the eighteenth century, the English monarchy, as divided as it was by religious strife, agreed that the press needed close watching. A series of press licensing laws were enacted which required getting material approved by the censor before publication. Gradually, however, this comprehensive scheme of prior restraint was viewed as a violation of the inalienable rights of free people to express themselves. And finally, in the eighteenth century, "prior restraint" died and Blackstone, the preeminent legal commentator of the time, was able to state:

> The liberty of the press is indeed essential to the nature of a free state; but this consists in laying no previous restraints upon publications, and not in freedom from censure for criminal matter when published. Every free man has an undoubted right to lay what sentiments he pleases before the public; to forbid this, is to destroy the freedom of the press; but if he publishes what is improper, mischievous or illegal, he must take the consequences of his own temerity. [1]

Blackstone's views live today in the First Amendment which forbids prior restraint as repugnant to the concept of freedom of expression. Why repugnant? Once material is published, there is an opportunity for public review and criticism. Prior restraint, however, completely eliminates the information at its source.

In addition, as a practical matter prior restraint is more damaging to free speech than post-publication penalties. It has simply proved to be easier to stop the media from airing or publishing a story beforehand than to punish the journalist after the same story is in the public domain. This is because any attempt at criminal punishment traditionally carries with it important procedural safeguards that are commonly not available when material is pre-censored. Experience with censorship in a number of societies leads most observers to conclude that prior restraint is easily abused once allowed. Simply put, it is as hard to unpublish a newspaper as it is to unring a bell.

C. Is Prior Restraint Unconstitutional?

Although the drafters of the First Amendment relied on Blackstone's view of the evils of prior restraint, they did not explicitly prohibit it. Surprisingly, it was not until 1931, in the *Near v. Minnesota* case, [2] that the Supreme Court considered the constitutionality of prior restraints. At issue was a Minnesota statute (called the "Gag Law") which provided that any person "engaged in the business" of regularly publishing or circulating an "obscene, lewd and lascivious" or a "malicious, scandalous and defamatory" newspaper or periodical "is guilty of a nuisance." The statute went on to allow the state "to enjoin perpetually the persons committing or maintaining any such nuisance."

A Minneapolis newspaper had printed a series of articles that "charged in substance that a Jewish gangster was in control of gambling, bootlegging, and racketeering in Minneapolis and that law enforcement officers and agencies were not energetically performing their duties." Under authority of the Gag Law, a state court perpetually enjoined the newspaper from printing the articles, but the U.S. Supreme Court held the statute to be invalid because it allowed prior restraint:

---

1. *Blackstone's Commentaries on the Laws of England*, Vol.4, pp.151-152.
2. 283 U.S. 697, 51 S.Ct. 525, 75 L.Ed. 1357 (1931). See Friendly, *Minnesota Rag* (1981) for a lively discussion of the *Near* case.

The exceptional nature of its limitations [the Gag Law] places in a strong light the general conception that liberty of the press, historically considered and taken up by the Federal Constitution, has meant, principally although not exclusively, immunity from previous restraints or censorship.[3]

As is often true with Supreme Court opinions, however, there was a little bad news with the good. The Court cautioned that the prohibition against prior restraint was not absolute and could be waived in "exceptional circumstances," such as the following:

National Security in time of war. ("No one would question but that a government might prevent actual obstruction to its recruiting service or the publication of sailing dates of transports or the number and location of troops.");[4]

Obscenity or "primary requirements of decency;"

Fighting Words when the public order is endangered by the incitement to violence and overthrow by force of orderly government;

Criminal Proceedings when, in the judge's opinion, statements which might be made would interfere with a criminal defendant's right to trial by an impartial jury (see Chapter 5); and

Libel and Invasion of Privacy when the individual proves that the story would be harmful to his reputation. (See Chapters 3 and 4.) It should be noted, however, that this justification for prior restraint is more theoretical than real, as no lower court gag order has ever been upheld involving either libel or invasion of privacy.

To properly grasp the law of prior restraint and what to do if it affects your ability to report a story, it is necessary to understand when the exceptions are likely to be upheld by a court. This can best be done by examining a little judicial history.

CENSORSHIP

---

3. *Ibid.* at 702-703.
4. *Ibid.*

D. Prior Restraint in National Security Situations

1. The Pentagon Papers

In the midst of the Vietnam War, perhaps our most unpopular war since the Mexican War of the 1840's, Secretary of Defense Robert McNamara ordered an historical study on America's role in the war. This was contained in forty-seven volumes collectively entitled *History of the United States Decision-Making Process on Vietnam Policy*. Subsequently, Daniel Ellsberg, one of the study's authors, had come to oppose the war. Ellsberg made a copy of the 7,000 page study (classified as "top secret" and now known as the Pentagon Papers) available to a *New York Times* reporter. In June 1971, after four months of debate, the *Times* decided to print it although the war was still in progress. After excerpts appeared for two days running, the U.S. Government sought to prevent further publication on the grounds that it was "directly prohibited" by the Espionage Act.

A new Nixon appointee, Judge Murray Gurfein, heard the case (his first) and issued a temporary restraining order barring the *Times* from further publication of the Pentagon Papers. This was the first time an American newspaper had been restrained by a court order from publishing articles and documents.

During the ensuing litigation, the government vigorously argued that publication would directly cause deaths of U.S. prisoners of war, soldiers, CIA agents, and employees of other governments. The government's case was injured when one of the documents it presented to the judge to demonstrate its "worse case of damage" was discovered by a reporter to be an officially published government document. This event, more than any sophisticated presentation of First Amendment doctrine, greatly helped the *New York Times*.

After studying the case further, Judge Gurfein reversed his position and decided in favor of the *Times*. After his decision, government lawyers raced to the Second Circuit Court of Appeals and successfully obtained an order continuing the restraint on publication, pending appeal. In the meantime, Daniel Ellsberg had made portions of the Pentagon Papers available to almost twenty other newspapers.

Not to be beaten by a photocopying machine, the government brought actions for injunctive relief against three of these — the *Washington Post, Boston Globe*, and the *St. Louis Post Dispatch* (no action was taken against the other newspapers, some of whom had no plans to publish the papers). The *Washington Post* alone was initially successful in defeating attempts by the government at restraint. The result was the anomaly that the Washington D.C. paper could legally publish the papers, while the New York, Boston and St. Louis papers could not.

The U.S. Court of Appeals for the Second Circuit decided to continue its restraint on the *Times* publication of the papers and the *Times* then asked the U.S. Supreme Court to review the case on an expedited basis. A week later, the Court allowed the *Times* to resume publication. The numerous issues raised in the case resulted in separate opinions by each Supreme Court justice — six concurring and three dissenting.[5] The only issue on which the six justices in the majority could agree was that the federal government, in seeking prior restraint, had failed to meet its "heavy burden of justification" for such action.

Most of the justices expressly agreed that the First Amendment permitted subsequent criminal punishment for publication of government secrets, assuming the existence of relevant criminal statutes and even though prior restraint would not have been permissible.[6] All of the

---

5. *New York Times v. United States*, 403 U.S. 713, 95 S.Ct. 2140, 29 L.Ed.2d 822 (1971).

6. As of this writing it is not a specific crime for a government official to disclose classified information to a reporter. However, the Reagan Administration has tightened procedures governing classified materials.

justices were concerned with the serious impact to national security interests.

The decision in the Pentagon Papers case therefore allows the government to try again, whenever it thinks it can meet the heavy burden of justification for such restraint. Unfortunately, the case provides no guidance concerning what kind of public interest would be protected against press publication, what weight should be given different public interests and the interests of the press, or what types of evidence would meet the government's burden.

What this case, as well as several others did, however, was to establish that limits may be imposed on the media's right to publish and the people's right to learn government secrets relating to national security.

HISTORICAL NOTE: The practical effect of the resumption of the publication of the Pentagon Papers had a great deal more significance than the legal decision. It led President Nixon to establish a group to patch up "leaks," later known as the "Plumbers." The Plumbers were initially responsible for the criminal break-in at the office of Daniel Ellsberg's former psychiatrist and the task of gathering information for the purpose of discrediting Ellsberg. Later they were involved in the Watergate break-in. The Pentagon Papers decision is credited by many with paving the way for the bold reporting of Watergate.[7]

"HOW TO BUILD AN H-BOMB WITHOUT REALLY TRYING"

2. How to Make Your Own H-Bomb — The Progressive Case

Following the Supreme Court's decision in the Pentagon Papers case, it was common for law school professors to give their constitutional law class the following hypothetical "hard" case: "If someone were about to publish the secret of the H-Bomb, would a prior restraint be constitutional?" In one more bit of evidence that history and fiction have merged in the twentieth century, exactly this question reached the courts when a publication, *The Progressive*, advertised an article entitled, "The H-Bomb Secret — How We Got It, Why We're Telling It."

---

7. It should be noted that there has never been a demonstration of harm resulting from the release of the Pentagon Papers. See Floyd Abrams, "The Pentagon Papers A Decade Later," *The New York Times Magazine*, June 14, 1981, p.27.

The editors of *The Progressive* had commissioned Howard Morland, a freelance writer with a long-standing interest in nuclear issues, to prepare an article on the American nuclear weapons program. With the knowledge and consent of the Department of Energy (DOE), Morland visited several nuclear weapons facilities and interviewed government employees.

The Progressive claimed that Morland identified himself as a journalist during all interviews and had no access to classified documents. In contrast, the government claimed he used pseudonyms to obtain the information. At any rate, there was no dispute about one thing — by piecing together what he read, saw, and was told, Morland managed to deduce the basic design of the American hydrogen bomb.

Eventually, a draft of the article was sent to the Department of Energy (DOE) for verification of certain technical details. The DOE promptly notified *The Progressive* that Morland's piece contained "restricted data" as defined in the Atomic Energy Act of 1954. *The Progressive*, in turn, maintained that the information on which the article was based came entirely from public domain sources. While refusing to specify which parts were restricted, the DOE offered to rewrite the article in sanitized form.

When *The Progressive* rejected this kind offer and reiterated its plans to publish the article in full, the DOE filed an action requesting prior restraint. The judge granted the request, stating: "I'd want to think a long, hard time before I'd give a hydrogen bomb to Idi Amin. It appears to me that is what we're doing here." As a legal justification for his decision, the judge held there would be a "likelihood of direct, immediate, and irreparable injury to our nation" if the articles were published (this was the test suggested by Justice Stewart in the Pentagon Papers case). [8]

While *The Progressive* appealed the decision, similar but independently acquired information about hydrogen bomb construction was published elsewhere. Because of this, the government abandoned its effort to prevent publication. Again, as in the *Pentagon Papers* dispute, *The Progressive* magazine injunction demonstrated that, in practical terms, prior restraints are usually useless. Once information exists in our media-rich society, it tends to get out, one way or another. And once it's been printed or aired anywhere, an order to prevent broader dissemination is, as one judge put it, like "asking us to ride herd on a swarm of bees."[9]

3. The CIA as Censor

The Progressive case raised the issue of whether the fruits of individual research and speculation based on publicly available sources of data can be subjected to prior restraint. What happens when the information in question comes directly from government files? This occurred when disgruntled former CIA agents revealed information which they had agreed to keep secret when they were first employed by the "Company."

---

8. *United States of America v. The Progressive*, 467 F.Supp. 990 (W.D. Wisc. 1979).
9. *Abrams*, op.cit. p. 78.

In 1972, the government successfully obtained a court order enjoining Victor Marchetti from publishing a book which allegedly disclosed information in violation of his CIA employment agreement. The Fourth Circuit Court of Appeals modified the restraint to apply only to classified information, but required Marchetti to submit any material he intended to publish to the CIA for its review in advance of publication.[10] Marchetti, in collaboration with John Marks, subsequently submitted a manuscript to the CIA entitled "The CIA and the Cult of Intelligence." The CIA agreed to reduce the number of deletions from 339 to 168 and the authors and publishers then went back into court seeking permission to publish the book in full.

After hearing the evidence, the judge concluded that most of the CIA decisions on classified items were made *after* rather than *before* the CIA read the manuscript, and accordingly upheld the CIA on only 26 of its deletions. Unfortunately, the same appellate court in the original *Marchetti* case disagreed with the district court's decision[11] and ruled the CIA's classification must be presumed correct and that material should still be considered classified even if already leaked to the public. The Appeals Court also said Marchetti had effectively relinquished his First Amendment rights when he entered into a "secrecy agreement" with the CIA. In sum, the CIA was given the power to decide what information may be published by its former employees through the presumption of correct classification of information.

Attempting to avoid Marchetti's fate, Frank Snepp, a former CIA agent who also signed a CIA contract requiring prior clearance, decided to publish and be damned. He was. The book, entitled *Decent Interval,* was published in November 1977 without prior submission to the CIA and contained information bearing on Snepp's contention that the CIA had been inept in Vietnam. Although the government conceded that the book contained no classified material, they asked for and were awarded a permanent injunction against any further publication of information obtained during his CIA employment, as well as an order requiring Snepp to pay it an undetermined amount of money as "damages" suffered by the government, including all book royalties, movie profits and other income which might result from the book.

The Supreme Court upheld this result,[12] viewing the case as involving a breach of contract by a faithless employee rather than a prior restraint by an overzealous court. In addition, the Court strengthened the overall ability of the government to obtain prior restraints. A footnote in the opinion would allow the CIA to protect governmental interests by placing restrictions on its employees' First Amendment rights, even in the absence of a contract.

Ironically, had Snepp not been a CIA agent, he would have been able to publish everything contained in the book with no legal penalty whatever.[13]

To summarize, prior restraints are unconstitutional unless:

- An actual showing of highly probable damage to national security is made; or
- A violation of a secrecy agreement with a government agency involved in national security matters is threatened; or
- A carefully drawn legislative scheme, designed to protect sensitive information relating to national security, authorizes them.

What does all this mean in the life of a working journalist? If you believe a government agency might try to censor your material if you ask them to review it first, your best bet is to

---

10. *U.S. v. Marchetti*, 466 F.2d 1309 (4th cir. 1972).

11. *Alfred A. Knopf, Inc. v. Colby*, 509 F.2d 1362 (4th Cir), cert. den. 421 U.S. 992 (1975).

12. 444 U.S. 507 (1980).

13. Security Decision Directive No. 84 (March 1983) required a number of other federal agencies to establish procedures similar to those employed by the C.I.A. for reviewing manuscripts. The purpose of the order was to stop unauthorized disclosures of secret material called Sensitive Compartmental Information (SCI). The order required some 100,000 federal employees having access to such material to sign agreements promising non-disclosure and advance submission of manuscripts to the government to "assure deletion" of all SCI. While this order did not prevent publication of SCI once it is obtained by the media, it did comprise a type of censorship by cutting off access to information at the source. This directive was rescinded early in 1984, due to opposition by Congress and many of the government officials subject to its provisions.

publish first and ask second. Of course, you, your news organization and its legal staff will have to arrive at your own ethical decision as to whether publication of the sensitive material will truly jeopardize the lives of individuals or the security of the nation.

E. Prior Restraint: Obscenity

The second exception to the general rule that prior restraints on publications are unconstitutional involves the publication of obscene material. The Supreme Court has always held that obscenity does not fall within the protection of the First Amendment but has never been very clear about what is and is not obscene. Here is its latest view:

> The basic guidelines for the trier of fact must be: (a) whether "the average person, applying contemporary community standards" would find that the work, taken as a whole, appeals to the prurient interest, (b), whether the work depicts or describes, in a patently offensive way, sexual conduct specifically defined by the applicable state law, and (c) whether the work, taken as a whole, lacks serious literary, artistic, political, or scientific value. [14]

The problem with these "guidelines," of course, is they are laden with value judgments. What is meant by "prurient interest," and "offensive," for example, or how does one decide whether something lacks "serious literary, artistic, political, or scientific value"?

Recognizing that its "guidelines" involve some slippery concepts, the Court established procedural rules that must be followed before "obscene material" can be censored. These include:

- The censor must institute judicial proceedings;

---

14. *Miller v. California*, 413 U.S. 15, 93 S.Ct. 2607, 37 L.Ed.2d 419 (1973).

• The court may restrain publication on an interim basis (e.g., issue a temporary restraining order) only after a hearing has been held in which the parties involved can present their views on whether the material is or is not obscene; and

• The publisher must be afforded a prompt trial and a final decision in the event publication has been restrained on an interim basis.

To see how this should work, let's examine what happened when a Rhode Island obscenity commission sent identical notices to booksellers informing them that it deemed certain books to be objectionable for minors. The notice additionally stated that copies had been sent to the local police, that the commission had power to recommend prosecution, and that it would be a good idea for the booksellers to cooperate.

Treating the notice as censorship, the Supreme Court[15] ordered it stopped, due to the absence of any prompt and effective safeguards against abuse (i.e., judicial review) and any way to verify whether or not the material was in fact obscene.[16]

HISTORICAL CONTEXT NOTE: The *Bantam* case involved, in essence, an administrative licensing system closely akin to the English prior restraint system in effect at the time of the American revolution and thus particularly objectionable in Anglo-American law. In truth, the danger of a government successfully censoring responsible print media on the basis of obscenity is by now almost non-existent.

As a result of a number of Supreme Court decisions, almost all written material that can claim any literary or artistic merit will be allowed. Pictures are another issue, however. As film and print have become bolder in visually depicting frank sexual conduct, most recent obscenity cases have involved this form of expression. If you are running photos that you think may come under attack, check your state obscenity statute. Many laws specifically refer to the parts of the body or sexual acts deemed to be obscene.

F. Prior Restraint: Incitement to Violence

Because "fighting words" have also been held by courts to fall outside the protection of the First Amendment, prior restraints on such speech is at least theoretically permissible.[17] However, because the definition of what constitutes "fighting words" has been drawn so narrowly, this exception normally has little or no practical effect on news reporting.

It is hard to imagine that the media would ever be censored on "incitement to violence" grounds. Although the strong influence of media is well-documented, there is no evidentiary basis to assert that riots have ever directly resulted from an article or program. Perhaps the fact that the media usually exhibits considerable self-restraint is part of the explanation. Also, reading and watching TV are, by their very nature, a private activity, whereas listening to a speech in public runs a greater risk of joining others in spontaneous collective acts of protest or expressions of outrage (some would refer to this as the "mob effect").

---

15. *Bantam Books, Inc. v. Sullivan*, 372 U.S. 58 (1963).

16. The Supreme Court, in *Miller v. California*, gave "a few plain examples" for what a state statute could define as "patently offensive":

(a) *Patently offensive representations or descriptions of ultimate sexual acts, normal or perverted, actual or simulated.*

(b) *Patently offensive representations or descriptions of masturbation, excretory functions, and lewd exhibition of the genitals.*

17. *Near v. Minnesota*, 283 U.S. 697, 51 S.Ct. 625, 75 L.Ed. 1357 (1931).

G. Prior Restraint: To Guarantee Fair Criminal Proceedings

Prior restraints in the context of criminal trials normally occur when judges issue gag orders on journalists which prevent them from publishing what happens in the courtroom. This is an area of great contemporary interest and we have therefore assigned the subject to its own chapter — Chapter 5 — where it is discussed in great detail.

H. Prior Restraint: Libel and Invasion of Privacy

The courts rarely prevent the publication of potentially libelous material (or that which might constitute an invasion of privacy). The reasons for this reluctance are the traditional aversion to prior restraints and the ability of the victims to file traditional damage suits. However, such judicial action is not unheard of and journalists should know their rights if it happens to them. For example, a federal district court ordered the *Los Angeles Herald Examiner* to refrain from publishing a serialized story on the marital life of baseball star Steve Garvey and his wife, Cyndy. The appeals court immediately reversed because it was a prior restraint.

If you face the threat of this situation, document your facts (see Chapters 3 and 4), protect yourself by creating a record of everything you have done, and publish. If a court issues a temporary order enjoining you from publication or broadcast, publicize far and wide this unconstitutional restraint on freedom of the press. You will get immediate help from concerned media organizations, and, when your story does appear (this shouldn't take long), it will receive a great deal more attention than if the court order had not been issued.

I. Prior Restraint: Book Banning

In Chapter 1 we emphasized the heavy historic role that governments have played in censorship of speech. However, history also has produced many examples of censorship arising from community based movements and campaigns. The post-Civil War activities of the Ku Klux Klan, and the seventeenth century persecution of witches by the good citizens of Salem serve as dramatic reminders of this fact.

So too in the 1980's, the most insidious form of censorship has not come from court orders or the decrees of federal or state governments. Rather, it has taken the form of a concerted grass roots campaign by an alliance of conservative political and religious organizations to limit the public's right to read. Almost before it was noticed, it took hold in dozens of communities. Unfortunately, this new wave of censorship is not confined to backwoods school districts and libraries — it's happening in the suburbs and the cities. In a very few years, special interest groups in thirty-eight states sought to ban more than 150 books, many considered English and American literary classics. Disturbingly, incidents of censorship have quintupled between 1980 and 1982, and have shown little sign of decreasing since.

Not surprisingly, people active in all aspects of media have become concerned. If you can ban a book today, the same reasoning is sure to be used on TV and radio shows tomorrow. As a matter of fact, the TV networks have already felt the heavy hand of right-wing pressure on potential advertisers to not support controversial TV programming. This even extended in November 1983 to a campaign designed to pressure ABC to cancel its plans for airing "The Day After," a portrayal of the effects that one hydrogen bomb would have on Kansas City.

Community based censorship has also occurred through school boards, political entities which often closely reflect local moral and ethical standards. Thus, in 1982, the U.S. Supreme Court considered the constitutionality of a school board's removal of books from high school and junior high school libraries. [18] The censored books were *Slaughterhouse Five*, *The Naked Ape*, *Down These Mean Streets*, *Best Short Stories of Negro Writers*, *Go Ask Alice*, *A Hero Ain't Nothin' But a Sandwich*, *Soul on Ice*, *A Reader for Writers*, and *The Fixer*. The school board of the Island Trees Free Unified School District in New York had justified the removal of these books in a press release which described them as "anti-American, anti-Christian, anti-semitic, and just plain filthy."

Several students went to court over this issue. The case ultimately led to the school board changing its mind after the U.S. Supreme Court determined that the First Amendment may have been violated. As often happens in First Amendment cases, a majority of the Supreme Court Justices could not agree on what exactly was wrong with the book banning. In fact, the nine justices took seven different positions (articulated in seven different opinions) which dramatically highlighted the tension between the First Amendment and the historic, virtually sacrosanct autonomy afforded local schools in this country.

The plurality opinion of five concurring judges, written by Justice Brennan, ruled that the discretion of school boards to remove books "may not be exercised in a narrow or political manner."

> Our Constitution does not permit the official suppression of *ideas*. Thus, whether [the board's] removal of books from school libraries denied [the students] their First Amendment rights depends upon the motivation behind [the board's] actions. If it intended by the removal decision to deny them access to ideas with which it disagreed, and if this intent was the decisive factor in its decision, the board has exercised its discretion in violation of the Constitution. [19]

This emphasis on motive allows books to be constitutionally removed if an "improper" motive cannot be proved. In addition, the decision applies only to the *removal* of library books, not *acquisition*. The plurality opinion also explicity excludes textbooks and required reading from First Amendment protection. The fact that even those justices leaning most heavily toward the First Amendment restricted their analyses to optional reading signals a reduced vigilance against censorship on the part of the Court.

Because the Court was so evenly divided in this case, it is impossible to predict the content of future decisions involving an interplay between book removals and the First Amendment. The only certainty is that until the Supreme Court issues another decision, supported by a majority of the Justices, there will be no coherent doctrine on which to rely.

LIBEL NOTE: Attempted book banning has recently occurred in the context of libel lawsuits. Governor William Janklow of South Dakota sued three bookstores because they refused to remove *In the Spirit of Crazy Horse*, by Peter Matthiessen from their shelves. Janklow claims the Matthiessen book is libelous and has included the bookstores in his $24 million suit. Although it is unlikely that Janklow will prevail, the suit has taken its toll on the bookstore. One store, Golden Mountain Books, is located in Hot Springs, population 5,000, and is one of the smallest bookstores in the state. Estimated costs of depositions alone are between $15,000 and $25,000.

---

18. *Board of Education v. Pico*, 454 U.S. 891, 102 S.Ct. 2799, 70 L.Ed. 1357 (1982).
19. *Ibid*.

Since Janklow filed his case, this tactic has been used in other libel cases around the country. Because of the sheer number of libel suits filed in recent years (see Chapter 3), this form of book banning may unhappily become extremely and rapidly prevalent.

J. Disclosing Identity of Government Agents Is a Crime

A deeply troublesome area for journalists is reporting on events possibly involving members of the U.S. Intelligence Community. A large number of persons operate undercover while in the employ of such agencies as the Secret Service, CIA, FBI, and the National Security Agency (NSA). Inevitably, these individuals become intertwined with newsworthy events. Intensive coverage of such events risks uncovering the agents' identities and either exposing them to danger or minimizing their future effectiveness.

An innocent disclosure in the course of a general story probably will not cause problems for the journalist. However, a knowing disclosure in the context of a story focusing even in part on the activity of the intelligence agency involved might lead to trouble.

The "Intelligence Identities Protection Act" of 1982 makes it a crime for anyone (not just former agents) to disclose "any information to any individual that leads to the identity of an individual as a covert agent." Even news reporters who engage "in . . . a pattern of activities intended to identify and expose covert agents and with reason to believe that such activities would impair or impede the intelligence activities of the United States" can be fined $15,000 or imprisoned for three years. The Act covers the FBI, military intelligence, and other agencies, not just the CIA. Furthermore, the Act makes no distinction between information which comes from classified sources and information which comes from unclassified sources.

The Act, originally drafted by the CIA, was primarily designed to extinguish a small magazine called *Covert Action Information Bulletin,* specializing in reporting on CIA activities abroad. Nevertheless, the law applies to all media. Enforcement of the Act has not occurred at the time of this writing and its legal interpretation is unclear. However, because of its lengthy legislative history, there are some indications of what Congress intended in passing this law. If you report in this area, it might do you well to get a copy of the law (P.L. 97-200) and the House-Senate Conference Report (Report 97-580). Here are a few words of warning:

• The phrase "pattern of activities" could mean even a one-time disclosure, but only if it follows "a substantial effort to ferret out names," e.g., seeking unauthorized access to classified information, and analyzing data for the purpose of identifying agents.

• The requirement of "reason to believe" that a reporter's acts would impair intelligence activities creates the problem of whether you should go to the agency to get its side, as you would with most stories. If you do, the CIA would probably request that you not print the story. This, of course, might then give you the "reason to believe" and get you in trouble if you publish. If you don't go to the agency, on the other hand, there may be a question of whether you reported the story in a fair and accurate way.[20]

If you feel yourself getting into these troubled waters, it might be wise to carefully document your activities and intent through memos to your editor and publisher outlining the reasons for your investigation and what you hope to find out. Advice from an experienced media lawyer would also be appropriate.

---

20. On the other hand, the conference report does focus on the "intent" of the disclosure. The report states the law does not affect "the First Amendment rights of those who disclose the identities of agents as an integral part of another enterprise such as news media reporting of intelligence failures or abuses."

SAMPLE MEMO #1

TO: Editor and Publisher
FROM: Reporter
DATE: 5 July 1983
RE: CIA infiltration of CISPES

On 29 June 1983, I received a phone call from the local office of the Committee In Solidarity with the Peoples of El Salvador (CISPES) that their national office had discovered that their files had been tampered with. According to the local spokesperson at CISPES, it looks like an inside job. The local office has been suspicious of a couple of its members on the steering committee and believes that it has enough evidence to substantiate their claim that these two individuals are government informants.

I intend to look at this evidence and investigate this further to complement our feature story last week on the government's attempt to discredit the nuclear freeze campaign.

SAMPLE MEMO #2

TO: Editor and Publisher
FROM: Reporter
DATE: 7 July 1983
RE: CIA infiltration of CISPES (Followup to Memo of 5 July 1983)

On July 6, an individual who identified himself as an ex-CIA agent (no name was provided) called on the telephone and identified one Juan Barrientos as a CIA operative who had been planted as a CISPES worker. Additional details from this source confirmed the information I received from CISPES directly. I then called Barrientos and asked whether he was employed by the CIA. He told me that was a ridiculous idea but that I should not publish anything about him or his connection with CISPES.

I think we have sufficient information to run a story about CIA infiltration into CISPES. Barrientos' identity will be disclosed as an indispensable by-product of the main story. This should not endanger him as he is already under suspicion by the CISPES staff. Because publishing Barrientos' name will be incidental to the story, and because the story is not focusing on covert operations as such but only on this one incident, we should be OK under the Intelligence Identities Act.

K.   Secrecy Agreements

In one of many of the Reagan Administration moves to plug news "leaks," the Defense Department asked reporters to sign a secrecy agreement before attending a background briefing held to discuss Soviet military capabilities. The secrecy agreement stipulated that the reporters must never disclose in writing, or broadcast, or make any verbal disclosure about the information they would hear. It also required the journalists to report to the Pentagon any effort made by others to obtain the sensitive information.

When the reporters balked at signing the agreement, senior defense officials settled for their verbal word of honor. [21] More of the same is likely in the future.

L. What Journalists Can Do to Maintain Free Expression

This chapter has focused primarily on the conflict in values between the free expression of information and ideas, and the interests of the government in such sensitive areas (as the government perceives them) as national security and domestic order. This conflict continues unabated as a result of the government's effort to censor its own employees and the government-engendered fear of reporters that they will face punishment in national security cases if they don't conform to governmental desires.

In this present era of sabre rattling, free expression and the dissemination of ideas suffer most not from government prior restraint, but because the media, fearing they will face government wrath, censor themselves.

One of the most eloquent arguments for the public's right to freely receive information was written, ironically, by the first judge in the U.S. who ever barred publication of a news article. In the *Pentagon Papers* case, Judge Gurfein wrote:

> The First Amendment concept of "free press" must be read in light of the struggle of free men against prior restraint of publication. From the time of Blackstone, it was a tenet of the founding fathers that precensorship was the primary evil to be dealt with in the First Amendment . . . If there be some embarrassment to the government in security aspects as remote as the general embarrassment that flows from any security breach, we must learn to live with it. The security of the nation is not at the ramparts alone. Security also lies in the value of our free institutions. A cantankerous press, an obstinate press, an ubiquitous press, must be suffered by those in authority in order to preserve the even greater values of freedom of expression and the right of the people to know . . . [22]

But how can you effectuate this role as the cantankerous press, given the climate of fear and uncertainty in which you operate? We suggest that you do what brave reporters have always done, which is keep a tight lip, stay within the law as best you understand it, and publish. When the government reads, hears, or sees all about it, it will be too late to restrain publication.

We hope that American editors and reporters will continue to follow their journalistic instincts to publish and not bow to censorship, government- or self-inflicted, when they honestly believe there is a public right to the material and that it will not endanger national security. If our press ever works out a cooperative relationship with the government, it will cease to be a free press. [23]

21. *The New York Times*, December 15, 1982.
22. *New York Times v. United States*, 444 F.2d 544 (2nd Cir. 1971).
23. Media Alliance — an organization of 2000 writers, editors, and broadcast media workers — has set up a project to oppose censorship. They can be contacted at Building D, Fort Mason, San Francisco CA 94123, (415) 441-2557.

Libel and
the Journalist

"The right of a man to the protection of his own reputation from unjustified invasion and wrongful hurt reflects no more than our basic concept of the essential dignity and worth of every human being—a concept at the root of any decent system of ordered liberty." *Rosenblatt v. Baer*, 383 U.S. 75, 92; 86 S.Ct. 669, 679; 15 L.Ed.2d 597, 609 (1966).

A.   The Media Under Attack

Nothing so effectively deters publication of a potentially controversial story as the threat of a libel suit. Only twenty years ago, libel verdicts rarely exceeded $20,000. In the last five years, however, juries have frequently returned record-breaking verdicts. Some observers feel that big awards may be even more common in the future, because jurors don't seem to like the news media. The impression that reporters are chronically careless with the facts and cavalier with people's reputations and private lives seems to be growing.

One case involving a large verdict was Carol Burnett's suit against *The National Enquirer*. On March 2, 1976, *The National Enquirer* ran the following headline about the entertainer: "Carol Burnett and Henry K. in Row." The story read:

At a Washington restaurant, a boisterous Carol Burnett had a loud argument with another diner, Henry Kissinger. Then she traipsed around the place offering everyone a bite of her dessert. But Carol really raised eyebrows when she accidentally knocked a glass of wine over on one diner—and started giggling instead of apologizing. The guy wasn't amused and "accidentally" spilled a glass of water on Carol's dress.

Burnett, denying the incident took place, demanded a retraction and apology. *The Enquirer* complied in its April 13th issue, but Burnett found the retraction inadequate. She later said it was "tantamount to my being run over by a hit-and-run driver and then they send me a bouquet of crab grass." In February 1981, a Los Angeles jury apparently agreed, as it awarded Burnett $300,000 in compensatory damages, largely for emotional distress, and $1.3 million in punitive damages.[1]

While the journalistic ethics of the *National Enquirer* might not be countenanced by most working reporters, successful libel suits are becoming more common against less flamboyant media organizations as well. In one case, for example, the *Alton Telegraph* originally lost a libel suit to the tune of $9.2 million which resulted in an ultimate settlement of approximately $1.5 million after the paper filed for bankruptcy. In another case, a jury assessed $26.5 million against *Penthouse* magazine in a libel suit brought by a former Miss Wyoming.

According to statistics compiled by the Libel Defense Resource Center (an information clearinghouse established by concerned news organizations), media defendants have lost approximately 85% of the 53 full-scale trials held during the past two years. Although 75% of these decisions were reversed or the awards substantially modified on appeal, for various reasons, the time and expense involved in this sort of litigation has been staggering. Thus, even though the appellate courts have imposed a number of limitations on libel suits in recognition of the adverse effects which such suits might have on freedom of expression, the mere threat of being sued at all has caused some publishers and broadcasters to become leery of reporting potentially controversial stories.[2]

B.   Libel and the Constitution

Although we define the term more specifically later in the chapter, libel essentially involves a false and damaging attack on another's reputation or character. Libel has traditionally been considered a personal injury or "tort" of the same order as a physical battery or false imprisonment. Since the definition of "tort law" has traditionally been left to the states, libel law has accordingly been considered a matter of state concern exclusively.

However, because imposing liability for libel necessarily "punishes" speech as such, a latent conflict always existed between state libel laws and the free speech provisions of the First Amendment to the U.S. Constitution. In 1964 this conflict was finally recognized and at least partially resolved.

In the case of *New York Times Co. v. Sullivan*,[3] the U.S. Supreme Court "constitutionalized" the state law of libel in respect to statements concerning public officials. (This was broadened in later cases to include "public figures.") We will examine the extremely significant effect of this case in more detail later in this chapter. For now, however, you should understand that since *Times v. Sullivan*, all journalists are governed by two sets of rules: 1) the old common law (state-by-state) libel statutes, when dealing with private individuals, and 2) the newer, federal constitutional standard, when dealing with public figures and officials.

The latter standard, usually referred to as the *N.Y. Times* rule, states that public officials and figures cannot recover damages for libel without proof that the libel was published with

---

1. Burnett's award was ultimately reduced from $300,000 to $50,000 in compensatory damages and $1.3 million to $150,000 in punitive damages.

2. In some situations, however, the media have not only fought a valiant defensive battle but have in turn required the plaintiffs to compensate them for at least part of their attorneys' fees incurred in defending the suit. This was true of *Time Magazine*, which successfully fought a libel suit brought by the Synanon Foundation arising from an article labelling that group a "kooky cult." See "Press Bites Back at Libel Suits," *The News Media and the Law*, Vol. 5, No. 2, June/July 1981, pp. 22-25.

3. 376 U.S. 254, 84 S.Ct. 710, 11 L.Ed.2d 686 (1964).

deliberate knowledge of its falsity, or with reckless disregard of the truth (known as "actual malice").

C.   What Is Libel?

1. A Working Definition

Enough background. Let's now examine what libel is and how to deal with the dichotomy between the rights of a free press to publish without fear, and the rights of the individual to be protected against unfair damage to her reputation.

Libel can best be defined as any false statement about a person which is communicated to one or more third persons and which tends to bring that person into public hatred, contempt, or ridicule, or to injure her in her business or occupation. Libel may be printed or broadcast.

2. Basic Requirements for a Libel Case

A person who claims she was libeled must prove the following in court:

a. **Publication:** The statement must be printed, broadcast, drawn, or photographed, and read or seen by someone other than the plaintiff.

b. **Identification:** A third person encountering the statement would reasonably believe it applies to the person claiming to have been libeled.

c. **Defamatory Content:** The statement must tend to injure the plaintiff's reputation or subject her to shame and ridicule in the community.

d. **Damages:** The person suing must show some kind of actual injury to her business or reputation in order to qualify for any substantial amount of damages.

e. **Fault:** The reporter must have been less than perfect in her reporting. The standard of journalistic conduct that reporters are held to in libel cases not involving public officials or public figures is extremely high. Put simply, the law allows you little room to be wrong. Nevertheless, the person suing must prove some degree of negligence on the part of the journalist (i.e., that the journalist did not behave prudently under the circumstances).

If you are sued for libel and any of these basic elements are missing, you are entitled to win the case.

3. The Difference Between Libel and Slander

Libel is one of two subcategories of the tort called "defamation" (a tort is a personal injury for which the law authorizes the award of damages). The other is "slander." Traditionally, libel has been defined as defamatory material presented in a written or visual form, whereas slander is oral or spoken defamation. However, most states[4] now define broadcast defamation as libel, since a written script often precedes the spoken word. For the purpose of media law then, libel is the more important tort and we will often use it in a broad sense to include slander.

4. State Variations

The definition of libel, the types of proof necessary in different contexts, and the categories of people whose statements are privileged (exempt from liability) all differ slightly among the states. Accordingly, the descriptions of law we provide here should be taken as working ones rather than as precise statements of every state's laws.

UNIFORM RULE NOTE: Happily, there is one important aspect of libel law which is true in all states: A journalist will only be held responsible for libel if her false statements were made with at least some degree of negligence. If a reporter is careless and relatively unconcerned with the accuracy of what is reported, the way *may* be open for a libel action. On the other hand, if the reporter takes every reasonable step to assure the accuracy of her reporting and still makes a mistake, the libel laws should not apply to her publication.

5. What Constitutes Publication?

a. Initial Publication

The first legal requirement for a libel action is "publication." Obviously, you can have false and nasty thoughts about a person without being held liable for them. You can even communicate them directly to that person without committing libel. Only when your defamatory thoughts are expressed to a third party does the possibility of injury to the person's reputation become an issue. Defamatory communication to a third party is known as "publication." As far as libel is concerned, publication is not limited to its ordinary meaning in the sense of printing and distribution of written material. In libel law, publication can also be accomplished by spoken[5] or written statements, photographs, drawings, gestures, and any other form of communication which would reasonably be understood to be defamatory by at least one other person.

---

4. California is a major exception; it treats defamation in broadcasts as slander (California Civil Code Section 48a).

5. As we discussed above, spoken defamatory statements have traditionally been referred to as slander. This is still true in some states.

b. Re-Publication and Single Publication Rules

Publication is usually not a contested issue when a media organization is sued for libel. Why? Because by definition, the media disseminates information to the world at large. But, assuming a libelous publication has been made, is each copy of a newspaper or each place a broadcast was seen or heard a "separate publication" and therefore the basis for yet another lawsuit? The answer is generally "No," under the "single publication rule." This rule provides that only one cause of action for defamation arises when the product of a press run or printing is released by the publisher for distribution, no matter how many separate transactions may result.[6] The reason for this rule, of course, is that otherwise one article might give rise to a million causes of action.

Re-publication becomes important when a defamatory statement is published again long after the original publication. In most states, there is a fairly short time period (called the statute of limitations) after a libelous statement is made within which a person may bring suit for libel (usually 1 or 2 years). This is because injuries from libelous statements tend to be relatively immediate (memories are short). But, what happens if a new edition of an old work is published?

For example, assume a softcover edition of a 1972 hardbound book is released in 1985. Is a person who is libeled by the book eligible to bring a law suit in 1985, even though she did not sue after the 1972 publication and thus has been barred from doing so by the statute of limitations for many years? The answer is "Yes." Why? Because under the re-publication rule, the second publication is considered a new publication with a new statute of limitations period. The theory is that each new tale bearer is as blameworthy as the original tale maker. Thus, if you report a statement by somebody which itself was defamatory, you may be subject to a libel action on the basis of such repetition even if the story comes from a "reliable source" or news service, and even if you don't endorse the truth of the statement.

Fortunately, the media can avoid actual liability for libel by taking the proper precautionary steps associated with responsible reporting. We suggest a number of these in Section J, at the end of this chapter. Basically, however, just following the accepted standards of ethical journalism will keep you safe in most instances. For example, publishing material from one of the major wire services which later turns out to be inaccurate will not be considered negligence unless circumstances dictated further investigation.

CAUTIONARY NOTE: When a local newspaper or station repeats a wire service story which is defamatory of a local person, the chances are higher that it will be sued than if the story involves somebody half way across the country. For this reason, wire service stories involving local people or issues should be subjected to greater scrutiny than would otherwise be the case. If you have any doubt at all as to the accuracy of what is provided, independent investigation is definitely warranted.

6. Identification of the Libel Victim

a. Generally

To be libelous, a publication must be able to be reasonably understood as referring to the plaintiff. Of course there is no problem if the plaintiff is named or depicted in a photograph. What happens, however, if a plaintiff's identity is hinted at by insinuation or innuendo? A

---

6. In California, an entire edition of newspapers is treated as a single publication instead of every single copy.

person need not be specifically named or depicted in the allegedly libelous material to have a case. But, she must establish that either:

- by clear implication the communication referred to her or
- outside circumstances not stated in the article would cause reasonable people who knew the plaintiff to connect the statement to her.

To better understand these rules, let's refer to the famous libel case *New York Times v. Sullivan*. In 1964, an ad was published in the *New York Times* describing how black students at Alabama State College were met with a "wave of terror" by local police. As the supervisor of the police in question, L.B. Sullivan claimed that anyone would know that he was the person responsible for the police action described in the article. The Court held that Sullivan was in fact adequately identified under these circumstances, despite the absence of his name or picture in the article, and therefore had fulfilled the identification requirement for a libel action.

b. Mistaken Identity

You don't have to intend to libel someone to do so. Mistaken identity may result in libel too. This is one reason why responsible media organizations must spend so much time checking facts. For example, if a newspaper publishes a correct story that Sarah Seidman was indicted for a crime, and then inadvertently includes a picture of the wrong Ms. Seidman, the result may be libel (if all elements are present).

c. Group Identification

An individual member of a group which has been libeled can bring an action under certain limited circumstances. Suppose, for example, a columnist after a Super Bowl game asserts that Dallas Cowboy fans are stupid and boorish. The general rule is that if a group is so large the reader or listener will be unlikely to understand specifically to whom the defamation refers, the courts will dismiss the action. The usual, but by no means absolute, rule of thumb is that a group of twenty five or more is too large to support a libel action.

On the other hand, the courts will permit actions by individual members of small homogenous groups. For example, the author of *U.S.A. Confidential* was sued for libel because he had called "some" models and "all" saleswomen employed by the Dallas Neiman-Marcus department store, "call girls." He also reported that "most" of the salesmen in the men's department were "faggots." At the time, Neiman's employed nine models, 382 saleswomen, and twenty-five salesmen. The court allowed the salesmen to sue, even though the accusation said "most" rather than "all," but dismissed the action by the saleswomen because there were so many of them.[7] See Section J at the end of this chapter for some tips on how to avoid group libel.

7. What Constitutes Defamatory Material

As we've seen, for a statement to be libelous, it must be published and must be understood on its face or by reference to outside (extrinsic) circumstances to refer to the person taking offense. In addition, the statement must contain defamatory material. What then is the definition of "defamatory?"

A statement must be false to be defamatory. True statements are not defamatory no matter how much they sting (but truth may not help you if you are sued for invasion of privacy, a

---

7. *Neiman-Marcus v. Lait,* 107 F.Supp. 96 (S.D.N.Y. 1952).

subject covered extensively in Chapter 4). What else beside falsity is required to make a publication defamatory?

The textbook definition of "defamatory" is anything which injures a person's reputation or good name, or holds him up to shame, embarrassment or ridicule in his community. Determining which statements do and don't do this can often be difficult. If you doubt this, make up a list of nasty statements about people. Include some public officials and famous people on your list. Make sure some of your statements are at least first cousins to the truth. Now ask your colleagues which statements they would consider to be legally defamatory. Did any two agree? We bet not.

What constitutes a defamatory publication is a most fluid concept depending heavily on the nature of the times as well as the position of the person libeled. Falsely labeling someone a "Communist" during the early World War II period, when the United States and the Soviet Union were in alliance, would probably not have been the basis for a successful lawsuit. However, the same false label was considered worse than that of "child molester" less than ten years later during the Cold War. How the label "Communist" would be treated now is unclear, but given the cooling of detente between the U.S. and Soviet Union, you obviously should treat it as one of those "red flag" words (i.e., a word you should avoid, if possible, unless you are absolutely sure of the truth of your statement).

Another good example of how the meaning of "defamatory" changes with the times involves imputing lack of chastity to a woman. In the 1980's, when the best seller lists are topped by such books as *Nice Girls Do, and So Can You*, implying that a woman has a sex life can hardly have the same impact as would have been true a generation or two ago. Indeed, today many women might be insulted if they were falsely referred to as "chaste" or "virginal."

Even so, the majority of judges are older men, and thus, traditional male attitudes towards women still play a large role in many of their decisions. For example, in Minnesota, the law still provides that the retraction of "any libel imputing unchastity to a woman" will not relieve the libeler of responsibility.

What is defamatory will continue to change as mores and attitudes evolve. It also varies somewhat from one community to another at any given time. This makes it useless and probably misleading for us to list all the words that have been previously held to be defamatory.

The important point is, words which have been held to be defamatory were so held because the average reader or listener reasonably understood the words to be so harmful and derogatory as to injure a person's reputation. If the statement is merely unflattering, annoying, irking, embarrassing, or just hurts the plaintiff's feelings, an action for libel should not be successful. Commonly, name calling and hyperbole fall into this category.

In understanding libel law, then, it is obviously crucial to distinguish between what is merely insulting and what actually injures reputation. For example, if you reported statements made by an irate citizen that a local public transportation head was a thief, whose decisions were typical of a demented and insane man, you would be dealing with defamatory material. Conversely, reporting an angry reference by a political candidate to his rival as "paranoid" and "schizophrenic" is probably okay, given the hyperbolic context of a political campaign. In fact, political campaigns have generally become so nasty that it's probably impossible for a candidate successfuly to sue his or her opponent for libel.

Unfortunately, while there are no hard and fast rules in this area, it is safe to say that the context in which particular words are used and the reasonable understanding of people at large are the keys to determining whether or not the statements would be subject to a lawsuit. How can you as journalists deal with this slippery subject?

First, remember that there are several types of reputation which, if impugned, are likely to cause injury:

a. **Honesty and Trustworthiness:** A reputation for honesty and trustworthiness is important. Calling someone dishonest, a thief, or a liar is likely to create libel suit trouble in a hurry;

b. **Law Abiding:** Never accuse someone of breaking the law unless you can back it up with a conviction record or other strong proof;

c. **Professional or Business Reputation:** A business reputation for competence and fair dealing is economically important to the person or enterprise enjoying it. An attack on this type of reputation can result in an instantaneous libel suit; and

d. **Physical and Mental Health, Virtue, Temperance, etc.:** All personal characteristics should be treated circumspectly. If you say someone has a drinking problem, V.D. or a long history of mental instability, you had better be able to back it up.

EMPATHY HINT: It never hurts to let empathy be your guide. Think how important your reputation as an honest reporter is to you economically and socially. What words, allegations, and charges would you feel are an unfair and hurtful attack on your reputation and personality? The goal of a good journalist is obviously to tell the truth without pulling punches, but to do so in a way that does not unnecessarily injure or destroy reputations.

WARNING! If a statement is ambiguous and capable of two or more interpretations, one of them innocent and the other defamatory, you are probably not in the clear. In New York, California, and most other populous states, the courts are under no obligation to interpret words in their mildest and most unoffensive form. However, Illinois, Missouri, Ohio and Montana have what is called the "innocent construction rule," which states that as a matter of law, words should be construed in their most innocent sense.

8. How Are Damages Computed in Libel Cases?

Even if a plaintiff can show publication, identification and defamatory material, there is little point in suing unless she can also establish that some kind of injury or damage resulted from the libel. There are several different categories of damages (monetary recompense for injury) a court can award. Each must be based on a different showing of harm.

a. Compensatory or General Damages

These are awarded as direct compensation for injury to reputation and are typically based on a showing that the plaintiff suffered injured feelings, humiliation, shame or insult, mental and physical anguish, or presumed injury to business or occupation. Generally, these types of damages cannot actually be proved but must be inferred from the circumstances. Thus, Carol Burnett was able to establish that the *Enquirer* article caused her to feel humiliated and insulted, and she was accordingly awarded general damages for such feelings.

b. Special or Actual Damages

These are meant to compensate for real, tangible monetary loss which is provable. For example, is a fast food restaurant could show a loss of business as a result of a publication that it uses worms in its hamburger meat, it would be entitled to special or actual damages measured by its provable business losses caused by the publication.

In most states, special damages must be shown if the libel is indirect (i.e., depends on extrinsic circumstances for its defamatory content).[8] For example, if a newspaper article erroneously reported that Mary Margaret McGillicuddy of 27 Langley Road had just given birth to quintuplets, this story would probably be libelous if Ms. McGillicuddy had been married only two months or was a nun and several readers knew this fact. But, in this situation, Mary Margaret would generally have to prove she had incurred actual out-of-pocket loss (i.e., special damages) to maintain a successful action.[9]

c. Punitive or Exemplary Damages

This type of damage award is intended to punish and make an example of those who libel intentionally or recklessly. The point, of course, is to discourage similar behavior by the defendant and others in the future. Because punitive damages are supposed to hurt the defendant, they can be quite high if the defendant is a wealthy corporation, since a lesser amount would only be a "slap on the wrist." Accordingly, the multimillion dollar jury verdicts consist largely of punitive damages and reflect the desire of juries to curb what they consider to be irresponsible behavior by the media.

Fortunately for the media, the First Amendment stands between media libel defendants and angry juries. The Supreme Court recognizes that "jury discretion to award punitive damages unnecessarily exacerbates the danger of media self-censorship." Thus, the Court requires that a libel plaintiff must establish clearly and convincingly that the publication was made with actual malice (knew or should have known statement was false), before punitive damages may be recovered. This is true whether the person is a private or public figure, or a public official. As an additional protection to the media against punitive damage awards, many state statutes (30) allow punitive damages only if the media has refused to print a retraction when requested to do so.[10]

---

8. At common law, this was known as libel *per quod* or libel by innuendo, implication, or due to an outside circumstance over which the writer has no control.

9. The two traditional categories of damages — compensatory and special — have now been at least partially blended because of a 1974 Supreme court case, *Gertz v. Robert Welch, Inc.*, 418 U.S. 323, 94 S.Ct. 2997, 41 L.Ed.2d 789 (1974). That case ruled 1) that a private plaintiff may only recover damages necessary to compensate for "actual injury," and 2) that "actual injury" includes the customary tapes of actual harm inflicted by defamatory falsehood (e.g., impairment of reputation and standing in the community, personal humiliation, mental anguish and suffering) as well as "out of pocket" losses.

10. Massachusetts, Pennsylvania, and Washington do not award punitive damages at all.

JUDGE FOR YOURSELF: TYPES OF DAMAGES

Suppose you, a journalist, receive a call from a local high school counselor accusing the School Superintendent, David Martin, of child neglect. The counselor tells you she received her information from Martin's eight-year-old daughter, who reported numerous incidents of food deprivation, lack of physical care and physical detention in her room for long periods of time. The counselor adds that she plans to contact the Child Protective Services division of the local welfare department.

With a little digging, you uncover the following facts: 1) the counselor who called you is locked in a battle with the school district over her job; 2) the daughter has been under the care of a child psychiatrist for the past year; and 3) the child has not been hospitalized or sent home from school for health related problems. You call Child Protective Services for additional information but they refuse to talk with you about the case, except to verify that they've received a complaint from the counselor.

Despite a nagging doubt about the story, you decide to publish. It turns out to be false. Are you guilty of libel? If so, what types of damages might be assessed?

—————Answer—————

Your story would most likely be considered libelous. Why? You "published" a false story injurious to another person's reputation under circumstances that warranted further investigation before publication. What about damages? To obtain special damages, School Superintendent Martin would have to show some loss of income, as would be the result if he was suspended without pay or lost his job. He could also sue for general and compensatory damages for the loss of reputation and shame experienced by him and his family. Finally, because of the surrounding circumstances, you might well be considered to have acted with actual malice (you acted with reckless disregard of whether the story was true or false). If so, Mr. Martin could recover punitive damages.

Now assume the facts were different. The Child Protective Services Division had completed an investigation and referred the matter to the police for possible criminal prosecution. The child had in fact manifested symptoms of malnutrition and general physical neglect and had been hospitalized.

In this situation, even if the story turned out to be false, punitive damages would probably be inappropriate since under these facts you would not be considered to have acted with actual malice. Indeed, you might even escape liability altogether if your report was a fair and accurate accounting of the charges and ongoing investigation and you could demonstrate exhaustive efforts to check the facts. [11]

---

11. A fair, accurate report of official proceedings is usually immune from a libel suit under state libel laws, due to the fact that statements made in the course of such proceedings are privileged. The subject of when police investigations may be considered "official proceedings," and other aspects of this topic, are discussed in more detail later in this chapter.

9. Fault as an Element of Libel

a. Some Fault Is Required

So far, we've seen that to make out a cause of action for libel, a plaintiff must show: 1) publication, 2) identification of the libel victim, 3) defamatory material, and 4) some kind of damage. Even if all these hurdles are met by a person claiming to be libeled, however, there is a fifth and final element which must be proved before a libel victim may collect from a journalist or media organization. The media defendant must have been at least unacceptably careless (negligent) in publishing the objectionable material, if liability is to attach. Put another way, the defendant must have violated a duty or standard of care imposed by law. As we mentioned earlier, this rule is true in all fifty states, although some states require a showing of even greater fault than mere negligence in order to hold a media defendant responsible for libel.

b. Fault When Public Officials and Figures Are Involved

If the plaintiff is a public official or public figure (these terms are defined and discussed later in this chapter), she must prove that the journalist was more than negligent, and that in fact she acted with actual malice (discussed fully later in this chapter).

c. Fault When Private Individuals Are Involved

If the plaintiff is a private person (defined later in this chapter), the journalist is on safe legal ground in all states, so long as reasonable care was taken under the circumstances to generate a truthful report, even if the report turns out to be false. Unfortunately, however, we can give you no accurate definition of what constitutes "reasonable care." This tends to be a slippery concept. In practice, it is defined by the judge and jury in each individual libel case.

In our first example of the school superintendent accused of child neglect, the journalist probably did not exercise reasonable care. Why not? The facts in the case tended to make both the counselor and the child unreliable witnesses. Publishing defamatory material solely on the basis of information gleaned from such people is not something a reasonably prudent person would do, absent extraordinary circumstances. It can thus be viewed as negligent reporting. On the other hand, in our second set of facts, the information from the counselor and daughter was supported and confirmed by additional *reliable* information. Thus, under the second set of facts, publishing the story would probably not be considered negligent.

Arizona, Arkansas, California, Florida, Hawaii, Illinois, Kansas, Kentucky, Maryland, Massachusetts, North Carolina, Ohio, Oklahoma, Tennessee, Texas, Washington, District of Columbia, and Puerto Rico are among those jurisdictions which have adopted a negligence standard. Other states require negligence or even a greater degree of fault for a plaintiff to prevail over a media defendant.

d. Fault When Publication Is of Public Interest

Alaska, Colorado, Indiana, and Michigan have applied the "actual malice" standard of knowing falsehood or reckless disregard of the truth to libel litigation between private individuals involving matters of public interest. As we discuss in Chapter 4 in relation to invasions of privacy, the concept of public interest is extremely broad and thus, for all practical purposes, actual malice must be shown to bring a successful libel action in these four states.

e. Fault Under the Prudent Publisher Rule

New York alone uses what is known as the "prudent publisher" standard of liability. Under this test, a media defendant is not liable unless a plaintiff can show a gross departure from journalistic standards. This essentially means that in New York, a private libel plaintiff must show a media defendant to be more than negligent but does not have to meet the "actual malice" standard. As is true with all these tests, what actually constitutes a "gross departure from journalistic standards" can only be determined on a case by case basis. Using our example of the school superintendent, such publication would probably have met the New York test under the first set of facts but definitely not under the second set.

f. Fault and Business Entity Plaintiffs

A corporation or business, like an individual, may recover general, special, and punitive damages for a libel, depending on the circumstances and the positions of the parties. To allege, for example, that a smoke shop is a front for a bookmaking and drug dealing operation is defamatory, and the owners of the smoke shop may bring suit. Whether the business is considered to be a public or private figure, and what fault must be shown to recover, depends on the state and the facts of each case.

IMPORTANT REMINDER: Although this discussion can be a little scary for you, the practicing journalist, remember that in all states a journalist is shielded from libel judgments so long as all precautions were taken which were reasonable under the circumstances.

THE BIG QUESTION: What is reasonable under the circumstances, or, how much fact-checking must you do before you feel secure that you haven't violated your state's standard of care? Again, there is no easy answer. Each fact situation is determined on its own merits. If you work for a daily, and you are under deadline pressure, you are in a different position than that of an investigative reporter who is writing an article for a monthly magazine. The general rule is, the more lead time you have before publication, the greater your duty to check and recheck your facts. For specific additional suggestions on how to steer clear of a libel suit, see Section J at the end of this chapter.

10. Collective Responsibility for Libel

Many people are usually directly involved in the publication or broadcast of material which becomes the target of a libel suit. The journalist, author, producer, director, photographer, cameraman, editor, publisher, corporate owner, distributor, broadcaster, channel, network, and news or book store may all be sued in the same libel case, depending of course on the nature of the publication. This is done for several reasons. An important one is simply that when a story appears, the person bringing suit commonly has no way of knowing where the true fault lies. She therefore needs to sue everyone connected with the publication to maximize her chances of recovering damages. As important, the plaintiff in a libel suit is looking for the "deep pocket" (the defendant best able to cough up a large damages award). Given journalists' wages, the "deep pocket" tends to be the corporate entity which owns the newspaper, radio or TV station.

A jury can make everyone involved in "publishing" the material jointly and individually liable for the ultimate award in the case. When this happens, the various defendants fight among themselves to see who is ultimately responsible, but the plaintiff can collect from any or all of them, so long as the total amount collected does not exceed the award. Libel insurance is discussed later in this chapter.

11. Visual Guide

Up to this point we have received the showing that a plaintiff must make in order to prevail in a libel suit against the media. Before we go on to some common defenses available to the media in these types of actions, however, a review of the following diagram should help cement in your mind the material we have covered so far.

A SUMMARY OF THE LEGAL ELEMENTS
A PLAINTIFF MUST PROVE TO WIN A LIBEL LAWSUIT

If a journalist is sued for libel, the person claiming to be injured (the plaintiff) must prove a number of legal facts (elements) to prevail. If he or she fails to do this, the journalist defendant prevails. If the elements are proven, the journalist may still offer defenses which are covered in the next section.

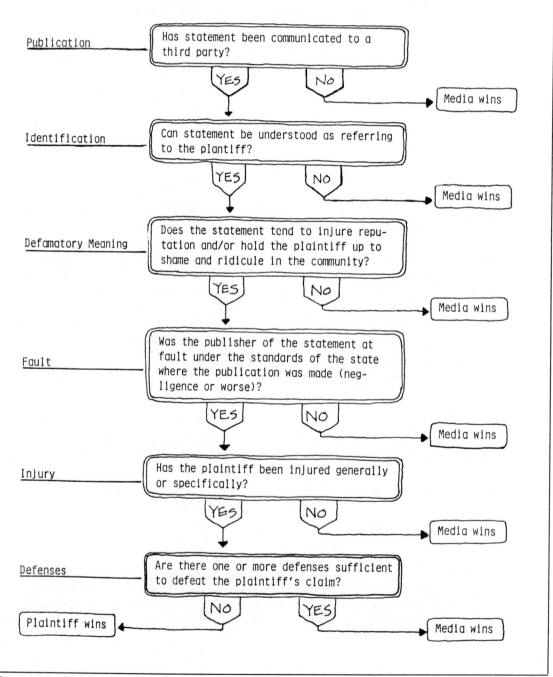

Publication — Has statement been communicated to a third party?
- YES ↓
- NO → Media wins

Identification — Can statement be understood as referring to the plantiff?
- YES ↓
- NO → Media wins

Defamatory Meaning — Does the statement tend to injure reputation and/or hold the plaintiff up to shame and ridicule in the community?
- YES ↓
- NO → Media wins

Fault — Was the publisher of the statement at fault under the standards of the state where the publication was made (negligence or worse)?
- YES ↓
- NO → Media wins

Injury — Has the plaintiff been injured generally or specifically?
- YES ↓
- NO → Media wins

Defenses — Are there one or more defenses sufficient to defeat the plaintiff's claim?
- NO → Plaintiff wins
- YES → Media wins

D. How to Defend Against a Libel Suit

1. Overview

The person who claims to have been libeled must prove the necessary legal elements of a libel action along the lines discussed in Section C above. If she fails to do so, you, as a media defendant, will win without lifting a finger. If, on the other hand, the plaintiff is able to establish each of the elements required for a libel judgment, it will be your turn to come forward and defend.

What does it mean to say a media defendant has a "defense"? Simply put, a defense is a state of facts which, *if proven by the defendant,* will entitle her to prevail in the action. This means that the burden is on the defendant to prove such facts. What specific sets of facts are allowed by the courts as defenses to a libel action depends on previous court cases, statutes, and the U.S. Constitution. The three primary types of defenses may be categorized accordingly as 1) common law defenses; 2) statutory law defenses; and 3) constitutional defenses (see Appendix A for a full discussion of these terms).

2. Common Law Defenses to Libel

Under the common law, the only defenses against a libel suit were "truth," "consent" and "fair comment." Then, *New York Times v. Sullivan* and later cases provided the media with the constitutional defense of privilege (immunity from liability unless actual malice is present) when sued by public officials or public figures. This is discussed fully later in this section. However, the common law defenses remain vital in cases involving *private figure* plaintiffs, and we turn to them first.

a. The Defense of Truth

Generally speaking, truth is a complete defense to a libel suit—that is, it will totally bar the plaintiff from recovery.[12] But don't wipe your brow and give a sigh of relief quite yet. Even though you made certain in your own mind your story was true, you are not home free. Why? Because knowing something to be true, and proving it in a court of law, are feathers from entirely different birds. Remember, since this is a defense, the burden of proof is squarely on you.

Sometimes the evidence to prove the truth of a statement is just not available. To establish your version of the facts, you may need documents, tapes and photos to which only the plaintiff has access and he will not readily turn over, even in a formal discovery proceeding (see Appendix A for a discussion of "discovery"). In short, truth can sometimes be a costly and hazardous defense. At the very least, a reporter in a potentially vulnerable situation would do well to think ahead and consider how the truth of a particular assertion might be proved if necessary.

In making truth your defense, it will not help to demonstrate that your report was an accurate repetition of a libelous charge. The truth of the charge itself must be established even though you were not the originator of the story. Although you only need to establish that a

---

12. For cases involving private plaintiffs, over half the states allow truth as a defense only if the communication was published with good motives and for justifiable ends.

statement is "substantially true," your defense will nevertheless fail if only a portion of the publication can be verified.

This is also true if you erroneously report a person guilty of one type of misconduct when in fact she is guilty of another. For example, if you falsely report that Kim McIntosh was charged with burglary, it is no defense to offer proof that she committed a murder. (Of course, Kim might have trouble getting much in the way of actual damages for injury to reputation). Or, if you carry a news story that Joe Schmoe is a habitual vice offender, you probably will not be successful in your truth defense if the only evidence you can offer is one conviction for a minor gambling violation that occurred fifteen years ago.

To determine whether or not a publication is true, the courts will consider it in its entirety and in relation to its structure, nuances, innuendo, and implications. For example, suppose you reported that Sue Gilliam shot Maria Cronin after finding Mr. Gilliam at Maria's house, but you neglected to mention that Mr. Cronin and several neighbors were also present and that the shooting was accidental. Although your story is literally accurate, this would be insufficient to defend against a rather obvious defamation.

b. Neutral Reportage

Much of the time "the news" which media people report consists of statements made by others. Sources such as wire services, news syndicates, and "rip and read" operations (used heavily in radio news), provide information which the journalist reports without establishing any actual personal contact with the story. In all types of media, statements by newsworthy individuals (i.e., the fire chief or mafia boss) and statements which themselves are newsworthy (e.g., an eyewitness account of a massacre) are commonly reported as such, without investigatory followup. Doesn't this raise potential libel problems? After all, we learned earlier that a journalist may be guilty of libel for accurately reporting the false or defamatory statements of others, no matter how responsible the spokesperson or how newsworthy the story.

Recognizing this as a problem, some courts have adopted a concept dubbed "neutral reportage." The first and best judicial articulation of this principle was made in relation to a *New York Times* article about birds. [13] The article repeated a National Audubon Society charge that segments of the pesticide industry and certain scientists lied when they said bird life in America is thriving despite the use of DDT.   The scientists sued the *Times* and the National Audubon Society. The court said:

> What is newsworthy about such accusations is that they were made. We do not believe that the press may be required under the First Amendment to suppress newsworthy statements merely because it has serious doubts regarding their truth . . . . The public interest in being fully informed about controversies that often rage around sensitive issues demands that the press be afforded the freedom to report such charges without assuming responsibility for them. [14]

The neutral reportage concept has not enjoyed much success. It has been adopted by an Illinois appellate court, a federal district court in Wyoming, and an appellate court in New York. Some other courts have rejected it. Most states have yet to decide whether they're for or against it. Unfortunately, there is no way to tell whether the courts in your state will adopt it or not if you raise it as a defense. If this is a problem area for you, consult the lawyer who represents your corporation or a good independent media lawyer.

---

13. *Edwards v. National Audubon Society*, 556 F.2d 113 (2nd Cir. 1977) *cert. den.* 98 S.Ct. 647 (1977).
14. *Ibid.* at 120.

c. The "Opinion" or "Fair Comment" Defense

Under the common law, comments and opinions have long been distinguised from bald statements of fact. The statement, "In my opinion, John is a thief," is different from the statement, "John is a thief." The former is self-qualified as a mere opinion and therefore not as inherently dangerous to reputation as is the latter, a definite accusation. Thus, if defamatory material could be fairly characterized as an opinion or comment rather than as a statement of fact, the plaintiff would have a more difficult time recovering under the rule which "protect[s] honest criticism of men, measures, and social institutions seeking public acceptance."

This distinction has been given constitutional status by the U.S. Supreme Court, which held that: "Under the First Amendment, there is no such thing as a false idea. No matter how pernicious an opinion may be, we must depend for its correction not on the conscience of judges and juries, but on the competition of other ideas.[15] Therefore, if you succeed in establishing your remarks as opinion or fair comment, you are provided a partial defense by the Constitution as well as by the common law.

The opinion or fair comment defense is not absolute. Thus, if you say, "In my opinion, John is a thief," and John can establish that you knew better, you would most likely be facing a libel judgment. What exactly is the opinion/fair comment defense?

Chief among its elements are:

1. The comment or opinion must be on a matter of public interest; and
2. The comment or opinion must be based upon specifically stated facts which are believed to be true; and
3. The comment must not be "malicious" (i.e., made with knowledge of its falsity or with reckless disregard for the truth).

If these elements are present, the law protects the publication even though it may contain exaggeration, illogic, sarcasm, ridicule, and even viciousness. The classic example is the critique of a vaudeville act by an Iowa newspaper drama critic:

> Effie is an old jade of 50 summers, Jessie is a frisky filly of 40, and Addie, the flower of the family, a capering monstrosity of 35. Their long skinny arms, equipped with talons at the extremities, swung mechanically, and anon waved frantically at the suffering audience. The mouths of their rancid features opened like caverns, and sounds like the wailings of damned souls issued therefrom. . . .[16]

As you might imagine, the sisters were upset and sued the Des Moines newspaper for libel. The Iowa Supreme Court, however, directed a verdict for the newspaper based on the right of the newspaper to critique.

The problem with this defense is that the line between fact and opinion is often blurred. Context is important (e.g., restaurant review, humor piece, column), but phrasing can also be determinative. How can you tell when opinion is opinion and nothing more? When is an opinion based on a false fact? When is a false fact presented in the sheep's clothing of an opinon? These questions must be answered when the fair comment/opinion defense is raised, since their answers will determine whether or not the defense properly applies to the defamatory material in question.

As an example of how the fair comment/opinion defense works, we will look at the facts of one reported case where the line between "fact" and "opinion" was hard to find. A *New York Times* reporter conducted an in-depth interview of Janis Ian in which the singer discussed the business problems of another singer, Phoebe Snow. In the ensuing article, Ian was quoted as

---

15. *Gertz v. Welch*, 418 U.S. 323, 94 S.Ct. 2997, 41 L.Ed.2d 789 (1974).
16. *Cherry v. Des Moines Leader*, 114 Iowa 298, 86 N.W. 323 (1901).

saying: "Her [Phoebe Snow's] record company and her manager and her lawyer all screwed her at once." The article, however, contained none of the context in which Ian's opinion was voiced. Snow's former manager sued *The New York Times*, the interviewer, and Janis Ian for libel, claiming that he could be identified as the manager referred to in the article, that Ian's statement was false, and that the statement injured his reputation in the entertainment and legal professions.

The trial court held that the base conclusions of managerial incompetence reported in the article could be considered libelous without the reporting of additional facts on which the opinion was based. Ian appealed and included a transcript of the entire interview with her appeal papers. The decision was reversed as to Ian on the ground the transcript established a factual basis for her opinion.[17] The *New York Times* and interviewer, however, could not escape liability, due to their failure to put the opinion in the proper context.

REMEMBER: When expressing your opinion or reporting somebody else's, state the factual context for the opinion and make sure that the statement in question is understood as an opinion and not as bedrock fact.

EXAMPLE: Fact: Supernut Machine Company has obviously been stealing the Pentagon blind through overcharging. Opinion/Fair Comment: On fifty different occasions in a two-year period between January 1983 and January 1985, Supernut Machine Company billed the Pentagon between 200% and 800% more for its parts than the market price would warrant. This, in our opinion, amounts to stealing the Pentagon blind.

d. The Libel Defense of Consent

Perhaps the simplest way to avoid a charge of libel is to get the subject of your report to review it prior to publication and to consent to it in advance, either in writing, on tape, or before responsible witnesses. A person who authorizes the publication of something about herself takes the risk it may or may not be defamatory. Consent, especially in written form, is a strong defense. Here are some examples of consent forms which might be used by the journalist to forestall future libel suits.

---

17. *Rand v. New York Times Co.*, 430 N.Y.S. 2d 271 (AppDiv 1980).

CONSENT TO PUBLICATION BY WRITTEN MEDIA

On _____(date)_____ I, _____(person's name)_____, carefully reviewed a ☐ transcript of an interview, ☐ an article, ☐ a photograph, ☐ _____ (other) involving ☐ me ☐ my business ☐ _____ (other) which is attached to this consent form. I hereby freely and without duress of any kind give my consent for the attached article, transcript, or photograph to be published as is. I have authority to give this consent on behalf of _____ (name of business or corporation, if applicable) _____.

CONSENT TO PUBLICATION BY ELECTRONIC MEDIA

On _____(date)_____, in the company of _____(name of witness)_____ I ☐ listened to a tape ☐ viewed a videotape ☐ reviewed a transcript ☐ _____ (other) of an anticipated publication involving ☐ me ☐ my business ☐ _____ (other). I hereby freely and without duress give my consent to the publication of such material, as is. I have authority to give this consent on behalf of _____(name of business or corporation, if applicable)_____.

Explicit consent is not always easy or practical to achieve, however. More commonly, such consent as exists is given by implication or is conditioned upon certain events happening, or limited to a particular time or for a particular purpose. Here is a possible form for obtaining conditional consent:

CONDITIONAL CONSENT

On _____(date)_____ I, _____(name)_____, was interviewed by _____(name of journalist)_____. The subject of the interview was _____ _____.

I was informed that the results of this interview might be ☐ published ☐ broadcast as follows: _____(intended program or media of publication)_____.

I hereby freely and without duress give my consent for the interview results to be published, on the express basis that such publication will be limited to the subject and to the program/media specified above.

As a general rule, if you go beyond the scope of the consent granted, whether explicit or implicit, your consent defense is lost.

Let's return to our example of School Superintendent David Martin who, as you will remember, was reported to have neglected his child. Let's assume now that a photographer obtained a signed consent form from him saying he was working on a story about staff competency in the schools. This consent or release will be of absolutely no value if the picture is run as part of child abuse allegations.

DEFENSE NOTE: Remember, consent is a *defense* and the defendant therefore has the burden to prove its existence. The more reliance on written or taped consents, the better.

e. The Right of Reply Defense

Traditionally, if you publish or broadcast a statement by one person defending against an attack by another, you are protected, even though the reply you published is false and defamatory. The defense does not apply, however, if you published with *actual malice*. Further, the reply must be reasonably related to, and not exceed the scope of, the attack.

For example, a newspaper can publish a Cabinet secretary's response to an attack on her for being a racist, even though the reply itself turns out to be defamatory ("Burns is the real racist. He apparently believes that others share his twisted and nazi-like attitudes towards all minority groups.") Again, however, the media must be free of "actual malice," and the response must be pertinent to the substance and proportionate to the size of the attack.

Broadcasters are compelled to extend the right of reply in certain circumstances—most particularly for a political candidate under the "equal time" provisions and when an individual or group is attacked under the "personal attack" rule of the Fairness Doctrine.[18] Because they are required to carry these speeches without censoring them, radio and television stations are relieved from liability for broadcasting libelous statements.

The print media, on the other hand, has no legal obligation to extend the right of reply.[19] The distinction made by the law between the electronic and print media centers on the fact that (theoretically) any citizen can start a newspaper, whereas the leasing of the airwaves is limited to a defined number.[20]

3. Statutory Defenses to Libel

a. Introduction

We have now covered the primary common law defenses available to the media in a libel suit. As is discussed in Appendix A these defenses have been fashioned by the courts over hundreds of years and are generally valid in all courts throughout the United States. In Appendix A we also observe that many common law precepts have been adopted in statutory form over the years, and the common law defenses to libel are no exception. Most states have gone even further, however, in providing additional statutory protections for the journalist. Let's examine some of these.

---

18. See Chapter 10 for further discussion of this topic.
19. The Case of *Miami Herald Pub. Co. v. Tornillo*, 418 U.S. 241, 94 S.Ct. 2831, 41 L.Ed.2d 730 (1974) concerned a Florida "right of reply statute" which granted political candidates the right to free and equal space to reply to newspaper attacks on their record. The court unanimously ruled that the Florida statute violated the First Amendment by, in effect, making the government the censor of what the people may read and know.
20. See Chapter 10 for further discussion of this subject.

b. "Privilege" as a Defense

The statutes of many states extend a shield against liability (called a "privilege" in legal jargon) to journalistic reports of statements made under certain circumstances. This statutory defense of privilege has been created because society feels it should be safe for anyone to rely on and publish certain types of public records and pronouncements without fear of a libel suit.

Reports of statements made or documents prepared in the course of 1) judicial proceedings (e.g., trials, motion hearings), 2) judicial-type proceedings (e.g., administrative hearings, inquests, grand juries), and 3) legislative, executive, or other official proceedings (whether at the federal, state or local level of government) generally are considered to be covered by this privilege.

This defense means that even if the statement or document later turns out to be legally libelous, the journalist will be shielded from liability if she has conveyed an accurate rendition.

Because this type of privilege is created by statute, the precise situations where it applies vary somewhat from state to state. For example, in Massachusetts the privilege does not extend to reports of statements contained in complaints, affidavits or other papers filed with the court unless and until such papers are presented to a judge or magistrate for some kind of judicial action. In New York on the other hand, the media is privileged to report statements in court papers which have been properly filed and served on the required parties.

In most states, reports of statements by officials and personnel of administrative or law enforcement agencies are generally not privileged until some definite official action has been taken. For example, a report of statements contained in a criminal complaint issued by a district attorney is generally privileged, whereas an article covering accusations made by the district attorney at a press conference prior to the filing of official charges is not.

In this regard, police proceedings are especially risky to report. It is safe to accurately report a crime has been committed and a particular person is being held for questioning. However, whether or not information on a police blotter, the record of a person's arrests and charges, and the oral reports of police officers is privileged, even if it later turns out to be wrong, varies according to the jurisdiction involved.

For example, in Washington, D.C., the police department has a one-way telephone line known as the "hot line" which summarizes information learned from various police sources. The media can subscribe to the service. In 1974, the hot line carried an item that Fannie Philips was shot to death during an argument and that her husband was charged with homicide. The *Washington Star* picked up the story and ran it. None of the subsequent police reports mentioned any argument. Subsequently the charges were dropped and the incident was recorded as an accidental shooting.

Mr. Philips sued the *Star* for libel because of the statement that his wife had been shot during a quarrel. The *Star* defended itself by stating that the story was an accurate summary of an official police report. The court found that although summaries of official reports are protected from libel suits, the hot line was not an official report. The court said:

> [The hot line] represents little more than an informal arrangement between the police and the media, a joint venture, which consists of nothing more sanctified than unofficial statements of police regarding a crime. [21]

IMPORTANT: In order to utilize the privilege defense, you must be able to establish that you gave a fair and accurate report of the official proceeding, statement, or document in question. Although your report need not be verbatim, make sure your summarizing is accurate. In many situations, oversimplifying or neglecting to mention an important qualifier can result

---

21. *Philips v. Evening Star*, 424 F.2d 78 (D.C. Cir. 1980).

in unfair or inaccurate reporting. An example of this, described in Appendix A, occurred when an article about a court decision reported that the judge found the plaintiff's allegations to be true, while neglecting to add this was only done for the purpose of deciding certain legal questions presented for resolution.

Also, remember that any defense of privilege can be destroyed if it is "abused." Thus, if you have reason to know that an otherwise privileged statement is inaccurate, or you are motivated to publish by ill will towards the human subject of the story, you may find yourself deprived of your privilege shield when you most need it.

YOU BE THE JUDGE

You are a reporter for a medium-sized daily newspaper and happen to be in the local courthouse. You are waiting in criminal session when a juvenile is brought before a judge for sentencing. The juvenile has been charged with sexual assault against a university student. The judge is explaining to the juvenile why she is about to throw the book at him.

By habit you start taking notes. This is what you get: "Ordinarily, we would not take a child of your age and punish you severely for your first offense. However, this case is different. I am convinced that unless I take severe measures now, you will prey on an ever increasing number of women and inflict on them your wanton disregard for all human decency." Later, in imposing the maximum sentence on the juvenile, the judge recommends a complete psychological evaluation on the ground that she could be wrong about her predictions, in which case the parole board should disregard them in deciding when the juvenile might be released.

Realizing the sensationalist nature of the quote you've picked up, you submit a story to your editor which includes the quote and subsequent comment upon imposing sentence.

The paper runs the quote but cuts the part containing the subsequent comment. The juvenile sues you, your editor, and the newspaper for libel, claiming that the story was inaccurate, exposed him to great public scorn, and greatly reduced his chance for a successful rehabilitation. All the defendants ask the court to dismiss the suit. What should the court decide and why?

The court should dismiss the suit as to you on the grounds *your* report was a fair and accurate account of remarks made in the course of a judicial proceeding, and therefore privileged. The article which was published, however, was arguably not a fair and accurate account of the judge's remarks since it failed to include the subsequent sentencing comment. On the other hand, the report of *the* remark itself was accurate, and the paper and editor may well have been privileged to report it without including the other comment.

Even if privilege did not apply, however, the article is probably not libelous. Why? Because all it did was report the judge's opinion, rather than fact.

c. Statutes of Limitation

Statutes of limitation are the laws which define the time span within which legal actions may be brought. The statute of limitations begins to run (like a meter begins to tick) from the date the libel is published. Any libel action must be initiated before the time fixed by statute has expired.

Failure by the plaintiff to comply with the applicable statute of limitation, no matter what the reason, provides an absolute defense against a libel action. Thus, even if you have libeled someone in the worst way possible (assume you have recklessly accused a teacher of sexually abusing his pupils), you will be off the hook if the teacher tries to sue you after the "statute has run."

The statute of limitations for libel actions is one or two years in all states except Arkansas, Delaware, New Mexico and Vermont, where it is three, and Hawaii, where it is six.

NOTE: Remember that re-publication starts the statute going again. Also, in March 1984, the Supreme Court handed down a libel decision (*Keeton v. Hustler Magazine, Inc.*) with important implications for the working journalist. The Court ruled that suit against a media publication can be brought in any state where the article containing the libelous statement is sold. Thus, an Ohio resident was permitted to sue the nationally distributed *Hustler Magazine* in New Hampshire, an important right since the suit was barred by the Ohio statute of limitations but not by the New Hampshire statute.

4. Constitutional Defenses to Libel
a. Overview

Prior to 1964, the common law and statutory rules which we have just considered governed media comment on the conduct of all newsmakers. Statements of fact had to be substantially true; comments or opinions had to be based upon true facts which fully and fairly justified the opinion. Mere negligence could result in liability and, in many cases, no fault at all was needed. It was enough that false defamatory material had been published. These common law principles accordingly resulted in self-censorship by the media and were thought by many to be incompatible with a system of freedom of expression protected by the First Amendment.

Then, as we mentioned in the introduction to this chapter, along came the *New York Times* case wherein the U.S. Supreme Court finally undertook the task of bringing the law of libel into harmony with the First Amendment.

b. Protecting Statements About Public Officials

It all began when a civil rights group purchased a full page advertisement in *The New York Times*, entitled, "Heed Their Rising Voices." The advertisement recounted the efforts of southern black students to affirm their rights at Alabama State College in Montgomery and told of the "wave of terror" they faced. It spoke of violence against the Rev. Martin Luther King, Jr. in his leadership of the civil rights movement, and asked for contributions to continue the fight for racial justice in the South. Some of the specific statements in the ad were simply not correct, including allegations concerning the Montgomery, Alabama police department.

As a result, L.B. Sullivan, Commissioner of Public Affairs, whose responsibility it was to supervise the operation of the police department, sued the *New York Times* company and four of the people who signed the ad. In accordance with Alabama libel law, Sullivan was awarded $500,000 in damages by the jury. On appeal, the Supreme Court of Alabama affirmed.

The U.S. Supreme Court reversed, holding that Alabama libel law was "constitutionally deficient for failure to provide the safeguards for freedom of speech and of the press that are required by the First and Fourteenth Amendments...." Justice Brennan, writing for the majority, felt the *Times* had been, at most, guilty of negligence in publishing the advertisement without verifying its accuracy. He felt that to subject the media to liability for honest mistakes or mere negligence which resulted in the defamation of public officials would inevitably lead to self-censorship regarding criticism of official conduct. In the Court's view, this would interfere with "a profound national commitment to the principle that debate on public issues should be uninhibited, robust and wide open . . ." To prevent this from happening, the Court established the *New York Times* rule:

> The constitutional guarantees require, we think, a federal rule that prohibits a public official from recovering damages for a defamatory falsehood relating to his official conduct unless he proves that the statement was made with "actual malice" — that is, with knowledge that it was false or with reckless disregard of whether it was false or not. [22]

This decision advances the concept that the First Amendment right of the press to publish in areas of public concern outweighs a public official's interest in his or her reputation. For the first time, the media was provided with a constitutional defense against suit by a public official for libel resulting from negligence.

BOLD REPORTERS HIT THE STREETS

As is so often the case when courts first establish new rules, there has so far been no consistent definition of "public officials." It appears that the phrase includes at least those in governmental hierarchies — past, present or future — who have or appear to have, substantial responsibility for the conduct of government business. It probably does not include minor governmental functionaries such as secretaries, clerks or others who work for a government agency but have no real power in its structure or decision making function.

After the *New York Times* case, public officials have had greater difficulty winning defamation cases against the media. Part of the reason for this is the difficulty in establishing a reporter's mental state of actual malice. The U.S. Supreme Court later recognized this difficulty and allowed libel plaintiffs to obtain a reporter's notes, "outtakes," and other evidence of the reporter's thought process which accompanied the piece in question. [23]

---

22. 376 U.S. at pp. 279-280.
23. *Herbert v. Lando*, 441 U.S. 153, 99 S.Ct. 1635, 60 L.Ed.2d 115 (1979).

Not surprisingly, this decision hasn't proved to be a popular one among journalists. Some have responded by destroying notes and outtakes which might prevent such destruction prior to the filing of a lawsuit, while others have kept selective records in the first place, omitting material they wouldn't want subpoenaed. The extent to which journalists may be required to disclose their materials and sources in libel suits against them is covered in detail in Chapter 6.

c. Statements About Public Figures

Recognizing that a "public official" category only covers a small number of people, the Supreme Court in 1967 extended the application of the *New York Times* rule to "public figures" in a case called *Gertz v. Welch.*[24]

Elmer Gertz, a well-known Chicago lawyer, was retained by a family of a slain youth to bring a civil suit against the policeman who killed him. The policeman had already been convicted of second degree murder in connection with the boy's death. The editor of the John Birch Society magazine *American Opinion* learned of the suit and published his perception that it was part of a nationwide conspiracy to undermine law enforcement in order to effect a Communist takeover of the United States.

Gertz sued *American Opinion* for libel. Although recovery was initially denied by the trial court on the ground that a public issue was involved and no actual malice had been shown, the U.S. Supreme Court reversed. The Court noted that Mr. Gertz was a prominent lawyer, author, law professor and civil rights leader, but nevertheless ruled he was still a private person under the circumstances of the case and could sue for libel without having to prove actual malice.[25]

In its opinion, the court reasoned that the private person is more in need of judicial redress than the public figure for two reasons. First, the private person has not voluntarily invited public comment and thus chosen to put his or her reputation at risk. Second, if a controversy does develop, the private person does not have the same access to media to correct the record as does the public figure.

What this all boils down to for the journalist is that a private (non-public) person can succeed in a libel suit without meeting the heavy burden of showing actual malice, whereas public persons must carry that burden to recover in a libel action.

But, there is a saving grace in all this, as far as the media is concerned. If a private person succeeds in a libel action, she can only recover the damages needed to compensate for actual injury to reputation, business, etc. *Punitive damages are not available unless actual malice is shown.*

Unfortunately for the working journalist, there are many Americans who are on the borderline between public and private status. As one lower court judge wrote, "defining public figures is much like trying to nail a jellyfish to the wall." If anything, the Supreme Court has, since *Gertz,* tended to signal the lower courts that they should narrow their interpretation of who has public figure status.

To help keep at least part of the jellyfish on the wall, here are several other examples of fairly prominent people who were defined by courts as private figures for purposes of libel suits. Remember, since we are dealing with court-made law in this area, we have no handy statute to refer to and must try to generalize from what courts have done, case by case.

● Mary Alice Firestone, a prominent socialite often mentioned in the press, was involved in a divorce action from her husband, Russell, of Firestone rubber fame. In characterizing the divorce case, the Florida trial judge described certain testimony as "bizarre and of an amatory

---

24. 418 U.S. 323, 94 S.Ct. 2997, 41 L.Ed.2d 789 (1974).
25. In April 1981, after a retrial, the jury awarded Elmer Gertz $100,000 in actual damages and $300,000 in punitive damages.

nature which would have made Dr. Freud's hair curl." [But then the judge said: "The court is inclined to discount much of this testimony as unreliable."] *Time* magazine reported the remark about the testimony being bizarre but left out the judge's followup remark, and was accordingly sued for libel. Despite Mrs. Firestone's social prominence and past penchant for publicity, the U.S. Supreme Court held that she was simply a private person availing herself of the judicial process and was not subject to the "actual malice" requirement.[26] This case made the media's hair curl.

• Dr. Ronald Hutchinson, a research scientist, sued Senator William Proxmire after the senator gave him the "Golden Fleece Award" for using a $500,000 government grant to study, among other things, why monkeys clench their jaws. The Supreme Court held that Hutchinson was not a public figure prior to the controversy engendered by the Golden Fleece Award, even though he was spending public funds in his research.[27]

• Ilya Wolston[28] pleaded guilty to contempt in 1958 for his failure to appear before a grand jury investigating Soviet espionage in the United States. In 1974, a book published by *Reader's Digest* falsely listed Wolston, among others, as having been indicted as a Soviet agent. Although Wolston's name had been on the front pages of America's press almost daily at the time he failed to appear before the grand jury, the U.S. Supreme Court stated:

> Petitioner's failure to appear before the grand jury and citation for contempt no doubt were "newsworthy," but the simple fact that these events attracted media attention also is not conclusive of the public figure issue. A private individual is not automatically transformed into a public figure just by becoming involved in and associated with a matter that attracts public attention. . . . A libel defendant must show more than mere newsworthiness to justify application of the demanding burden of *New York Times*.

Furthermore, the Court pointed out, Wolston did not try to engage the attention of the public. Although the defendant protested that of course a person accused of being a spy would not voluntarily attract attention, the Court ruled that Wolston was a private person for purposes of a libel action.

Other people who have been held to be private figures include: (1) two attorneys whose licenses to practice law were suspended, one after pleading guilty to a crime and the other after having been censured; (2) a major stockholder in a large shopping mall; (3) a harness racer who allegedly fixed races; (4) a criminal defendant; (5) a fundraiser for a charity; and (6) a retail firm engaged in the closeout sale of a prominent department store.

Fortunately, from a media standpoint, not all people are private figures. For example, the Meerpols (children of Julius and Ethel Rosenberg), diet author Dr. Robert Atkins, and *Playboy* magazine's "Miss December" have all been deemed public figures. So too were an emergency medical service and its owners, the former head of a supermarket, and two attorneys — one a private law school dean who became involved in a controversy over the school's accreditation and the other a former city attorney who joined in the controversy over his being fired and the subsequent selection of his replacement.

If you feel that no reasonable guidelines exist to help you determine whether a particular person is a public or private figure, you're right. However, here are two common themes:

• **Media Access:** Does the person who claims or might claim libel have ready access to the media to rebut accusations?

---

26. *Time, Inc. v. Firestone*, 424 U.S. 448, 96 S.Ct. 958, 47 L.Ed.2d 154 (1976).
27. *Hutchinson v. Proxmire*, 443 U.S. 111, 99 S.Ct. 2675, 61 L.Ed.2d 411 (1979). This case is also noteworthy because it held that a member of Congress's immunity for remarks made in the course of official proceedings did not extend to statements made off the floor or outside of committee rooms.
28. *Wolston v. Reader's Digest*, 443 U.S. 157, 99 S.Ct. 2701, 61 L.Ed.2d 450 (1979).

- **Voluntariness:** Did the person voluntarily involve himself in a particular controversy which existed independently of the reporter, publisher or broadcaster's efforts?

If famous persons, say Reggie Jackson or Henry Kissinger, voluntarily inject themselves into a hot public debate, you can be pretty sure they will be treated by the courts as public figures and the actual malice standard will apply. If they are brought into the spotlight more or less involuntarily, on the other hand, they will probably be treated as private figures and you will therefore need to tread more lightly. Do not assume, however, that a famous person is automatically a public figure or that a relatively obscure person is not.

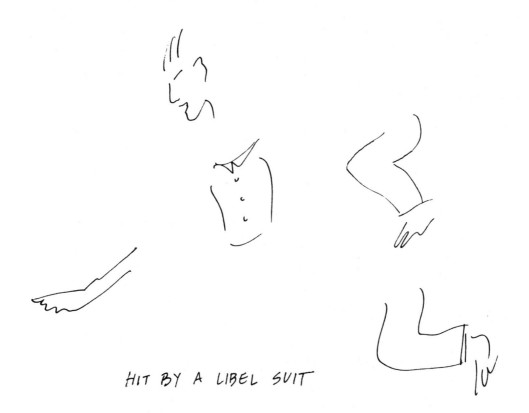

HIT BY A LIBEL SUIT

EXAMPLE: Let's say you write a story about Ali Blumross, a lawyer, charging her with having made unfair and illegal profits in certain real estate transactions. Since this is clearly defamatory, Ali would only have to show, to recover for libel, that the charge is false and that you acted unreasonably or unprofessionally in not verifying the reliability of your source and the truth or falsity of the statement.

But now suppose that Ali was a city attorney, as well as a lawyer in private practice. In this situation she would have more difficulty proving her case. As a public official, she would have to show that you wrote and published the reports knowing they were false, or doubting seriously that they were true (or that your source was known to be unreliable, but you didn't fact-check).

Finally, suppose that Ali was just a regular attorney but had recently been in the news for criticizing local rent control initiatives. Assume further that your article made the charges because their newsworthiness stemmed directly from Ali's position on rent control. In this case, Ali might well be treated as a public figure and required to establish "actual malice" to recover.

A JOURNALIST'S POSSIBLE DEFENSES TO A LIBEL LAWSUIT

Suppose you are sued for libel. What defenses can you present in court? Here is an analysis of your legal situation which summarizes in chart form the information in this chapter.

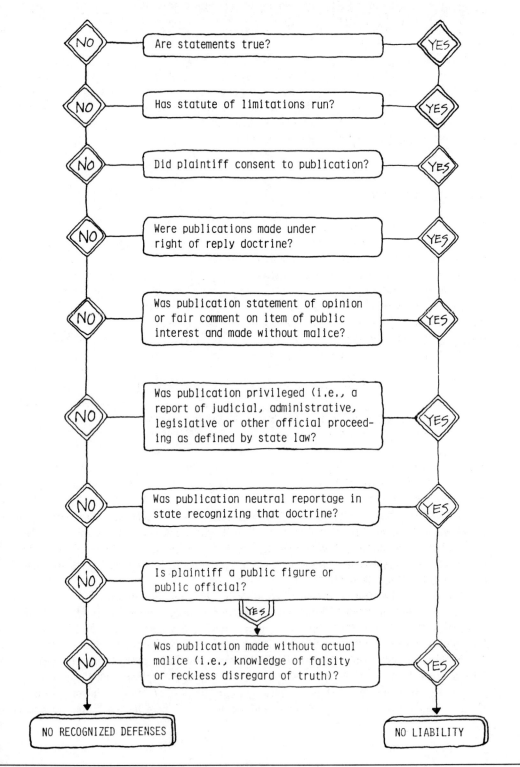

NO | Are statements true? | YES

NO | Has statute of limitations run? | YES

NO | Did plaintiff consent to publication? | YES

NO | Were publications made under right of reply doctrine? | YES

NO | Was publication statement of opinion or fair comment on item of public interest and made without malice? | YES

NO | Was publication privileged (i.e., a report of judicial, administrative, legislative or other official proceeding as defined by state law? | YES

NO | Was publication neutral reportage in state recognizing that doctrine? | YES

NO | Is plaintiff a public figure or public official? | YES

NO | Was publication made without actual malice (i.e., knowledge of falsity or reckless disregard of truth)? | YES

NO RECOGNIZED DEFENSES

NO LIABILITY

E. How to Limit Your Liability

1. Introduction

In prior sections of this chapter we have discussed the elements of a libel cause of action and available defenses under the common law, state statutes, and the U.S. Constitution. Now it is time to look at ways to cut your losses if you have made a mistake. Even if you do libel someone, you may still be able to limit the damages that person can recover. This is done under a legal doctrine known as "mitigation."

In a sense, mitigation is not a defense but rather a path of strategic defeat designed to demonstrate to a judge your good faith and lack of malice. It will not get a libel complaint dismissed, but it can reduce greatly the amount of damages recoverable by the plaintiff. Given the kind of verdicts being awarded these days, this can make an enormous difference as far as the ultimate consequences of libel are concerned.

2. Retraction

The best way to mitigate libel is by retraction, correction and/or apology. Although saying you're sorry and setting the record straight cannot get you off the legal hook, timely appeasement of the defamed person may avert the filing of a libel action altogether.

Be aware, however, that a demand for a retraction should be handled delicately with the advice of a libel attorney. The attorney must determine whether a retraction is warranted, the manner of publishing the retraction, and so on. A badly worded clarification of an ambiguous story may worsen your position in a subsequent lawsuit. For an example, let's return to the much maligned David Martin. Assume that after your story about Martin neglecting his daughter, you receive a demand for retraction and run the following:

> On March 8, 1984 we reported on charges that David Martin, head of the local
> school board, had seriously neglected his daughter. At present, no actual criminal or
> civil action has been initiated against Martin, and we regret any inconvenience that
> our earlier report may have caused Mr. Martin and his family.

This would not do you much good and in fact constitutes a re-publication of the original libel.

To date, thirty-three states have enacted statutes which govern the procedure to be followed in demanding and publishing a retraction and the effect of such a retraction upon the damages a plaintiff may recover. These statutes differ considerably in detail. Most apply only to statements which were broadcast or published in good faith and with reasonable grounds for belief in their truth. They also generally provide that the defamed person must serve written notice upon the publisher in order to give the publisher an opportunity to retract. Most states require that the notice and demand for retraction be served upon the publisher within a certain time limit, varying from ten days before an action is instituted (Mississippi) to three days (Indiana). A few states require that the defamed person serve notice — usually twenty days — after he has actual knowledge of the defamatory publication.

The time within which a publisher must issue a retraction ranges from 48 hours to 32 weeks. In some states, no time limit is prescribed. Some retraction statutes allow only special damages (see below) when a proper retraction has been made.

One sample statute is from California:

CALIFORNIA CIVIL CODE SECTION 48a. **Libel in newspaper; slander by radio broadcast**

1. **Special damages; notice and demand for correction.** In any action for damages for the publication of a libel in a newspaper, or of a slander by radio broadcast, plaintiff shall recover no more than special damages unless a correction be demanded and be not published or broadcast, as hereinafter provided. Plaintiff shall serve upon the publisher, at the place of publication, or broadcaster at the place of broadcast, a written notice specifying the statements claimed to be libelous and demanding that the same be corrected. Said notice and demand must be served within 20 days after knowledge of the publication or broadcast of the statements claimed to be libelous.

2. **General, special and exemplary damages.** If a correction be demanded within said period and be not published or broadcast in substantially as conspicuous a manner in said newspaper or on said broadcasting station as were the statements claimed to be libelous, in a regular issue thereof published or broadcast within three weeks after such service, plaintiff, if he pleads and proves such notice, demand and failure to correct, and if his cause of action be maintained, may recover general, special and exemplary damages; provided that no exemplary damages may be recovered unless the plaintiff shall prove that defendant made the publication or broadcast with actual malice and then only in the discretion of the court or jury, and actual malice shall not be inferred or presumed from the publication or broadcast.

3. **Correction prior to demand.** A correction published or broadcast in substantially as conspicuous a manner in said newspaper or on said broadcasting station as the statements claimed in the complaint to be libelous, prior to receipt of a demand therefor, shall be of the same force and effect as though such correction had been published or broadcast within three weeks after a demand therefor.

4. **Definitions.** As used herein, the terms "general damages," "special damages," "exemplary damages" and "actual malice," are defined as follows:

(a) "General damages" are damages for loss of reputation, shame, mortification and hurt feelings;

(b) "Special damages" are all damages which plaintiff alleges and proves that he has suffered in respect to his property, business, trade, profession, or occupation, including such amounts of money as the plaintiff alleges and proves he has expended as a result of the alleged libel, and no other;

(c) "Exemplary damages" are damages which may in the discretion of the court or jury be recovered in addition to general and special damages for the sake of example and by way of punishing a defendant who has made the publication or broadcast with actual malice;

(d) "Actual malice" is that state of mind arising from hatred or ill will toward the plaintiff; provided, however, that such a state of mind occasioned by a good faith belief on the part of the defendant in the truth of the libelous publication or broadcast at the time it is published or broadcast shall not constitute actual malice.

3. Previous Bad Reputation of Plaintiff

Basically, a person who is libeled is entitled to recover damages for aspersions cast on her character and harm done to her reputation. But, what if a libel defendant can show in court that the character and reputation of the person libeled is so bad that she could not as a practical matter be damaged by any further defamation? In this situation, a jury may award only nominal damages ($1.00 or some such paltry sum) to the plaintiff. In a sense, then, a libelous statement is mitigated by the previous poor reputation of the victim.

An extreme example of this would be Charles Manson. After all the negative press received by him, it is hard to see that he has much of a reputation left to protect. But what about a local diet doctor who has been convicted of defrauding his patients? If six years pass and the former doctor is out of jail and working as a therapist, chances are this person's reputation has been sufficiently rehabilitated so that he could recover damages for harm done to his reputation.

LIBEL! LIABLE TO EAT YOUR WORDS!

F. Is There Libel After Death?

A dead person cannot be libeled. Or as Justice Stephen wrote a century ago, "The dead have no rights and can suffer no wrongs."[29] Of course, if in a writing or broadcasting about a dead person references are made or implied to the character or reputation of someone living, that person can bring a libel action.

For example, a book (*Pennsylvania: Birthplace of a Nation*) included accounts of Henry Clay Frick, a then long deceased industrial magnate. Helen Frick, his daughter and sole survivor, objected to the depiction of her father as a stern and autocratic union buster who grossly mistreated his workers in a number of ways. Ms. Frick claimed that these were misrepresentations and reflected badly on her, since she was connected with the memory of her father through her philanthropies. She sued the author.

The trial court judge, after doing a bit of historical research on his own, agreed with the author's representation of Henry Frick. More to the point, he stated that as the daughter was not mentioned, no right of reputation or privacy was involved and she had therefore suffered no injury.[30]

However, there is some reason to think the reputation of the dead may be about to get some legal protection. For example, in 1981 Kenneth MacDonald sued Time, Inc. over an article which implicated him in the Abscam operation. MacDonald died before trial. The judge ruled that the family could bring the suit to clear his name and seek compensation for harm. Practical

---

29. *R. V. Ensor*, 3 L.T.R. 366 (1887).
30. *Frick v. Stevens*, 43 D. & C.2d 6 (Pa. 1964).

considerations, like the obvious ones that death makes a person a poor witness and eliminates all the harm they are likely to have suffered, will have to be dealt with in future cases.

The important thing to understand now is that, legally as well as ethically, you should use a reasonable standard of care when reporting about the dead. They cannot sue you, but their families may well be able to in the near future.

G. Libel in Fiction and Drama

At publishing firms and film companies lawyers can be heard dispensing advice such as: "The protagonist (a 35-year-old woman doctor who lives on Cape Cod with four lovers and an attractive poodle) in your 'lascivious' novel, better be changed to a 50-year-old male surgeon who lives in Los Angeles." Why? In one word—fear.

A widely publicized California case[31] has held that any time an individual is recognized and ridiculed in a work of fiction, the person can sue the publisher and the author of the work for libel. This is true even if the person is disguised by use of a false name, description, etc. The result has been for lawyers to counsel authors, film makers and dramatists whose characters are drawn more or less from a real person to add several extra layers of disguise. Even if this results in a 7'2" basketball player being depicted as a 4'10" Japanese woman jockey, the media lawyer would think the protection from liability is worth it. After all, there are probably too many basketball books on the market anyway, she might reason. Lawyers, being conservative folk, often tend to get carried away imagining problems.

Another type of novel or dramatization susceptible to libel actions has been dubbed "faction." Here, real people—say, the President of the United States, or a prominent movie actress, have fictional interactions with other real people or made up characters. Usually the "real people" pressed into this sort of fictionalized service are public figures. As such, they must prove "actual malice" to prosecute a libel suit successfully. This would not seem to be difficult, if in fact they are libeled, as by definition their activities are knowingly false because they are fictionalized. However, most writers are smart enough to use these real people as background, borrowing a bit of their life story or portraying them in an unobjectionable light. Of course, if the famous person is dead, an author has a great deal more legal license to involve them in the details of their story. Remember, the dead can't be libeled and the living can sue only if they are directly affected.

The subject of libel in fiction is covered extensively in *Author law*, Bunnin and Beren, Nolo Press.

H.   Libel Suits and the Journalist

1. Attorneys

If you are sued for libel, you and your media organization will need to respond. Presumably the radio, television station or newspaper involved will conduct and pay for the defense. If you are a freelance writer and expect no help defending the case, you will need to either

---

31. *Mitchell v. Bindrim*, 155 Cal. Rptr. 29 (1979) concerned a novel called *Touching* about two women who attend a nude encounter weekend and are adversely affected by it. In preparation of her novel, author Mitchell attended a nude encounter group run by Dr. Paul Bindrim. Bindrim sued for libel, claiming he was identifiable as the central character, Dr. Simon Herford. Despite the fact that Mitchell had been careful to camouflage her characters, Bindrim succeeded and was awarded $75,000.

represent yourself or hire a lawyer. You may also want to consult a lawyer even if your media organization will defend you. Why? In many cases your interests and theirs will not be the same. For example, if your media organization wants to put all the blame on you (throw you to the wolves, so to speak), their lawyer will be unable to provide you with independent advice in your own best interest.

If you need to contact your own attorney, either for advice about an article or to represent you in a libel suit, you would do well to find one experienced in media law. Like medicine, law has become highly specialized. Whether or not you are dealing with an "in-house" or an independent lawyer, however, here are a few tips.

Lawyers get paid big money to see threats on the horizon and give an early distant warning of possible trouble. Because many libel law concepts are difficult to pin down, the media lawyer is likely to spot potential liability in the most apparently innocent of circumstances. The good media lawyer is sensitive to the possibility that "good legal advice" can operate as an extremely effective form of censorship and will censor herself severely accordingly. Unfortunately, there are many media lawyers who are not so wise.

We do not suggest you ignore the lawyer who advises you of possible problems with your material. However, a "second opinion" is always a good idea. Also, lawyers can often be induced to give a percentage-type estimate regarding the likelihood of a successful libel suit against you. Ultimately, you should strive to meet your own journalistic standards, recognizing that on occasion these may come into conflict with the real or imagined difficulties envisioned by a lawyer.

2. Pre-Trial Discovery

We do not have space here to review all aspects of a civil suit for libel. However, there are two areas important to the rights of journalists which we do discuss. The first is called "pre-trial discovery," and the second is known as "summary judgment." These are discussed more generally in Appendix A.

Pretrial discovery means the techniques by which the parties to a lawsuit obtain information from each other prior to trial. Concretely, in a media case, this involves the circumstances under which the person suing you may conduct a "fishing expedition" through your notes, files, articles, etc. Similarly, discovery governs when you can obtain information from the plaintiff that will help you to prove your defenses (e.g., truth, privilege) and establish mitigation.

As we discuss in Appendix A, each side has the right to serve "interrogatories," take "depositions," request a party to admit facts and confirm the genuineness of documents, and request the production of documents and other evidence for inspection (e.g., tapes, notes, etc.), in order to prepare their case for trial.

In the normal libel case, a plaintiff will want access to documents in your files (and those of your media organization) in an effort to demonstrate shoddy and unprofessional investigative techniques necessary to establish your negligence. For example, in a suit brought against CBS, William Westmoreland was able, through the discovery process, to obtain an internal CBS report establishing that the journalists in question had violated in-house reportorial guidelines.

Again, if the plaintiff is a public person or a public figure, she will also need to provide specific evidence that the newspeople were acting with actual malice. This often means delving into and sifting through the defendants' editorial processes in a hunt for indications of the necessary mental intent (i.e., knowledge of falsity or reckless disregard).

Such things as informal conversations in the newsroom, conferences with sources, and outtakes become important. The reasons why the individuals connected with producing the material at issue included some facts and excluded others can provide the type of evidence necessary for a plaintiff to surmount the actual malice barrier.

HOW MUCH FISHING CAN ONE DO?

THIS LOOKS INTERESTING!

Needless to say, nothing is more distasteful to the journalist than having to account for her mental processes underlying a particular publication. In fact, it is easy to see that such a process might lead to profound self-censorship at the outset. On the other hand, a public official or public figure libel plaintiff has little other means of establishing actual malice. An inherent conflict therefore exists between free expression and the right of a libeled public official or figure to obtain recourse.

The only Supreme Court case directly dealing with this issue is *Herbert* V. *Lando*. There, a reporter had resisted questions in a deposition about his mental processes while investigating and writing the article in question. By the time the case reached the Supreme Court, the question was clearly defined: Did a public figure or official's right to recourse in the courts outweigh the chilling effect which forcing the disclosure of a reporter's mental processes would have on the full dissemination of information protected by the First Amendment?

Unfortunately for the media, the Supreme Court answered this question in the affirmative:

> Permitting plaintiffs such as Herbert to prove their cases by direct as well as indirect evidence is consistent with the balance struck by our prior decisions. If such proof results in liability for damages which in turn discourages the publication of erroneous information known to be false or probably false, this is no more than what our cases contemplate and does not abridge either freedom of speech or of the press. [32]

This issue was again raised in a lawsuit in which Dr. Carl Galloway, implicated by CBS in a medical insurance fraud scheme, successfully obtained the outtakes of a "60 Minutes" segment to demonstrate the journalist's negligence and unfairness in the resulting program. Not only did Galloway obtain the outtakes, he showed them to the jury during trial, the first time a libel plaintiff had done so. [33]

3. Avoiding a Long Law Suit

If you are ever a defendant in a libel suit, a favorable "summary judgment" should be sought as quickly as possible. As we point out in Appendix A, summary judgment means that the judge will examine the facts in the case as presented by each side in written statements under oath (declarations or affidavits) and decide whether there is any real dispute as to what occurred. In some libel cases, there isn't. The question is whether what happened constitutes libel. In such a case the judge will decide the case without a trial. On the other hand, if there is a dispute about important facts the answer to which will determine whether you win or lose (e.g., your

---

32. Op.cit.
33. Dr. Galloway lost and filed an appeal (pending as of January 1984).

state of mind as a journalist in a public official or figure case), the judge will deny summary judgment and a jury trial will eventually be held.

From a journalist's point of view, summary judgment is particularly useful and necessary to put lawsuits to rest at the earliest possible time. The longer a libel suit remains in the court, the greater the expense. Without the summary judgment procedure, one wealthy plaintiff such as a religious cult or large corporation could threaten the very existence of an alternative investigative newspaper or magazine by bringing any lawsuit, even if it had no real chance of success.

I.   Libel Insurance

It is more than likely that if you are working for a corporation, and you are sued for libel, the corporation will also be named as a defendant. This is permitted under a legal doctrine called "respondeat superior" which makes employers legally responsible for the acts of employees occurring in the normal course of their duties. Corporations are sued primarily because of their financial ability to pay money judgments. This ability, of course, is enhanced if they carry libel insurance. Not surprisingly, purchase of such libel insurance has surged in response to multimillion dollar damage awards and a hostile legal climate.

Still, about half of all media organizations do not have libel insurance. Even those which do may not be fully protected. For example, the *Alton Telegraph*'s $1 million policy did not meet the jury's $9.2 million judgment. Even after a settlement, the paper had to pay a substantial amount over the insurance coverage.

Also, insurance companies are refusing to cover the punitive damages portion of a libel award. One court in California upheld this position, ruling it against public policy for the *National Enquirer*'s insurance company to reimburse the publication for the punitive damages portion of Carol Burnett's award.

Even if your media organization is financially solvent and has insurance, however, there is no guarantee it will defend you. Many do, both because they genuinely feel an obligation to protect their people, and because it would be hard to get good employees if they didn't. Nevertheless, most reporters and broadcasters do not have contracts guaranteeing that they will be defended. This fact commonly causes even some courageous reporters sleepless nights. This can be especially true if the reporter had been with the corporation a short time or for some other reason isn't completely confident of being supported by management. Also, because media people frequently change jobs, a suit quite possibly may be filed after a journalist's employment with the organization has ended. In such a case, the journalist might be on her own.

In March 1984 in a case involving the nationally distributed *National Inquirer*, the Supreme Court ruled that a California resident was permitted to sue the individual journalists in the California courts even though the publication and the journalists are based in Florida (*Calder v. Jones*). This means that an individual journalist can be sued in any state where the publication was intended to be sold and thus be required to travel long distances to defend the action. Libel insurance would be most helpful in this situation.

Philosophically, libel insurance has its proponents and opponents. It can embolden a reluctant editor, since the best of the policies cover punitive damages and the exhorbitant pretrial attorneys' fees and court costs. On the other hand, there can be problems with insurers instead of publishers being ultimately at risk. There may be a tendency for insurers to pressure the press to take fewer risks, make less waves. Because of this, the *New York Times* has, to date, chosen not to be insured. This position may change in the future. Even the *Des Moines Register and Tribune Co.*, which defended sixty-two libel suits without a loss, decided to purchase insurance. Without insurance, a newspaper can spend thousands of dollars and much time either getting a frivolous claim dismissed in court or accepting an out-of-court settlement, even in cases where integrity and freedom of press is attacked.

LIBEL CHECKLIST

We've covered a lot of ground here. Hopefully you have a basic understanding of the law of libel as it affects the work of a journalist. If you can answer "yes" to any one of the following questions, then your piece is not, legally, libelous. Since there are fifteen questions, you have at least this many chances to defeat a libel action, even if you happen to be sued.

1. Did you fail to communicate your statement (i.e., publicize it) to a third person?
2. Did you avoid identifying the plaintiff, either expressly, by implication, or "per quod" (with the assistance of external facts)?
3. Given current social mores and political attitudes, did your publication lack a defamatory meaning?
4. Did you conform to the duty of care placed on journalists by your jurisdiction (i.e., without legal "fault")?
5. Did your publication fail to cause any actual or implied damage to the plaintiff?
6. Can you prove the truth of your publication?
7. Was the plaintiff's complaint filed after the Statute of Limitations had run on your publication?
8. If your publication was a report on official proceedings, was it a fair and accurate account (i.e., privileged)?
9. Could your publication properly be characterized as fair comment or opinion on a matter of public interest and made without actual malice?
10. Was your broadcast affording another the "right of reply?"
11. Did the plaintiff either expressly or impliedly consent to your publication?
12. Was your publication "neutral reportage" in states which recognize this doctrine?
13. If the subject of your publication was a public official or figure, did you lack actual malice (i.e., a knowledge of the story's falsity or a reckless disregard for its truth)?
14. Will the plaintiff be unable to show that any actual harm resulted from your publication?

J. How to Avoid a Libel Suit

In the previous sections we have outlined the basic law of libel as it affects the working journalist. In this section, we include several practical suggestions for how to do your job without being stuck for libel damages in the bargain.

1. Using Outside News Sources

When a newspaper, radio, or T.V. station repeats a defamatory wire service story involving a local person or business, the local impact of the publication or broadcast will greatly increase the chance of a lawsuit being filed. Such wire service stories should therefore be subjected to greater scrutiny than would be the case if the person or business were located half-way across the country. If you have any doubt at all as to the accuracy of what is provided, independent investigation is definitely warranted.

2. Handling Pictures and Film

Carefully caption every photograph and print you make before turning it over to the ultimate user of the photo. Be particularly careful when common names are involved.

Editors should double check pictures and film of criminals, indicted persons, and anyone else depicted in situations which might prove seriously unflattering. Especially, make sure the right names are attached to the right people. The great majority of the material you use will not result in a libel suit if you make an innocent mistake. Still, anything having to do with crimes, sex, communism, etc. should always be double checked.

In one photograph appearing on the front page of a metropolitan daily, a group of suspects in a suspected prostitution ring were portrayed with their lawyers. The caption suggested that one of the attorneys was a suspect. Although the attorney decided not to sue, the paper should not have allowed such confusion to occur.

3. Group References

When making statements about groups, especially small ones, be sure of your facts. Unless you are absolutely sure your statement applies to every group member, qualify it with phrases such as "some," "a significant number," and "many." When you proof-read your piece, ask yourself whether you would feel singled out if you were a member of the group. If your ears burn a little, at least figuratively, you may want to word your material differently.

4. Documenting Your Process

When you are dealing with potentially sensitive material, make a habit of keeping logs of each call and visit you make in an effort to check out your story. If you are later accused of not meeting your journalistic standard of care, documentation of your efforts will be of tremendous help. Likewise, lack of documentation can lead to problems, should you later end up in litigation. Here is a sample journalist's log and memorandum. We call attention to the careful documentation of telephone calls, sources of information, times and dates. These items can be invaluable when you are later asked to reconstruct your investigatory technique.

SAMPLE MEMORANDUM:

TO: Tom Landry, City Editor
FROM: Laura Seldin
Date: 6/20/85
Re: School asbestos story

I received a letter from a Mary Simpson, who is a widow. John Simpson died in December, 1984 of Mesothelioma Aninciabile — a disease directly related to asbestos exposure. Simpson worked for Ace Construction Company as an applicator of asbestos for insulation purposes. Before he died, Simpson brought a lawsuit against the Construction Company and others. That suit is now a wrongful death action brought by Simpson's family. Mrs. Simpson says her husband insulated many city buildings including the school. She says Simpson alerted school authorities when he learned he was ill, but nothing has been done. Mrs. Simpson thinks there is a cover-up.

From my investigation, I agree. I've attached a copy of my log which documents my efforts so far. I think we should run this story soon before OSHA does something to cover itself.

SAMPLE LOG:

6/15: Called Karen Sloven, Simpson Attorney. Asked questions about asbestos case. Told me it was on appeal, deps and documents at appeals court. Suspected my motives. Told her was looking into complicity of school board. She opened up and provided background into re asbestos effects and current laws regarding.

6/16: Visited appeals court, viewed record in Simpson v. Johns-Manvill et al, No. 82-1038, filed 3/6/82. No decision. Found following:

Dep of Simpson—talks about installation of asbestos in Jefferson Jr. High, Washington High, King Elementary and others;

Dep of president of Ace—Jack Sprague—acknowledges knew of asbestos harmful effects;

Medical studies since 1934 re asbestos;

Medical reports re Asbestosis in Simpson 9/80;

Autopsy report cause of death Mesothelioma.

6/17 a.m.:

Met w/Mrs. Simpson. Told me of Simpson's illness. Gave me copy of letter dated 10/15/80 Simpson sent to Pres School Board (John Nathan). Also, gave me letter from Nathan stating committee set up to investigate.

11:00 Called Sprague—in conference—left message.

1:00 p.m. Called Sprague—another line—left message.

2:00 Went to school board to check minutes of meetings from 10/15/80 on. No record of committee but discussion regarding OSHA citation of 12/8/81. Also saw original contract of Ace with City re insulation in schools. Made copies of pertinent entries.

4:00 Called OSHA re citation. Talked with Ray Montross. Said informed city of asbestos in schools but then told to turn it over to his supervisor, Owen McLean. Said McLean didn't push it and gave school board extensions because of ongoing study. Montross told to keep a lid on but uneasy cuz his kids are in one of affect schools.

5:00 Called Sprague—gone—left message.

6/18

8:30 a.m. Spoke with Sprague—referred to his lawyer Morris Cohen. Cohen said litigation on appeal, can't talk, client knows nothing.

Check out files on Sprague and Nathan. Both members of same golf club. On executive committee of boys club together, same church, lunch together at men's club dining room

10:00: Called Nathan—not in—left message.

11:00: Called Nathan—in conference—left message.

11:30: Called Nathan—out for rest of day—left message.

12:00: Called McLean at OSHA. Said he gave extension to Board cuz no money to remove. Said didn't think a problem and agreed with Nathan it would panic parents for no good reason. Said no intention of enforcing citation in near future.

1:00: Spoke to Atty Kay Widess in enforcement division re extensions. Was unaware of situation. Indicated not normal procedure to grant extension in such cases. Said Enforcement situation was grim as new administration had cut legal staff.

2:00: McLean called—furious at meddling.

2:30: Spoke to Jenny Silver—staff of school board memb. Sullivan. Said would talk to Sullivan.

6/19 8:00: Called Nathan—on vacation for week—left message.

9:15: Sullivan called—said to come to office at noon.

12:00: Meeting at Sullivan's office—Sullivan, me, former Board member Eriksen. Eriksen speaks off the record, I agreed not to take notes or tape. Says Nathan convinced committee to cover up, because didn't want parents to know. Also Erikson thinks Sprague influenced Nathan to keep lid on because of lawsuit.

Right to Privacy and the First Amendment

A. What Is the Right of Privacy?

This chapter focuses on the inevitable conflict between an individual's right to be left alone and a reporter's right to inform the public. Generally speaking, how you handle the area of personal privacy has more to do with journalistic ethics and good taste than it does with law. Nevertheless, in this field, as in almost every other area of our society, the law does intrude and it's essential you understand its impact.

The legal rules governing privacy are very similar to, and sometimes even overlap, those having to do with libel. There is, however, a fundamental difference between the legal rules for libel and privacy. Libel law is generally intended to protect the character and reputation of an individual from false attack, whereas the right of privacy generally seeks to protect how individuals feel about themselves, their peace of mind, spirit, sensibilities, feelings, etc.

It's no secret that the ability of an individual to maintain privacy consistently gets more difficult as our population increases and becomes ever more dominated by technology. Significant violations of privacy increasingly occur in many contexts — eavesdropping and surveillance of all sorts (including cameras on spacecraft), unreasonable searches and seizures,[1] data-gathering by government bureaucracies, the maintenance of huge computer databanks, CIA and FBI activities, credit bureaus, psychosurgery, body cavity searches at the border, and on and on. We cannot deal with all of these areas here. But, as we focus on rights of individuals to privacy in the context of rights attendant to a free press, it is important to remember there are many areas involving personal privacy which need airing.

---

1. See *Marijuana: Your Legal Rights* by Richard Moller, Addison-Wesley Publishing Co. (1981) for a solid overview of search and seizure law under the Fourth Amendment.

The legal definition of the right of privacy is elusive. It has been called the right "to be left alone" and defined as "the claim of individuals, groups, or institutions to determine for themselves when, how, and to what extent information about them is communicated to others."[2] Perhaps the best definition is that of First Amendment scholar Thomas Emerson, who wrote, "The purposes of a system of privacy is, in the broader sense, simply to maintain the oneness of the individual despite the demands of the collective."[3]

Issues of privacy can evoke reactions as strong as those involving prayers in the schools or abortion. But, while feelings are strong, there is also a great deal of confusion when it comes to defining exactly what the right of privacy entails. For example, large segments of the public and many lawyers and judges fail to distinguish between the "right of individuals" to be free from intrusive media prying and other types of government interference with individual activity, such as the Fourth Amendment right to be free from unreasonable search and seizure.

B. Origins of the Right of Privacy

The right of privacy was not among the pieces of common law baggage the English colonists brought with them to America. It was first proposed in 1890 by Louis Brandeis and Samuel Warren in an influential *Harvard Law Review* article[4] written about the time the phrase "yellow journalism" was coined.

In the 1880's the press had begun to gossip about the private affairs of the social elite in ways that were unheard of a generation or two before. Samuel Warren, a prominent Boston lawyer, and his family were members of this elite, and when the press reported the wedding of Warren's daughter in embarrassing detail, Samuel Warren had had enough. Reacting to what they considered the impropriety and indecency of the reports, Warren and Brandeis (his law partner) collaborated in presenting their argument for the vindication of "the right to an inviolate personality:"

> The press is overstepping in every direction the obvious bounds of propriety and of decency. Gossip is no longer the resource of the idle and of the vicious, but has become a trade, which is pursued with industry as well as effrontery . . . . The intensity and complexities of life, attendant upon advancing civilization, have rendered necessary some retreat from the world, and man . . . has become more sensitive to publicity, so that solitude and privacy have become more essential to the individual. . . .[5]

Interestingly, while the two lawyers recognized limitations on the right of privacy, including the right of the press to publish matters of general interest, they did not agree that truth should be an absolute defense in a suit based on invasion of privacy. Truth, they maintained, could exacerbate an invasion of privacy.

---

2. Alan F. Westin, *Privacy and Freedom* (New York, Athaeneum, 1967).
3. Thomas I. Emerson, *The System of Freedom of Expression* (New York, Random House, 1970) p. 546.
4. "The Right to Privacy," 4 *Harvard Law Review*, 193 (1890).
5. *Ibid.*

C. Invasion of Privacy

1. An Overview

Invasions of privacy are generally classified into four broad categories. These are:

False Light: This invasion occurs when you portray someone in a false light that you know, or should know, is false. For example, an honest taxi driver won a privacy suit when his photo was used by the *Saturday Evening Post* to illustrate a story about corrupt cabbies.

Truthful Embarrassing Private Facts: This invasion occurs when you publicize details about someone's private life which are both offensive and lack newsworthiness. For example, if you publish a list of school teachers with herpes you would most likely be invading the teachers' right of privacy.

Intrusion: This invasion usually occurs in the course of the newsgathering process itself. Intrusion claims fall into three general sub-categories: a) surreptitious surveillance, i.e., eavesdropping, bugging, etc.; b) traditional trespass, i.e., unauthorized physical intrusions onto property; and c) abuse of consent to enter, i.e., instances where consent to enter into a secluded setting for one purpose has been exceeded by the newsgatherer.

Commercialization: Misappropriation and the Right of Publicity: This claim usually arises when there is an unauthorized use of a name or picture for an advertisement or other commercial purpose.

In the next four sections of this chapter, we examine each of these invasions of privacy in greater detail.

2. False Light Claims

a. Introduction

"False light" claims commonly occur as a result of journalistic carelessness. The coincidental misuse of a name, the poor disguise of real people in fiction, and the distortion of photographs accompanying otherwise legitimate news stories all give rise to false light claims. When this invasion of privacy not only injures a person's feelings, but also his reputation, an action for libel may exist in addition to the privacy claim.[6] If the invasion is also libelous, the case will tend to be brought primarily on that ground since judges and lawyers tend to be more familiar with the law of libel than with theories surrounding false light claims. If you haven't already done so, read Chapter 3 on libel for further explanation of that concept.

b. What Constitutes a False Light Claim?

The major elements of a false light claim are similar to what you have encountered already in libel. The communication must be:
1. Made public;
2. About the plaintiff;
3. False in a substantial and material way.

An oft-cited false light example is a newspaper photo of a child being helped to her feet after having been knocked down by a car which ran a stoplight. The photo was reprinted twenty

---

6. In California, a plaintiff must choose between a defamation and a "false light" claim.

months later in the *Saturday Evening Post* under the caption "They Asked to Be Killed." The article erroneously implied that this particular child pedestrian had been at fault. A trial court judgment of $5,000 was sustained on the ground that the original publication was newsworthy but the later misuse of the photo offensive.[7]

Claimed distortions amounting to false light can also arise because a journalist has omitted facts, or because captions or headlines are misleading. For example, in the course of investigating alleged police harassment of the Louisville drug community, two *Louisville Times* reporters tape recorded a prospective client's talks with her lawyer concerning possible representation in a criminal case. The lawyer guaranteed that for $10,000 the woman would not go to prison. The *Louisville Times* published the following headline on the front page: "'Lawyer's Guarantee' to Keep Woman Free for $10,000 Unethical?"

Although the article concluded that on the basis of the entire tape, there was no evidence of a fix, the lawyer sued the *Times* for casting him in the false light of a person willing to engage in the crime of bribery. The Kentucky Supreme Court agreed and found the average person could interpret the *Times* headline as indicating the lawyer offered to fix the case or bribe a judge.[8]

c. Constitutional Defenses to False Light Claims

What about the First Amendment's guarantee of free speech? Are courts really going to award damages when a reporter makes an innocent mistake that by coincidence depicts someone in a false light? No. Just as in the libel area, courts have moved to protect journalists' rights of free expression. In fact, a reporter has even more protection in "privacy" cases than in those concerned with libel. Thus, in several false light cases the Supreme Court has ruled that actual malice on the part of a journalist must be proved, even though the plaintiff is neither a public figure or official.

To get a better feel for this area, let's look briefly at the Supreme Court's most famous invasion of privacy decision. *Time v. Hill*[9] grew out of an incident in 1952 in which three escaped convicts held James Hill, his wife, son and daughter hostage in their home for nineteen hours. The family was not physically harmed. The story was widely reported at the time, and Hill, attempting to avoid the publicity, moved his family to another state.

The following year, a novel entitled *Desperate Hours*, purported to describe the dramatic episode, but with the fictionalized addition of considerable violence by the captors against father and son, as well as a verbal sexual assault on the daughter. The novel did not mention the Hill family. However, the novel led to a Broadway play and the play led to a promotional picture-story in *Life Magazine*. The article referred to the original episode, named the Hills, and characterized the play as a "heart-stopping account of how a family rose to heroism in a crisis."

Hill sued for damages under New York's privacy statute, alleging that the *Life* article had revived a painful episode, and caused a serious emotional and nervous illness in his wife. In addition, Hill claimed the *Life* article was false or "fictionalized" in that it gave the impression that the play mirrored the family's actual experiences, and that *Life Magazine* knew the article was "false and untrue." The jury awarded Hill $50,000 compensatory and $25,000 punitive damages.[10]

---

7. *Leverton v. Curtis Pub. Co.*, 192 F.2d 974 (3rd Circuit, 1951).
8. *McCall v. Courier-Journal & Louisville Times*, 623 S.W.2d 882 (1981).
9. 385 U.S. 374, 87 S.Ct. 534, 17 L.Ed.2d 456 (1967).
10. This was later reduced to $30,000 compensatory damages.

FALSE LIGHT OVERVIEW

Here we assume the plaintiff has filed a complaint alleging you invaded his privacy by publishing an article and photograph casting him in a false light.

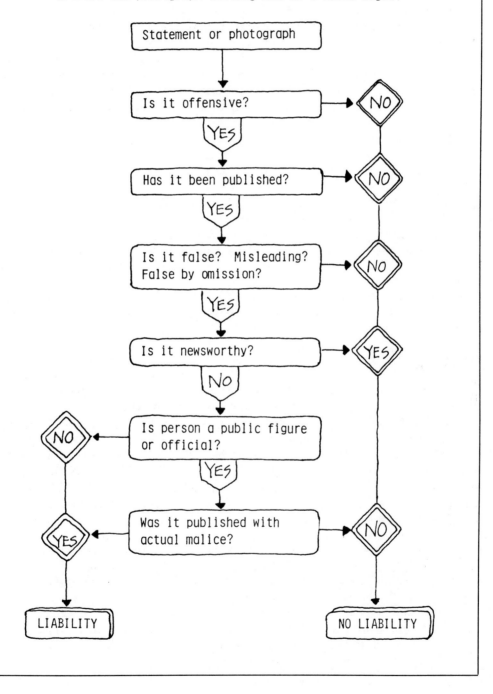

The U.S. Supreme Court reversed. In the clearest statement of the Constitutional restrictions on the false light doctrine, Justice Brennan wrote:

> We hold that the constitutional protections for speech and press preclude the application of the New York statute to redress false reports of matters of public interest in the absence of proof that the defendant published the report with knowledge of its falsity or in reckless disregard of the truth . . . We create a grave risk of serious impairment of the indispensable service of a free press in a free society if we saddle the press with the impossible burden of verifying to a certainty the facts associated in news articles with a person's name, picture or portrait, particularly as related to nondefamatory matter.

Many legal scholars have called for the merger of libel and false light privacy claims on the ground the "interest protected is clearly that of reputation with the same overtones of mental distress as in defamation."[11] However, we believe there is enough of a difference between the two to justify journalists being aware of and protecting against both.

For example, compliments and flattery may constitute a false light invasion of privacy, whereas if made genuinely such items would never constitute libel. To illustrate, Elizabeth Taylor sued to prevent the broadcast of an ABC dramatization of her life, arguing that no matter how flattering it turned out, it would present her in a false light. "They plan to use my name throughout the show, to hire an actress who supposedly resembles me, and to have her speak lines which they want the public to believe I used in numerous personal and private conversations."[12]

For some tips on guarding against false light claims, read the last section of this chapter.

3. Private Embarrassing Facts

a. The Tort

This second type of invasion of privacy squarely focuses on the original concerns of Brandeis and Warren, i.e., publicizing a matter concerning the private life of a person which would offend ordinary sensibilities. Here, invasion of privacy as a tort departs radically from libel law. Truth is not a defense to the disclosure of private embarrassing facts. Nor can damages be limited by publishing a retraction. Once embarrassing information is out it cannot be recalled. In addition, because the "privacy invading" statement is usually truthful there is often nothing to retract.

b. Defenses

A journalist may defend against a privacy claim based on private embarrassing facts if he establishes the material as newsworthy. Thus, when dealing with a case of this kind, judges and juries must weigh the public's right to know (i.e., newsworthiness) against someone's personal sensibilities and the value society places on their protection.

Lawsuits involving publication or airing of facts that invade a person's privacy are therefore difficult to pursue. Why? Because the defense that the story is newsworthy normally protects the journalist. In a society that is interested in how far frogs can jump and who can swallow the

---

11. Prosser, "Privacy," 48 *Cal.L.Rev.* 383 (1960).
12. *New York Times*, November 21, 1982, Section 2.

most goldfish, it can be quite a job to find something that isn't newsworthy. Nevertheless, invasions of privacy have been found to have occurred in extreme situations where the following criteria have been met:

- The facts are private;
- The facts are highly offensive to a reasonable person;
- The matter is not of legitimate concern to the public, i.e., it is not newsworthy.

Let's examine each of these criteria individually.

Private Facts: The facts that are publicized must in fact be private. This means that if you are considering publishing or airing particular information that could be subject to a claim that you invaded someone's privacy, you should first consider whether these facts:

- were already known in the community;
- are matters of public record;
- are of "general interest;"
- were revealed or published by the person who may claim that his privacy was invaded;
- took place at a public location;
- took place at a semi-public location in view of the general public.

Generally speaking, if you can answer "yes" to any of these questions, you can feel secure about publishing because the information, while it may be embarrassing, isn't private.

Reporting what goes on in a public place is rarely considered to be an invasion of privacy. Thus, if you take a photograph or news film of a street scene, no one present has cause for an invasion of privacy lawsuit. Similarly, reporting on what occurs in such semi-public places as restaurants and theatres will not invade privacy so long as what is reported occurs in view of the general public.

An odd legal case arose from a situation where a happily divorced couple invited friends and relatives to their "unwedding ceremony." It was held on a hillside which, though located on private property, was visible to passers-by. Several strangers attended, including a reporter and photographer employed by the *Hartford Courant*. Dressed in a lovely wedding gown, the former bride removed a noose from her neck as the former bridegroom removed bonds from his ankles. Without the consent of the celebrants, the newspaper subsequently published an article and a picture portraying the negative nuptials. The jury found that the paper had not invaded the couple's privacy because the ceremony had occurred in a public manner. [13]

The "public place" rule is not inviolate. For example, a woman emerging from a "fun house" at a local fair was photographed when a fan beneath the exit blew her dress above her waist. The resulting picture was published on the front page of the local newspaper. The Court recognized that the photograph was taken at a public place. Because the plaintiff was a private individual and the very reason for publication of the photograph was its embarrassing nature, however, the Court decided that an invasion of privacy had occurred. [14]

In sum, it would seem that journalists following even minimum standards of decency should have no problem photographing or reporting public or semi-public events.

Embarrassing or Offensive Facts: William James Sidis was a child prodigy who graduated from Harvard College at the age of sixteen amid considerable public attention. A shy and retiring person, Sidis lived a reclusive life until the *New Yorker* published a brief biographical sketch of him entitled "Where Are They Now?" The sketch accurately and sympathetically recounted Sidis' unusual background, traced his attempts to conceal his identity through the years, and detailed his pattern of menial employment and unusual behavior. Sidis sued the magazine for destroying his anonymity, but was ultimately denied relief. [15]

The Court recognized that "revelations may be so intimate and unwarranted in view of the

---

13. *Rafferty v. Hartford Courant*, 36 Conn. Supp. 239, 416 A.2d 1215 (Sup.Ct. 1980).
14. *Daily Times Democrat v. Graham*, 276 Ala. 380, 162 So.2d 474 (1964).
15. *Sidis v. F-R Publishing Corp.*, 113 F.2d 806 (1940).

CHEEKY HEADLINES

victim's position as to outrage the community's notions of decency" and thus be actionable under privacy standards even if otherwise newsworthy. Applying this test to the Sidis case, however, the Court held that an invasion of privacy had not been established. Why? Because the story simply wasn't that embarrassing or offensive.

Cases where plaintiffs *have* successfully met this stiff test of offensiveness have often involved photographs. They include:

- A woman whose disfigured face was photographed while she was semi-conscious;
- A photo of a worker's mangled thigh; and
- A picture in *Time Magazine* of a hospital patient who was photographed against her will and presented to the world as the "starving glutton" who "eats for ten." The woman, it turned out, was afflicted with some kind of disorder which caused her to lose more weight the more she ate.[16]

However, in most cases which involve "embarrassing private facts," the courts have ruled that the broad defense of "newsworthiness" protects the right to publish and outweighs any embarrassment which may have been caused the plaintiff.

Unnewsworthy: In order to be successful in a case brought under the "embarrassing private facts" theory, the plaintiff must prove that the facts disclosed are not of public interest. As noted, this tends to be rough sledding, since an almost limitless range of matters are of general interest. Also, in practice, many courts tend toward the attitude that publication of the item makes it a matter of public interest almost by definition.

There are, however, a few areas where the reporter should tread with care. Often you can make a preliminary determination of whether you are on shaky legal ground by thinking for a moment about the position the subject of your story occupies in the world. The general rule is

---

16. *Barber v. Time, Inc.*, 348 Mo. 1199, 159 S.W.2d 291 (1942).

that if you are reporting about a person who is involuntarily in the news, you must be more careful than if the subject of your story is a public figure.

For example, if a woman was raped and had brought charges against the alleged assailant, you should probably stick to the story of the crime. Digging up dirt on her other sexual relationships would not be of legitimate concern to the public. On the other hand, you could legitimately report on the kinky sex life of a congressman or an anchorperson on the evening news.

NOTE: Even the most public person is probably entitled to protect some area of his or her private life, although the more public the figure, the more limited the area of protection. The court in the *Sidis* case described the distinction as follows:

> . . . when focused upon public characters, truthful comments upon dress, speech, habits, and the ordinary aspects of personality will usually not transgress this line. Regrettably or not, the misfortunes and frailties of neighbors and "public figures" are subjects of considerable interest and discussion to the rest of the population. And when such are the mores of the community, it would be unwise for a court to bar their expression in the newspapers, books, and magazines of the day.

Can a line be drawn between legitimate news and maudlin curiosity? Mike Virgil was interviewed for an article in *Sports Illustrated* on the sport of body surfing as practiced at the "Wedge," a public beach near Newport Beach, Califorina. Virgil revoked his consent for the story when he discovered that the article would include a description of his lifestyle, one which could only be described as a bit bizarre. The magazine published it anyway and a law suit ensued. The following are quotes from the article:

> Every summer I'd work construction and dive off billboards to hurt myself or drop boards of lumber on myself to collect unemployment compensation so I could surf at the Wedge. Would I fake injuries? No, I wouldn't fake them. I'd be damn injured. But I would recover. I guess I used to live a pretty reckless life. I think I might have been drunk most of the time . . . I love tuna fish. Eat it all the time. I do what feels good. That's the way I live my life. If it makes me feel good, whether it's against the law or not, I do it. I'm not sure a lot of the things I've done weren't pure lunacy. Cherilee [plaintiff's wife] says, "Mike also eats spiders and other insects and things."

The case wound up in the Ninth Circuit Court of Appeals, which sent it back to the U.S. District Court to be analyzed under the following standard:

> In determining what is a matter of legitimate public interest, account must be taken of the customs and conventions of the community; and in the last analysis, what is proper becomes a matter of community mores. The line is to be drawn when the publicity ceases to be the giving of information to which the public is entitled, and becomes a morbid and sensational prying into private lives for its own sake, with which a reasonable member of the public, with decent standards, would say that he had no concern. [17]

The trial court granted summary judgment to *Sports Illustrated* on the ground that although the facts were embarrassing, they were not "morbid" or "sensational" and were not published "for their own sake." The Court said:

---

17. *Virgil v. Time, Inc.*, 527 F.2d 1122 (9th Cir. 1975).

Any reasonable person reading the *Sports Illustrated* article would have to conclude that the personal facts concerning Mike Virgil were included as a legitimate journalistic attempt to explain Virgil's extremely daring and dangerous style of body surfing at the Wedge.[18]

The Passage of Time: We have seen that by definition a "newsworthy" story does not invade privacy. Furthermore, the passage of time between an event and the publication about it will generally not defeat a claim of newsworthiness. However, where publicity has had the great potential for interfering with a felon's rehabilitation efforts, the passage of time has proved to be an important factor.

For example, in one case a former prostitute had become a respectable housewife after being acquitted of murder. Her friends did not know of her past until seven years after the trial when a motion picture entitled "The Red Kimono" was released,[19] truthfully depicting the woman's story and using her maiden name. The woman sued for invasion of privacy and the Court awarded damages, outraged that the woman's real name had been used and concerned about the negative effect of the disclosure on the woman's rehabilitation.

In another case, the California Supreme Court ruled that a convicted truck hijacker, who had subsequently lived a rehabilitated life, had a cause of action against *Reader's Digest* for describing the event in an article eleven years later. The Court emphasized the importance of rehabilitation in this particular case, but also recognized the general rule that a public figure remains a matter of legitimate recall to the end of his days.[20] The rehabilitation exception to this rule may no longer be valid, as we discuss in the next section.

c. Public Record Defense

But for the "rehabilitation exception" discussed above, the truthful and accurate publication of material contained in public court records open to public inspection cannot generally be the basis for an invasion of privacy lawsuit.[21] This defense applies regardless of how much time has passed between the publication and the occurrence reflected in the court record. The only problem, of course, is in determining what is and is not a public court record.

Forty-seven states (plus the District of Columbia and Puerto Rico) have laws restricting public access to certain types of criminal records (e.g., juvenile court records, misdemeanor records) by a sealing or expungement process.[22] The expungement or sealing of records almost always occurs after a period of time has elapsed and the person has shown evidence of rehabilitation. Although records have been expunged or sealed, they still usually continue to exist physically and accordingly may fall into a journalist's hands. In such a case, does the public records defense protect the journalist if embarrassing private facts contained in such records are published?

---

18. *Virgil v. Time, Inc.*, 424 F. Supp. 1286 (D.C. Cal 1976).

19. *Melvin v. Reid*, 112 Cal. App. 285 (1931).

20. *Briscoe v. Reader's Digest Association, Inc.*, 4 Cal. 3d 529, 483 P. 2d 34 (1971).

21. *Cox Broadcasting v. Cohn*, 420 U.S. 469, 95 S.Ct. 1029, 43 L.Ed.2d 328 (1975). In *Cox*, the U.S. Supreme Court ruled that the father of a seventeen-year-old rape/murder victim did not have a claim for invasion of privacy against a television station which published the victim's name after obtaining it from an official indictment. However, the Court expressly refused to state how it would rule in the event that information taken from sealed court records or closed judicial proceedings were published.

22. In *Smith v. Daily Mail*, 443 U.S. 97, 99 S.Ct. 2667, 61 L.Ed.2d 399 (1979) the Supreme Court struck down West Virginia's penal statute making it a crime to publish the name of a juvenile involved in court proceedings. In so ruling, the court stated that "[I]f a newspaper lawfully obtains truthful information about a matter of public significance then state officials may not constitutionally punish publication of the information, absent a need to further a state interest of the highest order." In this case, the Court held that the policy favoring anonymity of juvenile offenders was insufficient to justify the statutory penalty.

OVERVIEW OF PRIVATE EMBARRASSING FACTS

Here we assume the plaintiff has filed a complaint alleging you invaded his privacy by publishing an article and photograph disclosing private embarrassing facts.

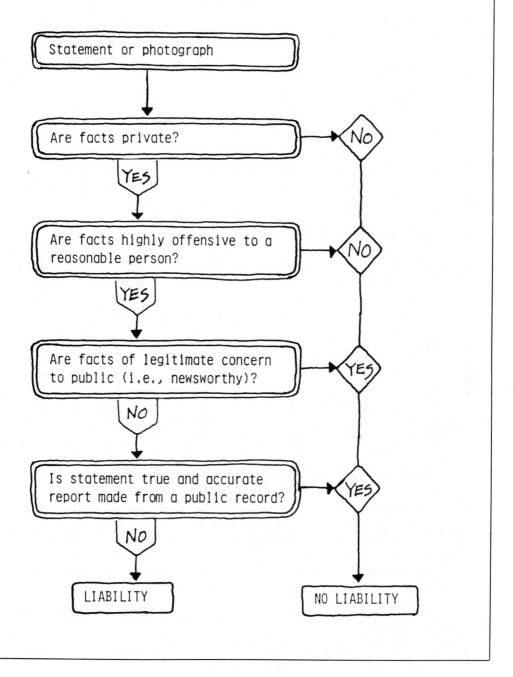

Due to the absence of statutory or case law on this point, we are unable to provide you with an answer. We can only recommend that you tread lightly and get specific legal advice where you know a record has been subjected to a sealing or expungement process, since society has indicated its desire to make them less "public" after the passage of time.

Although state requirements differ on access to juvenile proceedings,[23] federal courts are required to safeguard juvenile court records from disclosure and to seal them upon completion of the proceedings.[24]

4. Intrusion

a. Overview

To many people, invasion of privacy means Greta Garbo under a floppy hat protesting to the press, "I vant to be alone," or Jackie Kennedy in dark glasses avoiding photographers. The unreasonable intrusion upon the solitude or seclusion of another is what is at issue here. The type of information which is published is irrelevant. In many ways, therefore, intrusion resembles the concept of trespass more than it does invasion of privacy by publication.[25]

Intrusion as associated with newsgathering often involves the wrongful use of tape recorders, microphones, cameras and/or other electronic recording or eavesdropping devices to record a person's private activities. It also commonly occurs when a reporter misrepresents himself to gain access to a place or person.

A classic case of the latter type of intrusion occurred when two employees of *Life Magazine* gained access to the home of A.A. Dietemann by pretending to be friends of a friend. Dietemann was a plumber who practiced "healing" with clay, minerals and herbs. One of the employees complained to Dietemann that she had a lump in her breast and while Dietemann examined it, the other employee took pictures and relayed tape recordings to law enforcement officials waiting outside. The whole affair was a cooperative venture of *Life* and the public officials to aid in what *Life* characterized in its article as the "Crackdown on Quackery."

Dietemann pleaded "nolo contendere," or "no contest," to practicing medicine without a license and then sued *Life* for invasion of privacy by intrusion. A U.S. District Court awarded him $1,000, and the Ninth Circuit Court of Appeals upheld the verdict,[26] observing that the First Amendment has never been construed to accord newspersons immunity from the consequences of torts or crimes committed in the process of newsgathering.

The following paragraphs discuss other types of intrusion.

b. The Statutory Rules Against Bugging

While authorized physical entry onto another's property in search of a story sometimes occurs, electronic surveillance is a far larger problem. Phonebugs, hidden tape recorders, and even lasers are routinely used to get information. Often the journalists who use these techniques are breaking the law.

A growing number of statutes regarding surreptitious surveillance may give rise to an increasing number of intrusion lawsuits. The federal eavesdropping statute applicable in all fifty

---

23. For details concerning these laws, see "State-by-State Guide to Expungement Laws," *News Media and the Law*, Oct-Nov 1981, p.31.
24. Justice and Delinquency Act of 1974 (Public Law 93-415).
25. Trespass is the entering onto another's property without his or her consent. It can be a crime and/or a tort.
26. *Dietemann v. Time, Inc.*, 449 F.2d 245 (9th Cir. 1971).

states restricts the situations in which conversations may be electronically recorded.[27] In addition, thirteen states[28] place additional restrictions on the secret or nonconsensual recording of another's conversation. Remember, therefore, that even if the federal statute allows you to record a conversation, the law of your state may not.

The federal statute places greater restrictions on radio-activated recording devices (broadcast to another location for recording) than on non-radio-activated devices (normal tape recording). These restrictions are greater in respect to conversations occurring in private places (home, hotel room, car) than in the case of those taking place in public areas (e.g., the street, courthouse, bus) and semi-public places (e.g., restaurant, theatre). In the most restricted situation, both parties to a conversation must consent to its being recorded, whereas in the least restricted situation, only one of the parties need consent. Basically, here is the way it works.

• If the listening device is radio activated and the conversation is held in a public or semi-public place (e.g., restaurant, theatre), only one party to the conversation needs to consent (i.e., one person to the conversation can be bugged without the other person knowing about it).

• If the listening device is radio activated and the conversation is held in a private place, then both parties must consent.

• If the listening device is non radio-activated, and the conversation is not recorded for the purpose of later broadcast, then only one party to the conversation needs to know, regardless of where the conversation is broadcast.

• If the listening device is non radio-activated but the conversation *is* recorded for the purpose of later broadcast, then both parties need to consent.

WARNING: As we mentioned, the Federal Eavesdropping Act places the minimum recording restrictions on a journalist. Thus, in all states, the journalist must at least comply with these federal guidelines. The individual state laws in thirteen states, however, are stricter than these federal guidelines.

In one case, members of an investigatory team of a Congressional Select Committee on Aging posed as prospective purchasers of cancer insurance while American Broadcasting

27. Section 2510 of Title III of the Omnibus Crime Control Act.
28. California, Delaware, Florida, Georgia, Illinois, Maryland, Massachusetts, Michigan, Montana, New Hampshire, Oregon, Pennsylvania, and Washington.

SUMMARY OF THE LAW OF ELECTRONIC INTRUSIONS
UNDER THE FEDERAL PRIVACY ACT

The Federal Privacy Act makes certain types of electronic surveillance illegal.

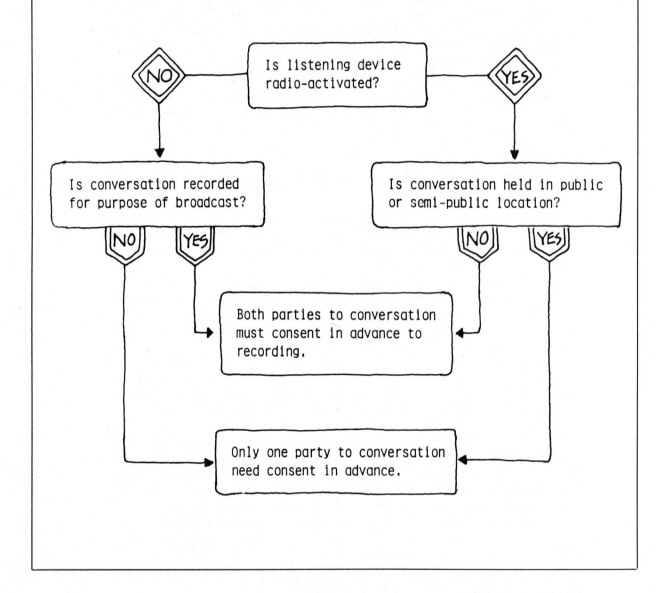

Company employees surreptitiously taped the insurance agent. The tape was later played on the ABC nightly news. The insurance agent filed suit for violations of the Maryland Wiretapping Act, the Federal Eavesdropping Statute, and invasion of privacy, among other things. ABC asked the court to dismiss the privacy claim. The court refused, stating that, at the very least, ABC would have to show that its only purpose in taping the meeting was to aid the Congressional subcommittee.[29] The implication was that if the taping was for newsgathering only, then there would be no protection.

Not surprisingly, media people are more sensitive to unauthorized taping when they are the tapees. For example, Hedrick Smith, Washington bureau chief for *The New York Times*, filed an invasion of privacy suit against Nixon and members of his administration after learning that his home and office phones had been tapped by the government in an attempt to discover leaks that led to a story about secret negotiations with Japan.

Many reporters routinely record telephone conversations with news sources without informing the party on the other end of the line. Since these conversations almost always occur in a private context (i.e., telephone in a home or business office) the federal law permits such taping only if a non radio-activated device (such as a tape recorder) is used and the conversation is used for background only. Further, although such a recording may or may not be illegal under the state's law as well, it does violate telephone company tariff regulations.

A good general rule for the journalist is that if you can hear something in a public place (unless in a courtroom or legislative chamber where rules forbid using tape recorders), you can record it. However, if you enter a person's business office or home with a concealed electronic device, you are probably guilty of illegal behavior and are also vulnerable to a civil lawsuit for invasion of privacy.

c. Trespass: Entering Another's Property Without Consent

This form of intrusion occurs when you invade someone's property without his or her consent. You don't have to enter the property physically. Sticking a microphone or camera into someone's property could be considered trespass.

Journalists are on shaky legal ground when they do any of the following to get a story:

• Enter private property in a situation in which they have been told to keep out or where the common practice of society is sufficient to indicate that they shouldn't enter. Surreptitiously entering a person's residence is a good example. A harder situation occurs during protests on private property such as nuclear power or defense plants.

• Misrepresent their identity to gain a person's trust and get a story. The rule seems to be that if the story is sufficiently newsworthy (i.e., "Congressman Steals 10 Million Dollars from Poor"), the journalist might get away with it. But otherwise, the reporter and his or her organization are vulnerable to big judgments. Expert legal advice is a must here.[30]

In general, intrusion should be looked upon as a newsgathering wrong. As we mentioned, the newsworthiness of a report or whether it is published with reckless disregard of its truth or falsity is not a legal issue (although newsworthiness may as a practical matter get a journalist off the hook). Further, courts are generally unwilling to extend First Amendment protection to intrusive activities. You would do well, therefore, not to feel secure when publishing reports based on illegal entry, stolen documents, illegally taped conversations, and so on.

It is important to know, however, that courts tend to reject a plaintiff's "intrusion" claim

---

29. *Benford v. A.B.C.*, 502 F.Supp. 1148 (D.Md. 1980).
30. A reporter for *The Daily Record* of Morristown, New Jersey, was convicted of impersonating a government official when, for the purpose of obtaining information for a story, she represented to the family of a murder victim that she was "from the morgue," *New York Times*, October 30, 1983.

brought under the trespass theory when the media is not directly involved in the illegal act, but instead receives and publishes the products of another's intrusion. An example of this involved four of the late Senator Thomas Dodd's ex-employees, who removed documents from his office and gave copies to Drew Pearson and Jack Anderson.[31] Stories then appeared in the Pearson column based on these documents.

The Court held that even though one columnist knew that the documents were stolen, the subsequent publication did not give rise to an action for intrusion-trespass against him because he himself did not participate in the unlawful reproduction of the documents.

d. Defenses to Intrusion Claims

Hot Pursuit: Journalists in "hot pursuit" of a story frequently enter private property to obtain information or photographs without first obtaining permission. Technically, this constitutes trespass, but the law seems settled that there is no unlawful trespass when peaceable entry is made, without objection, under common custom and usage. Once an objection is raised, however, the "trespasser" should leave.

For example, a photographer accompanying a fire marshall into a home destroyed by fire was held not liable for intrusion under the theory of implied consent based upon the "common usage, custom and practice for the news media."[32] If the householder had been there to object, the same protection would not apply.

On the other hand, journalists were convicted of trespass when they followed demonstrators into a power plant site in Oklahoma. The power company had provided an on-site viewing area for the press, but the reporters could not see or hear the protestors being arrested.

Consent: Where feasible, it is considered best to enter private property with permission, even if it is generally accessible to the public, as the courts will tend to uphold the rights of property owners to be free from unauthorized entry. Thus, even though a theatre implicitly authorizes members of the public to enter the premises for the purpose of viewing a film, it has not thereby authorized a camera crew to enter for the purpose of reporting on the patrons' reactions or behavior.

For instance, when CBS television reporters entered an expensive New York City restaurant without consent and with cameras "running" following the announcement of a health violation, the court ruled that although the restaurant was open to the public, the reporter and cameraman had entered without intent to purchase services, and no consent to telecast had been granted.[33] (Persons lunching with persons other than their spouses were reported to have ducked under their tables while the cameras were rolling.)

Public figures are often considered to have consented (by implication) to substantial news coverage simply by virtue of their status. Such consent can be exceeded, however. In a case involving America's "paparazzo," Ronald Galella, and Jacqueline Kennedy Onassis, a federal District Court held that the photographer's antics were not protected by the First Amendment, but constituted actionable assault, battery, harassment, a violation of the civil rights statute and "infliction of emotional distress."[34] It said:

> When Galella suddenly jumped from behind the wall in Central Park, frightening
> John and causing him to lose control of his bicycle, Mrs. Onassis described her state
> of mind as having been "terrorized." The Santa Claus pursuit in and around the

31. *Dodd v. Pearson*, 279 F.Supp. 101 (D.D.C. 1968).
32. *Florida Pub. Co. v. Fletcher*, 340 So.2d 914 (Fla. 1976).
33. *Le Mistral, Inc. v. CBS*, 61 A.D.2d 491, 402 N.Y.S. 2d 815 (First Dep't. 1978).
34. *Galella v. Onassis*, 353 F.Supp. 196 (S.D.N.Y. 1972), 487 F.2d 986 (2nd Cir. 1973).

Collegiate School in December 1970 left Mrs. Onassis extremely upset. Galella's outrageous pursuit of Mrs. Onassis on the night of "Two Gentleman of Verona" terrified her and left her in an "anguished," "humiliated" and in a "terribly upset" state. Numerous times, and at dangerous speeds, he has followed cars in which the children were passengers, violating the rules of the road, and the Secret Service agents assigned to protect the children have frequently expressed concern for the safety of their principals as a result of Galella's activities.

We conclude that the First Amendment does not license Galella to trespass inside private buildings, such as the children's schools, lobbies of friends' apartment buildings and restaurants. Nor does the Amendment command that Galella be permitted to romance maids, bribe employees and maintain surveillance in order to monitor plaintiff's leaving, entering and living inside her own home.

The Court ordered Galella and his agents to keep their distances from Mrs. Onassis and her children by several hundred feet.[35]

D. Stealing or Commercializing Another's Identity

1. An Overview

The law allows the individual the right to prevent others from trading on his or her name or likeness. In a sense, the courts have considered the name or likeness of many people to be a type of property which itself can be utilized for commercial purposes. Consequently, if a name or likeness can be utilized to make money, it is unlawful for another to use it (called "appropriating" it, in legal jargon) without permission.

Appropriation is an offense which can be of concern to journalists but which much more frequently arises in the advertising and personal promotion business.

How do you defend against a claim that you have stolen something of value from a person about whom you are writing or talking, or whom you are filming? The best defenses are either written consents or a claim that your report was newsworthy. The latter is used most often, since in most circumstances the fact that a journalist reports a story makes it "newsworthy." However, there are times when a particular story is so sensitive that either explicit or implied consent should be arranged, if possible. See Section E of this chapter for sample consent and release forms.

An example of where a journalist's report was held to appropriate impermissibly another's name or likeness involved Hugo Zacchini, the "Human Cannonball," who shot himself from a cannon in a dramatic act lasting about fifteen seconds. Despite his specific refusal to be filmed, the entire act was shown on television news. Zacchini sued the Cleveland television station involved, claiming it had appropriated his professional property without his consent.

The Supreme Court ruled for Zacchini, emphasizing in its decision that: "The effect of a public broadcast of the performance is similar to preventing petitioner from charging an admission fee." The Court held that despite the newsworthiness of Zacchini's act, the First

---

35. The Court of Appeals upheld the lower court's decision but sharply cut down the distances. Mrs. Onassis has since asked the court to hold Galella in contempt for not obeying the order.

Amendment did not bar him from recovering damages for a violation of his right to privacy under Ohio common law.[36]

The *Zacchini* case leaves open some questions. Was the basis of the Supreme Court's decision the fact that Zacchini's entire act was filmed? If so, would it be all right to broadcast only part of the performance? Couldn't this be considered "free advertising" for Zacchini? Or, does it really amount to the fact that Zacchini withheld his consent to be filmed? This is certainly an example of a situation where "newsworthiness" alone wasn't adequate.

The lesson seems to be that if you are dealing with an area in which the person or group charges for the performance or other activity you want to picture, or otherwise directly reproduce, you'd better get their consent. If you are dealing with a group or event of importance, this consent should be in writing. A number of states, including New York, have statutes which protect a person's commercial privacy where the injured person's commercial purpose is clear and primary and the use is substantial as opposed to incidental. These statutes have been interpreted to protect direct news reporting but not always to allow the commercialization of entertainment features.

2. Advertising and Promotion

The unauthorized use of someone's name or likeness for purposes of advertisement or promotion gives rise to one of the most common types of commercialization claims. For example, the 4th Circuit U.S. Court of Appeals ruled that Johnny Carson's publicity rights had been violated by a Michigan corporation named "Here's Johnny Portable Toilets, Inc.," even though his name or likeness was not used. The clincher for the Court was that the corporation used the phrase in conjunction with "The World's Foremost Commodian."[37]

Basically, you simply can't legally use a living person's likeness or name to promote any commercial product or venture without his consent.

3. Non-Advertising Use of Name or Likeness

In general, courts do not like to recognize claims of appropriation by people who are not involved in the commercial promotion of their own name or likeness. Courts only uphold such claims if the name or likeness specifically identifies the person, and its use is a principal part of a media presentation which is made with a commercial (e.g., advertising) rather than a news-gathering intent.

For example, a federal court in New York dismissed an appropriation claim, based on thirteen references to a private person's name, brought against the author and publisher of *The Blood of Israel* (an account of the 1972 attack on the Israeli Olympic Team). The judge reasoned that the plaintiff was not the primary subject of the allegedly fictitious work and the use of his name was merely incidental.[38] However, if a TV producer had without consent used still and movie footage of the same person as part of a made-for-television movie, the result might have been different.

---

36. *Zacchini v. Scripps-Howard Broadcasting*, 433 U.S. 562, 97 S.Ct. 2849, 53 L.Ed.2d 965 (1977).

37. *Carson v. Here's Johnny Portable Toilets, Inc.*, 698 F.2d 831 (4th Cir. 1983).

38. *Ladany v. Morrow*, 465 F.Supp. 870 (S.D.N.Y. 1978).

4. Photographs and Illustrations

Appropriation claims arise frequently with the use of photographs, both for advertising purposes and non-advertising uses. If a person's likeness is used in advertising, the same principle applies to photographs that applies to names — if the commercial purpose is clear and primary and the use of the photograph is not incidental, consent is required. If no consent is obtained, the media people and organizations involved are wide open for a successful "appropriation" suit. See Section E of this chapter for sample consent and release forms.

When advertising is not involved, the general rule is that use of a picture reasonably related to an article or book on a matter of public interest will not be actionable. This is really just another way to say the use is newsworthy.

EXAMPLE: A man's photo appeared on the cover of the *New York Times* "Sunday Magazine" to illustrate an article (in which plaintiff was not mentioned) concerning the upward mobility of the black middle class.[39] The man brought appropriation suits against the *New York Times*, the free-lance photographer who had taken his picture and the photographic agency which had sold the picture to the *New York Times*.

The Court rejected the claim against the *New York Times* on the ground that the *Times* used the photo for news purposes and that no appropriation therefore occurred. However, the Court also held that the man stated a valid claim against the free-lance photographer and the photographic agency because they had operated independently of the publisher and had "commercialized the photograph in furtherance of (his) trade."

ANOTHER EXAMPLE: Although neither his actual name nor a photograph was used, a New York court sustained Muhammed Ali's cause of action and granted him a preliminary injunction to stop distribution of an issue of *Playgirl Magazine*. The issue contained an "illustration falling somewhere between representational art and a cartoon" of a frontally nude black athlete with Ali's facial features in a boxing ring with an accompanying piece of verse referring to "The Greatest." One court said there was "no informational or newsworthy dimension to Playgirl's use of Ali's likeness. Nor did Ali's status as a public personality preclude liability."[40]

This aspect of privacy law can get quite abstract. To make it more concrete, let's look at several hypothetical situations.

Assume Fred, an aspiring photographer, snaps a photograph of Lillian Jones, a well known fashion model, as she is walking into a Kennedy International Airport terminal. The photograph luckily highlights all Ms. Jones best features and hides the worst ones. Fred gives the photograph to a friend of his who publishes a small computer magazine. The friend puts the picture on the cover of the next issue under the caption, "You Don't Have to Be Beautiful to Enjoy Computers." Appropriation by Fred and the computer magazine? You bet. Even though the picture was taken in a public place, it is being used for solely commercial purposes (i.e. to make Fred some money and to sell the computer magazine). Since Ms. Jones makes commercial use of her likeness, she is entitled to damages. If she were a computer programmer instead of a model, however, she might have difficulty collecting damages since she would not use her likeness for commercial purposes.

Suppose that instead of giving the photograph to his computer magazine friend, he rushes the photograph to the *New York Post*, which runs it the next day over the caption, "New York Loses Lillian Jones." Appropriation by the *Post*? Absolutely not. In this case Ms. Jones was photographed in a public place and the photo is being used in a "news" context. Even if the photo were used as part of a gossip column about the jet set life of the top models, it would not be appropriation because of the "newsworthiness" of the accompanying story. Fred, however,

---

39. *Arrington v. New York Times*, 434 N.E.2d 1319 (1982).
40. *Ali v. Playgirl, Inc.*, 447 F.Supp. 723 (S.D.N.Y. 1978).

AN OVERVIEW OF THE INVASION OF PRIVACY LEGAL DOCTRINE

In this chart we start with the assumption that a journalist has broadcast a statement or either published or televised a pictorial image which someone claims has invaded their privacy. The purpose of the chart is to give you an overview of the law in this area.

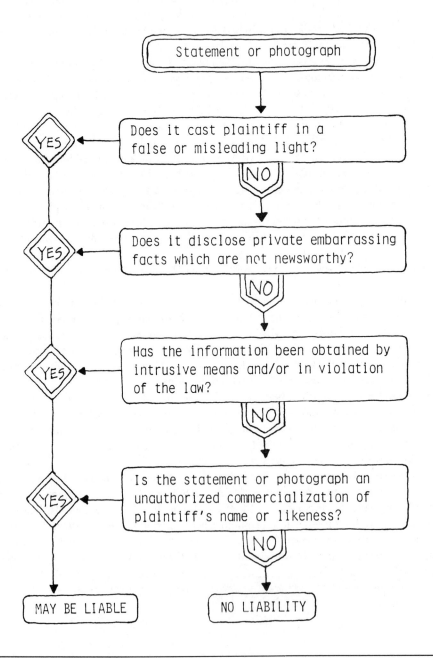

Statement or photograph

Does it cast plaintiff in a false or misleading light? — YES / NO

Does it disclose private embarrassing facts which are not newsworthy? — YES / NO

Has the information been obtained by intrusive means and/or in violation of the law? — YES / NO

Is the statement or photograph an unauthorized commercialization of plaintiff's name or likeness? — YES / NO

MAY BE LIABLE

NO LIABILITY

being a freelancer, might be held liable for appropriation.

For some suggestions on how to avoid being liable for appropriation turn to the last section of this chapter (Section I).

E.   Written Releases and Consents

Simply put, a release is a written statement absolving specified persons and institutions of liability for acts specified in the document. Thus, a typical release utilized by journalistic photographers absolves the journalist and his media organization from any liability arising out of how or for what purpose the photograph is ultimately used.

A written consent form does not expressly absolve anyone of liability as such. It does establish proof that the subject of the photograph or article did in fact consent to the piece. For the most part, forms used in the business combine the consent and release paragraphs into one document. Thus, typically a person is asked both to consent to the use of his name or likeness and to release the media from liability in the event of misuse.

It is possible that written consent and/or release forms arguably obtained under fraudulent conditions may not hold up later (i.e., the person claims you misrepresented your purpose when you asked him to sign the release). However, the burden is on the person who signed the release to prove he was mislead in some way. Thus, it makes good sense to obtain a written consent and release when feasible, especially if the circumstances indicate the possibility of trouble down the road.

If you could get a release from every adult who turns up in your stories, commentaries, pictures, or films (and from parents of every minor), you would have no problems with right of privacy suits. Obviously, though, getting wholesale releases isn't practical or even possible. Also, as we noted in the previous sections, it isn't generally necessary if you are reporting or otherwise dealing with a newsworthy person or event.

If you do need to get a release, here are a few short rules of thumb:
- Get the release in writing or on tape.
- If the subject is a minor, have the release signed or voiced by a parent or guardian.
- Don't exceed the limits set forth in the release.
- Don't secure the release by trickery or fraud. A release will protect you only if you present honestly the facts of how you plan to use the material.
- Make the release as specific to your purpose as possible. For example, if you want to use a famous person's picture in an ad for a symphony or charity or commercial product, say so.

NOTE: Generally speaking, candid shots of people for illustrative purposes taken in public places do not require releases, but if the shots are unknown to the subject and are embarrassing, privacy lawsuits may result.

For advertising purposes, some state laws require the photographer to obtain the subject's prior *written* consent. In New York, where this is the case, courts have held defendants liable where there is no written consent, even though they had reason to believe written consent had been obtained.

Here are some examples of releases and consent forms:

RELEASE FOR PHOTOGRAPHS

In exchange for good and valuable consideration I have received:

I hereby give _____(your name)_____, his associates, publishers, employers, and any other person or entity with whom he or she may contract for the use of the product covered in this release, the absolute right and permission to use without restriction any photographs of me which were taken on __(date of photographs)__ at _____(city)_____. I also consent to the use of any printed matter in conjunction therewith.

I hereby release and agree to hold harmless all such persons and entities from any liability connected with an accidental or intentional distortion of said photographs that may occur in the taking of said picture, in the subsequent processing thereof, or in the publication thereof.

I hereby waive any right I may have to inspect and/or approve the finished product which results from said photographs, or the use to which they are put.

I understand that by signing this form I am waiving any right of privacy which might be infringed upon as a result of the publication of the said photographs.

I make this authorization, release and agreement on the basis of the representation by _____(your name)_____ that the photographs are intended for the purpose of _____

_____

_____.

I am of full age and have every right to contract in my own name. I have read the above authorization, release and agreement prior to signing it and am fully familiar with its contents.

Dated: _____   Name: _____ (L.S.)

Witness: _____   Address: _____

RELEASE FOR FILMS, VIDEOTAPES, AND AUDIOTAPES

In exchange for good and valuable consideration I have received:

I hereby give _____(your name)_____, as well as his or her employer, station, network, film company and any other person or entity with whom he or she may contract for the use of the product covered in this release, the right and permission to record me, my acts, poses, statements and performances on film, videotape and/or audiotape.

I also give all such persons and entities the right to use such film, videotape and/or audiotape throughout the world, as well as my name, likeness and biography, in connection with the production, exhibition, advertising, promotion or other exploitation of the following program: _____(name of program)_____.

I hereby release and agree to hold harmless all such persons and entities from any liability connected with an accidental or intentional distortion of said film, videotape, and/or audiotape that may occur in its recording, in the subsequent processing thereof, or in its use.

I hereby waive any right I may have to inspect and/or approve the film, videotape and/or audiotape or the use to which it is put.

I understand that I am waiving any right of action which I might otherwise have for an invasion of my privacy caused by the use of said film, videotape and/or audiotape.

I make this authorization, release and agreement on the basis of the representation by _____(your name)_____ that the film, videotape and/or audiotape is intended for the purpose of _____

_____

_____.

I am of full age and have every right to contract in my own name. I have read the above authorization, release and agreement prior to signing it and am fully familiar with its contents.

Dated: _____ Name: _____ (L.S.)

Witness: _____ Address: _____

F. The Right of Publicity After Death

Here we deal with whether or not fame can be inherited. Five states with statutes prohibiting commercial use of a peson's name or likeness say that the right of a living person to control her likeness for publicity purposes passes to her heirs upon the person's death.[41] Six states have statutes to the opposite effect.[42] The rest are controlled by the common law, and most of these have refused to recognize this right. As one lawyer put it, "You have to draw the line somewhere, so you won't have Napoleon's heirs stopping the sale of Napoleon brandy."

Those states allowing the right of person's heirs or next of kin to inherit the value of a famous person's name or likeness stress the right of each person to enjoy and pass to one's heirs the fruits of one's efforts. Those states which do not allow the heirs to "inherit" the value of a name or likeness emphasize the personal nature of the right not to have others capitalize on one's name and likeness, and the difficult questions inherent in treating such a right as independent of the person himself (e.g., How long should it survive? Is the right taxable? If so, how much is it worth at death?)

Court decisions in this area have also been confusing. For example:

Count Dracula Dolls:[43] The widow of Bela Lugosi (the actor who played the original "Count") brought suit against Universal Studios for marketing Count Dracula figurines, jigsaw puzzles and other novelties. She lost when the California Supreme Court decided the right to exploit one's name and likeness was personal to Lugosi and could only be exercised by him.

Martin Luther King Statues:[44] The heirs of Martin Luther King were found to have no right to royalties for little statues of the civil rights leader marketed after his death.

Stan Laurel and Oliver Hardy Impersonations:[45] Heirs were successful in suits based on TV programs which presented imitations of the dead actors complete with typical costumes, mannerisms and voice imitations. According to the Court, "the protection from intrusion upon an individual's privacy, on the one hand, and protection from appropriation of some element of an individual's personality for commercial exploitation, on the other, are different in theory and scope." The Court distinguished the Laurel and Hardy case from the Lugosi one on the basis that Laurel and Hardy had portrayed themselves and developed their own characters, whereas Lugosi's fame had come from portraying fictional characters (some have argued, however, that Count Dracula actually existed).

Elvis Presley Paraphernalia: Two cases involve Elvis Presley. During his lifetime, Presley entered into a contract with Boxcar Enterprises, in which he conveyed the exclusive right to use his name and likeness for commercial purposes. Since Presley's death, Boxcar has been involved in several suits relating to the exploitation of Presley's attributes by others. One court enforced the Presley-Boxcar contract and stopped the sale of Presley posters. Although the court declined to rule that the right of publicity in general can be inherited, it held that the "exclusive right to exploit the Presley name and likeness, because exercised during Presley's life, survived his death."[46] On the other hand, a court in another case involving Elvis concluded that the right of publicity, while properly recognized during a person's lifetime, should terminate at his death under all circumstances.[47]

---

41. Florida, Nebraska, Oklahoma, Utah and Virginia.

42. California, Massachusetts, New York, Rhode Island, West Virginia, and Wisconsin.

43. *Lugosi v. Universal Pictures*, 25 Cal.3d 813, 603 P.2d 425 (1979).

44. *Martin Luther King, Jr. v. American Heritage Projects*, 508 F.Supp. 854 (N.D. GA. 1981).

45. *Price v. Hal Roach Studios, Inc.*, 400 F.Supp. 836 (S.D.N.Y. 1975), and *Price v. Worldvision Enterprises, Inc.*, 455 F.Supp. 252 (S.D.N.Y. 1978) aff'd, 603 F.2d 214 (2nd Cir. 1979).

46. *Factors Etc. v. Pro Arts, Inc.*, 579 F.2d 215, *cert. den.*, 440 U.S. 908 (1979).

47. *Memphis Development Foundation v. Factors Etc., Inc.*, 626 F.2d 956 (6th Cir.), *cert. den.*, 449 U.S. 9063 (1980).

How can this aspect of the law be best summarized? With difficulty. The law in the various states differs over whether the heirs of a famous person have some kind of proprietary right to commercial proceeds based on the deceased's name or likeness. Even where there is such a potential right, often it will not be recognized unless the famous person commercially exploited his name or likeness while alive.

A NIGHTMARE TO THE JOURNALIST

G.   Privacy and Fiction

In fiction, the key to whether or not a person's privacy has been invaded is whether or not he can be identified. If the person's real name is used, then of course there is not as much problem with identification, and a law suit based on invasion of privacy will very likely succeed, if the other elements are present. Even so, it must be established by the plaintiff that the use of his name is something more than an amusing coincidence or peripheral. Thus, the average reader must suspect that a supposedly fictional character is in fact the plaintiff. Assurances that a work is fictional will not be sufficient to protect an author or publisher from invasion of privacy actions if it is apparent that this isn't true.

If a person is recognized in a work of fiction, the four common types of invasion of privacy claims discussed in this chapter apply with even more vigor than is true with other journalistic endeavors, since fiction is almost never considered newsworthy. These include situations in which:

1. People feel that recognizable depictions of their character are untrue (they are presented in a false light);

2. People feel that a novel or other fictional piece not only portrays them in such a way that they will be recognized, but discloses intimate personal matters which they want to keep private (embarrassing private facts are disclosed);

3. People claim that facts depicted in fiction were obtained by intrusive and perhaps illegal ways, such as by trespassing on private property or wiretapping (intrusion);

4. People don't want their personal "right of publicity" misused in fictionalized accounts (appropriation).

NOVELISTS' NOTE: If any character in a story is based, even loosely, on a real person, you will be wise to change enough facts so that the connection is not apparent. Further, it is wise to take reasonable care to be sure that you have not accidentally used the names of real people. For example, if you write a mystery story in which a New York police inspector is cast in unfavorable light, you would do well to check to be sure that there is not a real inspector with the same name. This is even more necessary if you are writing about a singer or performer who lives by exploiting the value of her name.

In some privacy cases, there is a practical restraint against plaintiffs filing lawsuits. Many individuals who do truly value their privacy are unwilling to admit to being the individual depicted in a novel or play about whom personal, intimate and often embarrassing facts are disclosed. However, this restraint has its own limitations. Some people may be proud of their present status and sue because they are angry that some unflattering incident from the past has been thrust into the present.

See *Author Law*, by Brad Bunnin and Peter Beren, Nolo Press, for a complete treatment of the law as it affects the writer of fiction.

H.   The Docudrama Dilemma

Many disputes arising in the privacy context occur when fact and fiction are mixed in what is called the "docudrama" or the "non-fiction novel." Here, it is common for a public figure to be involved. If the author makes incidental use of a famous person's name or story, say as background, he or she will probably not be succesful in a privacy suit. However, if the public figure is made the protagonist of the story, the legal situation changes. Public figures may be more likely to sue for violation of their right to publicity on the ground that cashing in on the use of their name unjustly enriches the author and publisher.

We mentioned earlier the case of Elizabeth Taylor, who claimed a violation of her right to publicity in her lawsuit against ABC for their docudrama, "The Elizabeth Taylor Story" or "Liz." "Some day I will write my autobiography, and perhaps film it, but that will be my choice," Miss Taylor said. "By doing this, ABC is taking away from my income."[48]

The very characteristics that go to make up a docudrama—invented dialogue, impersonation, and the impression that the scenes portrayed really happened—make them also vulnerable to false light invasion of privacy claims, on which Elizabeth Taylor also sued ABC. The argument is that mixing fact with fiction and calling it a life story, no matter how flattering it is, is showing the subject in a false light and creating a wrong image.

Where the real people who appear as fictional characters are clearly public figures, or the events portrayed are matters of public concern, false light claims are generally dismissed because the plaintiffs cannot establish actual malice. The Rosenbergs' sons' privacy allegations concerning statements about them in Louis Nizer's book *The Implosion Conspiracy* were dismissed, with the court noting that it was "immaterial . . . whether Nizer's book is viewed as a historical or fictional work. In either case, the *New York Times v. Sullivan* test of reckless disregard of the truth is applicable since we are dealing with "public figures."[49]

Likewise, a New York court dismissed the false light claims of aides of the late Senator Joseph McCarthy, whose activities were portrayed without their consent in a television movie.[50]

In a case concerning the film *Dog Day Afternoon*, the real-life family of the bank robber played by Al Pacino sued for invasion of privacy. The New York courts rejected their claims on

---

48. *The New York Times*, Nov. 21, 1982.
49. *Meerpol v. Nizer*, 560 F.2d 1061 (2nd Cir. 1977), *cert. den.*, 434 U.S. 1013 (1948).
50. *Cohn v. NBC*, 67 A.D.2d 140, 414 N.Y.S.2d 906, aff'd 50 N.Y.2d 885, 430 N.Y.S.2d 265, *cert. den.*, 66 L.Ed.2d 484.

the ground their real names were not used in the movie.[51] The absence of a real name did not prevent recovery in the widely reported *Bindrim* case, however.

There, a well known psychologist who conducted nude encounter therapy groups claimed his reputation as damaged by language and conduct attributed to the character, Simon Hereford, in the novel *Touching*, despite the use of a different name, different physical description, and different credentials. Although the action was for libel, it was essentially a false light claim. To prove that he was identified, Bindrim introduced videotapes of his nude marathons and drew parallels between incidents depicted on the tapes with those depicted in *Touching*. The court found that the portrayals of the character cast *Bindrim* in a disparaging light, depicting his language and conduct as crude, aggressive and unprofessional.[52]

The potential for a claim of inadequate disguise of a fictional character will depend, in part, on whether the character is central or peripheral, whether the real person was "depicted," or merely "suggested," how well the person is known, and the effectiveness of the disguises.

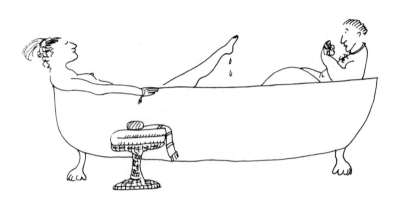

I. Some Practical Tips on Avoiding Privacy Claims

1. Avoiding False Light Claims

What can a working journalist do to guard against false light claims? As always, rigorous fact-checking is most important. Beyond that, be particularly careful in the following situations:

• Photos run with stories which may be unflattering. For example, if you do a story on unemployment, be sure the people standing in line in an accompanying picture are really waiting for unemployment checks and not lined up for the automatic teller at the bank next door.

• Name Identification as part of any story involving crime, disease, or other sensitive or unflattering material. It's one thing mistakenly to drop the mayor's name in a story about a flower show and quite another to list it among people who have an unpopular disease.

---

51. *Wojtowicz v. Delacorte Press*, 43 N.Y.2d 858 (1978).
52. *Mitchell v. Bindrim*, 92 Cal.App.3d 61, 155 Cal.Rptr. 29 (1979).

2. Avoiding Misappropriation Claims

Here are some do's and don'ts you may find helpful when dealing with another person's name or likeness:

- Photos and descriptions of people in public places are protected as long as used in a "news" or "feature" context.
- Photos and descriptions of public people (those who routinely trade commercially on their own name or likeness) used for advertising or other commercial purposes are not protected and may well give rise to a successful lawsuit.
- If you are in doubt as to whether you are infringing on another's commercial privacy, arrange for his or her consent.

3. Avoiding Intrusion Claims

- Film surreptitiously or without consent only when the subject is in a public place (e.g., street, public park, public buildings) or a semi-public place (e.g., theatres and restaurants).
- Do not film where people ordinarily would not be deemed to have consented. In a semi-public place, film only areas which can be seen readily by members of the public.
- Never record a conversation unless one of the parties knows you are doing it and consents. Do not record any conversation unless you know the law of your state regarding whose consent is required.

4. A Counseling Checklist

The questions on this checklist are designed to focus your attention on the sensitive areas of journalistic practice as regards possible invasion of privacy claims. Your answers should help you use the material presented in this chapter to assess whether you might be risking committing a privacy invasion.

COUNSELING CHECKLIST

I. *Status of Potential Claimant*
   1. Age: minor?
   2. Disability—mental or emotional condition; prison inmate? under influence of drugs, etc.?
   3. Is the subject alive? Did the deceased exploit his right of publicity during his lifetime? Do heirs have standing to assert claim?
   4. Public figure status, if any?
   5. Prior publicity?
   6. Receipt of compensation for material in question or for similar material on prior occasions?

II. *Status of Person Who Obtained Questioned Material*
   1. Employee?
   2. Independent contractor?
   3. Unrelated third party—was the person authorized or solicited or encouraged by any agent to obtain material?
   4. Was there a duty of confidentiality (e.g., doctor, social worker)?

III. *Interviews*
   1. Was potential claimant (the subject of the interview) the source of information to be used?
   2. Was the subject aware that interview was for publication? For which publication?
   3. Where was interview granted (home, public place)?
   4. How did reporter obtain admission to subject's home?
   5. Were any conditions imposed on interview? Approval? Confidentiality? How much of interview is used? Is there a copyright problem or a "droit moral" problem?
   6. Was interview recorded? Tape? Notes? If not, who was present?
   7. Do any of the circumstances surrounding the interview raise an issue of a statutory violation (e.g., impersonation, fraud, eavesdropping, bribery, theft, trespass)?
   8. Does the published form of the interview contain fictionalized conversation or speculative thought processes attributed to the subject?
   9. Was consent withdrawn prior to publication?

IV. *Photographs*
   1. How was the photograph taken? Was it posed? Taken with the knowledge of the subject that it was intended for publication? Surreptitiously? In a matter frightening to the subject? Is there any witness to the taking of the photo?
   2. Where was the photograph taken (private or public setting)?
   3. In what context will photograph be published (news article, magazine cover or book jacket, promotional material)? Will the photograph be "cropped" or altered?
   4. Does the context of the photograph, its caption, or related "teasers" or headlines imply any false fact about the subject?
   5. If the context is not clearly part of the editorial content of the publication, is there a need for a release from the subject? Are the subjects entitled to modeling fees? Do paid models appear in the same photograph?

6. Have all necessary rights from the photographer been obtained?

V. *Private Documents, Personal Letters, and Intimate Information*
1. How was the material obtained? Openly? Surreptitiously? In a manner violative of statute?
2. How old is the information? Has the subject's status changed since the information was documented?

VI. *Fiction*
1. Does a character suggest or depict a real person? Is the character a central or peripheral figure?
2. Are the disguises adequate? Age? Physical description? Personality traits? Ethnic origin? Locale? Other parallels in story? Use of real person's name in role other than that of character in question?
3. Are the disguises defamatory?
4. If name of the real person is used, does the context suggest a defamation or false light problem? Is the reference central or peripheral?

Free Press and Fair Trial

A.   The Conflict

> Free speech and fair trials are two of the most cherished policies of our civilization, and it would be a trying task to choose between them.
> —Justice Black
> U.S. Supreme Court

The First Amendment to the U.S. Constitution guarantees free speech and the Sixth Amendment guarantees a fair trial. The inherent conflict between these two laudable goals has been encompassed by the broad phrase, "free press v. fair trial." Before dealing with the details of this conflict and what it means to the working reporter, let's examine the texts of the two amendments:

FIRST AMENDMENT: Congress shall make no law respecting an establishment of religion, or prohibiting the free speech exercise thereof, or abridging the freedom of speech or of the press; or the right of the people peaceably to assemble, and to petition the Government for a redress of grievances.

SIXTH AMENDMENT: In all criminal prosecutions, the accused shall enjoy the right to a speedy and public trial, by an impartial jury of the State and district wherein the crime shall have been committed, which district shall have been previously ascertained by law, and to be informed of the nature and cause of the accusation; to be confronted with the witnesses against him; to have compulsory process for obtaining witnesses in his favor, and to have the assistance of Counsel for his defense.

The Sixth Amendment guarantee of an "impartial jury" often conflicts with the First Amendment's prohibition against "abridging the freedom of speech or of the press." The problem commonly arises when the media so publicizes a trial that the impartiality of the jury is prejudiced. The solution put forward by some courts and commentators is to allow an individual's Sixth Amendment right to a fair trial to override the First Amendment right of the public to know. This has resulted in photographers, TV reporters and sometimes even print journalists being excluded from courtrooms. It has also given rise to reporters being told what they can and cannot report, and the closure of preliminary criminal hearings to all media representatives. Not surprisingly, those who make their living reporting the news view these steps as a perversion of the fundamental freedoms upon which America was founded (on the other hand, those whose freedoms are threatened rely on them as means of preserving a fundamental right).

This chapter has three objectives. First, we briefly sketch the historical background of the fair trial/free press controversy. Second, we tell you as best we can what the current state of the law provides. And finally, we offer some practical suggestions as to what you can do if you find your freedom to report unreasonably restricted.

NOTE: As with most media law topics governed by the U.S. Constitution, this one also is difficult to "nail down," due to confusing and conflicting pronouncements by the U.S. Supreme Court. However, we have done our best to extract some basic principles.

B.   Historical Background

Let's start with one of the most famous trials of the twentieth century — one that has not unfairly been described as a "trial by newspaper." The Lindbergh case involved the 1932 kidnapping and murder of the 19-month old son of Charles and Anne Lindbergh. As the first person to make a solo air crossing of the Atlantic Ocean, Charles Lindbergh was a genuine world hero. The kidnapping was front-page news for weeks, long after the murdered child's body was found in a shallow grave.

More than two years after the child was abducted, Bruno Richard Hauptmann was arrested and subsequently tried for the kidnap-murder. In an atmosphere more closely resembling a carnival than a court of law, as many as 800 journalists and photographers tried to cram into a small courtroom in Flemington, New Jersey. Headlines such as "Bruno Guilty, But Has Aides, Verdict of Man in Street" and descriptions of Bruno Hauptmann as "a thing lacking human characteristics" were epidemic. Hauptmann was both quickly convicted and promptly executed.

Before long, however, a disquieting question arose. Had Hauptmann been afforded a fair day in court or was his execution predetermined by a totally unfair trial by headline? To answer this and a number of more technical questions, a Special Committee Between the Press, Radio, and Bar was established. Its specific mandate was to deal with the effect of bias-inducing publicity during trial. In a scathing report, the Committee referred to Hauptmann's trial as "the most spectacular and depressing example of improper publicity and professional misconduct ever presented to the people of the United States in a criminal trial."

Despite a plethora of other trials in which "yellow journalism" was similarly claimed to have prejudiced the right of the defendant to receive a fair trial, the Supreme Court did not squarely consider the issue until 1961. In that year, the Court overturned a state criminal conviction specifically because pretrial publicity prevented a fair trial before an impartial jury. The case developed like this.

Leslie Irvin, a parolee, was arrested on April 8, 1955 on suspicion of burglary and writing bad checks. A few days later, Evansville, Indiana police and the Vanderburgh County prosecutor issued press releases asserting that "Mad Dog Irvin" had confessed to six murders, including three members of one family.

Because of the wide media attention on the "confessed slayer of six," Irvin was able to obtain a "change of venue" (change in the place of trial). However, the trial was moved only to an adjoining county. Because Indiana law permitted only one change of venue, the court in that area denied Irvin's additional request to be tried in another county much further away.

Trial began November 14, 1955. Of 430 prospective jurors questioned by the prosecution and defense attorneys, 370 (i.e., 90%) expressed their belief in Irvin's guilt. When twelve jurors were finally seated by the Court, Irvin's attorney attempted to challenge them on grounds that they were all biased. He failed. Irvin was found guilty and the jury sentenced him to death. His conviction was upheld by the Indiana Supreme Court.

However, a unanimous U.S. Supreme Court ruled that Irvin had not been accorded a fair trial before an impartial jury because of prejudicial news reporting.[1] In addition, the Court ruled that the U.S. Constitution required a second change of venue under such circumstances, regardless of the Indiana law. Irvin was eventually retried in a less emotional atmosphere. He was found guilty again, but this time he was sentenced to life imprisonment.

If the Supreme Court thought the Irvin decision settled the issue of pretrial publicity, they were mistaken. Two years later, the question of whether media coverage prejudiced the rights of a defendant was again before them.

This time the defendant, Wilbert Rideau, was charged with bank robbery, kidnapping and murder. The day after his arrest, a twenty-minute "interview" between Rideau and the Parish sheriff was broadcast over the local television station at three different times; it was seen by an estimated 97,000 persons out of a local population of 150,000.

Rideau's request for a change of venue was denied. Similarly, his request to remove three jurors who had seen the television interview was rejected. Rideau was convicted and sentenced to death. The U.S. Supreme Court again reversed, stating in part:

> What the people of Calcasieu Parish saw on their television sets was Rideau, in jail, flanked by the sheriff and two state troopers, admitting in detail the commission of the robbery, kidnapping, and murder, in response to leading questions by the sheriff. The record fails to show whose idea it was to make the sound film, and broadcast it over the local television station, but we know from the conceded circumstances that the plan was carried out with the active cooperation and participation of the local law enforcement officers. And certainly no one has suggested that it was Rideau's idea, or even that he was aware of what was going on when the sound film was being made.[2]

Now we come to the quintessential case of Dr. Sam Sheppard. Suspected of brutally bludgeoning his wife to death in the upstairs bedroom of their lakeshore home, Dr. Sheppard, a Bay Village, Ohio osteopath, claimed he was innocent. He was nonetheless treated as the prime suspect in the case by local law enforcement personnel. Indeed, the coroner was reported to have said, "Well, it is evident the doctor did this, so let's get the confession out of him." Sheppard was pressed by the police either to take an "infallible" lie detector test or an injection of "truth serum," or to confess. When he resisted, the local press played up his refusal, as well as claiming a "protective ring" had been thrown up around him by his family.

On July 20, 1954, a local newspaper ran a front page editorial charging someone was "getting away with murder." The following day another front page article was headed: "Why No

---

1. *Irvin v. Dowd*, 366 U.S. 717, 81 S.Ct. 1639, 6 L.Ed.2d 1751 (1961).
2. *Rideau v. Louisiana*, 373 U.S. 723, 83 S.Ct. 1417, 10 L.Ed.2d 663 (1963).

Inquest? Do It Now, Dr. Gerber." A coroner's inquest was indeed held the same day in a school gymnasium. It was televised live to the viewers in the Cleveland area, and covered by a swarm of reporters and photographers. After three tense days, it ended in a public brawl.

The newspapers emphasized facts tending to incriminate Sheppard and highlighted discrepancies in his statements. Much of the "evidence" the press relied on was never admitted into evidence at trial. Meanwhile, editorials proclaiming Sheppard's guilt became increasingly insistent. Late in July, newspaper editorials appeared bearing titles such as "Why Don't Police Quiz Top Suspect?" and "Why Isn't Sam Sheppard in Jail?" Another headline shrilled: "Quit Stalling — Bring Him In."

The night the latter headline appeared, Sheppard was arrested and charged with murder. He was taken to the Bay Village City Hall where hundreds of spectators, including many reporters, photographers, and newscasters, awaited his arrival.

Publicity intensified. Stories about Sheppard's extramarital affairs were emphasized, and suggestions were made that the affairs were a motive for the murder. Press comment, much of it both sensational and undocumented, continued without let-up. By the time of trial, the media were firmly in control.

The great majority of the very limited number of seats was occupied by reporters. Private telephone lines were installed in other rooms on the same floor of the courthouse, and a radio station was allowed to broadcast from the room next to the jury room. Although photographs were allowed in the court only during recesses, reporters moved in and out while the court was in session, sometimes making it difficult for witnesses and lawyers to be heard. Because of crowding, it was almost impossible for Dr. Sheppard and his lawyers to hold confidential discussions. Generally, reporting was flamboyant, and the jury was indirectly exposed to considerable testimony and other evidence which was inadmissible.

Dr. Sheppard was found guilty of first degree murder and sentenced to life imprisonment in December 1954. His appeals were unsuccessful and he served ten years in the Ohio penitentiary. Finally, he obtained a review of his conviction in federal District Court. The district judge found that Sheppard had been deprived of his constitutional right to a fair trial by the prejudicial publicity and referred to the trial as a "mockery of justice." Press clippings from the three Cleveland newspapers alone filled five volumes of the court record. The issue finally reached the U.S. Supreme Court, which reversed Sheppard's conviction and ordered a new trial.[3]

In a second trial, Sam Sheppard was acquitted. He was released from prison in 1966. He married again twice, gave up osteopathy for wrestling, and died of undetermined causes in 1970.

C. The Judicial Response:
The Reardon Report

As a result of the decisions just discussed, as well as the massive publicity which surrounded both President Kennedy's assassination and the arrest and shooting of Lee Harvey Oswald,[4] the American Bar Association established an Advisory Committee on Fair Trial and Free Press. This committee eventually issued the "Reardon Report" establishing categories of pretrial publicity the Committee believed should be prohibited. Included were publication of prior criminal records, character references, confessions, lie detector and other test results, and the

---

3. *Sheppard v. Maxwell*, 384 U.S. 333, 86 S.Ct. 1507, 16 L.Ed.2d 600 (1966).
4. The American Bar Association charged that "widespread publicizing of Oswald's alleged guilt, involving statements by officials and public disclosures of the details of 'evidence,' would have made it extremely difficult to impanel an unprejudiced jury and afford the accused a fair trial."

out-of-court opinions of lawyers and witnesses on guilt or innocence, or on the merits of the evidence.

The Reardon Report also recommended a number of methods to insure a defendant's right to a fair trial. These included granting changes of venue, "continuances" (postponements), waiver of the right to trial by jury (trial by a judge), "sequestration" (keeping the jurors together and away from outside influences), a new trial when publicity prejudiced the first trial, and juror challenges (removing individual jurors who have been biased by pretrial publicity).

The report addressed itself primarily to attorneys, police officials and other officers of the courts, and recommended that they restrict their comments to the press during pretrial and trial periods. More pertinent to the rights of the media, it also recommended that courts use their contempt power to punish anyone who willfully disseminates extrajudicial statements designed to affect the outcome of a trial or who violates a valid order not to reveal information from a closed judicial hearing.

By mid-1974, joint meetings of the bench and the bar on the one hand, and news organizations on the other, resulted in the promulgation of voluntary fair trial–free press agreements in nearly half the states. These attempted to establish standards of responsible conduct acceptable to all interests.

D.   Current Restraints on the Right to Report

1. The "Voluntary" Guidelines

Although the guidelines resulting from the Reardon report are voluntary, they have often been perceived by judges, prosecutors and policemen as having the effect of a judicial mandate. The result has been that many participants in the criminal justice system are increasingly reluctant to talk to reporters about certain types of crimes. In addition, some courts have relied on these guidelines to justify issuing wholesale gag orders to "protect the rights of the defendant."

As many reporters have noted, however, restrictions on reporting often serve the ends of the law enforcement bureaucracy rather than the rights of the defendant. For example, when it suits the interests of a prosecutor, reporters are routinely told all, but when a prosecutor thinks his or her position would be better served by silence, the rights of the defendant are trotted out to justify closed hearings, gag orders, and the like. Not surprisingly, many journalists have long and bitterly repented voluntary agreements limiting the media's right to report. Indeed, in the last several years, many press groups have formally withdrawn from them.[5]

2. Gag Orders in Pretrial Hearings

In many cases trial judges have tried to "resolve" the fair trial/free press conflict by issuing court orders directly prohibiting the press from publishing certain types of information. The press has

---

5. This has resulted in part from the U.S. Supreme Court decision not to review the Washington state case of *Federated Publications v. Swedberg*, 96 Wash.2d 13, 633 P.2d 74 (1981). In that case, the Washington Supreme Court ruled that a trial judge could force reporters to state in writing that they would be bound by the state's "voluntary" guidelines as a condition to allowing them into a preliminary hearing. The press across the country widely considered the ruling to be a blatant prior restraint.

ZIP YOUR LIP AND PUBLISH

steadfastly fought all such prior restraints on its ability to report criminal proceedings. Not so affectionately referred to as "gag orders," these restraints have been violated by more than one reporter at the cost of days, weeks, and in a few situations, months behind bars.

The gag order controversy came to a head in a Nebraska multiple murder case where the prosecuting attorney and the defendant's attorney jointly asked the judge to enter a gag order against the press. Incorporating the Nebraska bar-press voluntary guidelines, the judge issued a sweeping order stopping publication of material from the public pretrial proceedings. He then went on to forbid the press to talk about what he had done. The press was infuriated by what they called a "gag on a gag" and how the "voluntary guidelines" had become part of a formal court order.

Unlike the conduct of journalists in other situations, the press obeyed the gag order and pursued its appeal efforts, eventually to the U.S. Supreme Court. On June 30, 1976, some eight months after the original order was issued, the Supreme Court unanimously struck down the Nebraska court's restrictive order as an unconstitutional prior restraint.[6]

The Court's decision reaffirmed the general prejudice against all prior restraints discussed in Chapter 2. It held that gag orders were only permissible where there is a clear demonstration of the potentially harmful effects of publicity on the jury. In addition, the Court placed the burden on the party desiring the gag order to establish 1) the probable effectiveness of such an order and 2) the absence of alternatives less destructive of First Amendment rights.

3. Barring the Press from Hearings

Unfortunately, two alternatives to gag orders against the press have become popular:
*   Gag orders against non-press, i.e., lawyers, court personnel, and law enforcement officers; and
*   Exclusionary orders barring the public, including the media, from the courtroom.

Although the decision in the *Nebraska* case has slowed the flow of gag orders as such, judges have become more likely to close judicial hearings altogether, thereby shutting off information at its source.

---

6. *Nebraska Press Assn. v. Stuart*, 427 U.S. 539, 96 S.Ct. 279, 49 L.Ed.2d 683 (1976).

There are two stages of the trial process from which courts have barred the press—pretrial and trial. At the pretrial stage, judges (and often defense counsel) argue that public disclosure of potentially tainted evidence will threaten a defendant's right to the empaneling of a constitutionally impartial jury. At the trial stage, they fear that the jurors, who normally go home at night, will be prejudiced by daily reports of the trial.

We need to examine several Supreme Court cases to determine which types of press exclusion are permitted and which forbidden as violative of the First Amendment. Unfortunately, we cannot provide you with any hard and fast rules. Why? As we mentioned at the beginning of this chapter, the rulings of the Supreme Court itself are often confusing and contradictory.

a. Closed Pretrial Hearings

Let's start with an important point. In 1979, the Supreme Court held that the press and public have no independent constitutional right to attend pretrial hearings when the defense requests and the prosecution and judge agree to close the proceedings in order to assure a fair trial.[7] The court ruled that the Sixth Amendment guarantee of a "public trial" is personal to the defendant; it is not an independent right of the press and public.

This seems simple enough. Why then is the law confused? Because in that case (*Gannett v. DePasquale*) the Court was sharply divided, and the reasons of the individual justices for the decision were very diverse. In fact, the Court could only muster a plurality opinion, i.e., less than a majority of the justices agreed on the precise reasons for the decision. Indeed, many experts feel the *Gannett* case has left the law in so much confusion as to beg for clarification in the near future.

The practical effect of the *Gannett* decision has been disastrous to reporters' access to pretrial hearings. In the twelve months following *Gannett*, judges closed some part of a criminal proceeding more than 260 times. In some cases, judges even closed entire trials and sentencings to the press. Commonly, the press, but not the public, was barred from the courtroom. The ruling was particularly onerous for the press, since full-scale criminal trials are extremely rare in the United States. With the widespread use of motions before trial and plea bargaining (an agreement to plead guilty in exchange for a promise of a reduced sentence, probation, or dropping of other charges), well over 90% of all criminal prosecutions are terminated at the pretrial stage. In effect, then, the *Gannett* case has been read by many to give trial judges almost unlimited discretion to bar reporters from what amounts to the entire criminal adjudication system.

Not surprisingly, the Supreme Court came under heavy attack by the press for its ruling. Many journalists went so far as to accuse the justices of presiding over the birth of a police state. Stung, several justices uncharacteristically issued public statements, disagreeing among themselves as to the meaning of *Gannett*. Chief Justice Burger, for example, insisted that the opinion applied only to pretrial proceedings: "Maybe judges are reading newspaper reports of what we said, rather than the Court's majority opinion . . . ." Justice Blackmun, on the other hand, told a group of federal judges, "I think it is an outrageous decision, totally in error. Despite what my colleague, the Chief Justice, has said, the opinion authorized the closing of all trials." Finally, at an American Bar Association meeting, Justice Powell said that judges might be "a bit premature" in interpreting *Gannett* to mean that actual trials can be closed. Nevertheless, the Reporters' Committee for Freedom of the Press identified 434 cases after *Gannett* in which defendants sought to close the courtroom, with about a 60% success rate.

---

7. *Gannett Co. v. DePasquale*, 433 U.S. 368, 99 S.Ct. 2903 (1979).

b. Closed Trial

In an attempt to clarify this confusion, two Richmond, Virginia newspapers challenged a closure order after they were barred from covering an entire murder trial.

In July 1976, John Paul Stevenson was convicted in a rural Virginia Court of second-degree murder of a local motel owner. The Virginia Supreme Court reversed the conviction and sent the case back for retrial. The retrial ended in a mistrial when a juror became ill and no alternative juror was available. Again in June 1978, a second retrial was declared a mistrial when one of the jurors read a newspaper account about the first trial and told other prospective jurors about it.

At the start of the fourth trial, Stevenson's attorney moved to close the courtroom to the press, "because," he stated, "I don't want any information being shuffled back and forth when we have a recess as to who testified to what." The prosecution did not object. The judge granted the request without a hearing, and cleared the courtroom. The closure was challenged by the two newspapers. The Virginia Supreme Court relied on the *Gannett* case to uphold the closure, and the issue found its way back to the U.S. Supreme Court.

This time, the Supreme Court struck down the closure order. [8] Its reasons were expressed in six separate opinions produced by a seven justice majority. The essential holding of the *Richmond* case is that the press and the public do have a First Amendment right to attend trials. Before any criminal trial can be closed to the public and the press, the defendant must demonstrate "an overriding interest." Chief Justice Burger, who wrote the majority opinion, does not specifically define what this "overriding interest" is, but he does indicate that it cannot be found to exist if there are alternate methods, such as jury sequestration (i.e., keeping the jury isolated during the entire trial) to deal with the possible prejudicial effect of publicity on a defendant's right to a fair trial.

E.   Questions after Richmond

Despite the jubilation with which the *Richmond* decision was received by the press, several important questions were left unanswered:

1. Does the *Richmond* ruling apply to trials only, or also to pretrial proceedings?
2. Has *Richmond* established a right of newsgathering under the First Amendment, as some have argued?
3. Does the ruling apply to civil as well as criminal trials?
4. Under what circumstances exactly is a closed trial permissible?

One of the problems with defining important legal issues by court decision is that a court generally deals only with the particular narrow issue before it. Dozens of related questions are typically left in limbo, to be answered by future courts. Thus it may be years before all issues surrounding closed judicial proceedings will be known. There have been some post-*Richmond* cases, however, which may give a glimmer of future developments.

The most important of these is a 1982 decision in which the Supreme Court struck down a Massachusetts statute because it barred the press and public on an across-the-board basis from every trial involving a rape victim who is a minor. The decision (*Boston Globe Newspaper Co. v. Superior Court*[9]) relied heavily on *Richmond* in holding that criminal trials must generally be open to the press and public even though the right of access is not absolute.

Massachusetts argued that it had an interest in protecting minors from the stress and

---

8. *Richmond Newspapers v. Commonwealth of Virginia*, 448 U.S. 555, 100 S.Ct. 2814, 65 L.Ed.2d 973 (1980).
9. *Globe Newspaper Co. v. Superior Court for Norfolk County*, 102 S.Ct. 2613 (1982).

embarrassment of testifying about the details of sexual assault. The Court agreed that the state's interest was a "compelling" one but said it did not "justify a mandatory closing rule," and that "a trial court can determine on a case-by-case basis whether closure is necessary to protect the welfare of the minor victim."

The *Globe* decision appears to have voided all state laws that mandate *automatic closure* of criminal judicial proceedings or portions of them. However, a judge still has the discretion to close criminal proceedings to the press if she feels that reporting will deny the criminal defendant a fair trial.

A 1984 Supreme Court decision established the right of the press and public to be present during examination of prospective jurors, further expanding press access to the courts.

ALTERNATIVES TO CLOSURE

1. Voluntary agreement between the press and the court about the timing and scope of coverage, with an agreed-upon delay being as brief as possible.

2. Change of venue — request (motion) to the court that the trial be moved to another location.

3. Continuance — request (motion) to delay the proceedings to a later date.

4. Voir Dire — questioning of jurors at the outset of the trial to ascertain any bias or prejudice.

5. Judge's instructions to jurors — warning (admonishing) jurors not to read about the case nor discuss it with others or among themselves until actual deliberations are begun.

6. Sequestration — isolating and keeping jurors together to shield them from harassment and to preclude any direct or indirect communications from others about the case.

7. Additional peremptory challenges — allowing the defense to dismiss additional jurors without having demonstrated actual bias (a limited number of such challenges are provided as a matter of course).

8. Severance of multi-defendant cases — conducting separate trials in cases involving multiple defendants, so that publicity about one defendant will not prejudice the other defendants.

9. Change of venire — changing the entire jury, which really results in a new trial.

10. In-chamber hearings — conducting pretrial and trial discussions about the admissibility of evidence in the judge's office (chambers) outside the hearing of the press, jury and public.

F.   Coverage of Juvenile Trials

Before we go on to consider what you can do to fight gag orders and courtroom closures, let's look briefly at the rules in force in juvenile court proceedings. Juvenile proceedings are not, by definition, criminal, mostly because of their rehabilitative goals. Further, many states have special rules restricting media access to these proceedings on the ground that the potential for publicity would hurt the interests of the minors coming before the court.

Thirty states bar any individual from juvenile hearings who does not have a "proper interest" in the case or in the workings of the court. Most states do not define the phrase "proper interest," although the District of Columbia and Wisconsin have designated the media as being properly interested and able to attend juvenile proceedings.

Statutes in eleven states[10] presume that juvenile hearings will be open, though they allow judges wide discretion to close the proceedings if closure would be in the best interest of the juvenile.

California, Illinois, New Mexico, and South Dakota have provisions allowing press attendance at juvenile hearings even in cases from which the general public is excluded.

In Maine, Montana, New Mexico, and Virginia, on the other hand, the seriousness of the charge determines whether a hearing will be presumed to be open or closed (the more serious the crime, the more likely the press will be allowed in).

Are journalists prohibited from publishing the names of juveniles involved in juvenile court proceedings? If there is no statute closing juvenile case files, you may always publish the juvenile's name, even if you cannot attend his hearing. Even if there is such a statute, if you can ascertain the name of the offender through other investigatory means, you can report it without fear of judicial reprisal.

G.   The Press Organizes to Defend Its Rights

The negative court decisions restricting the rights of journalists have resulted in a project known as "Court Watch." Initiated by the Reporters' Committee for Freedom of the Press, and ten other professional journalism associations, Court Watch catalogs closure motions and what happens to them.

Between July 1979 and May 1981 the Reporters Committee compiled summaries of more than 400 closure motions in pre-indictment, pretrial, trial and post-conviction hearings. Almost two-thirds of the motions were made on the basis of potential jury prejudice from pretrial publicity. The rest were based on a variety of other reasons, including: embarrassment to victims, defendants, witnesses and even third parties; potential harm to the trial participants; a defendant's Fifth Amendment rights against self-incrimination; the defendant's prominence in the community; unwillingness of reporters to sign a pledge to follow a bench/bar/press agreement; national security; protection of victims who are minors; and, in one case, potential disruption of the trial by the defendant's family.

The Court Watch study is intended to continue until the full effect of the *Richmond* decision can be ascertained.

---

10. Arizona, Colorado, Florida, Kansas, Michigan, New York, North Carolina, Ohio, South Dakota, Tennessee, and Iowa.

H. What You Can Do to Fight Trial Closure Motions

The following is a suggested procedure for challenging a court order excluding you from a hearing:

1. State your objection to the order for the record. This means that a court reporter should be present to take down your remarks. If there is not one present, request one ("Your Honor, would you please have a reporter present so I can make some remarks for the record?") Once a reporter is present, you will want to say something like the following:

> Your Honor, I respectfully object to your Honor's decision closing this hearing/trial and respectfully request that I be permitted to remain throughout the course of this proceeding for the reason that I'm entitled to be present as a member of the public to observe the administration of justice by your Honor and Counsel for both sides. I base this objection on the First Amendment of the U.S. Constitution.

2. Tell the judge you may wish to appeal her order to the state Supreme Court and ask her to postpone the hearing until you can talk to your editor about it. Ask that your request and the judge's response to it be set out in the record.

3. Ask that the judge direct the court reporter to give you a written transcript of the court order closing the hearing and your objection to it, as well as your request for postponement and her response to it. (You will probably have to pay for the transcript. However, since the part you'll be interested in is not very long, it shouldn't cost more than about $25.00).

If after making your objection the judge still orders you to leave, we suggest you make the following statement: "Your Honor, I am obeying your order, but I am doing so unwillingly and under protest."

4. Report the event to your editor, and give her the transcript as soon as you receive it. The editor will decide whether she wishes to contact the company's legal department for consideration of legal action.

If you are unable to follow the procedure outlined above because you have not been admitted to the proceeding and the door is locked or guarded, do the following:

a. Write out you objection and request that it and the judge's response be entered in the court record.

b. Deliver your written statement to a bailiff and ask that she present it to the judge at once. If no bailiff is available, or if she refuses your request, find another judge and deliver the statement to her with the request that it be taken at once to the judge hearing the proceeding. If no judge is available, deliver it to the clerk of the court with the same request. Be sure you get the name and position of the person to whom you deliver the statement.

c. Report the event to your editor.

d. Keep careful notes of everything you and others do and say.

Obey the judge's direct orders, even if you think they are unconstitutional, unless you wish to risk being jailed. You can be held in contempt of court even if the judge's order is patently wrong and is so held on appeal.

HOW TO AVOID A CONTEMPT CITATION

Given the range of unanswered questions as to when gag orders are constitutional and when they are not, any reporter who covers the courthouse will face the decision of whether to obey a gag order or risk contempt by going ahead and publishing or broadcasting. If you find yourself in the sort of situation in which your professional ethics demand that you do more than button your lip, start by getting competent legal advice.

If you decide to publish in contravention of a court order, here are general guidelines of what a lawyer is likely to do to prevent you from being jailed:

1. Go to a state appeals court judge and ask for a temporary stay of the order pending the filing of your formal appeal.

2. If the appeals judge believes the lower court order is wrong, the judge may grant the stay pending the full appeal.

3. If the appeals court judge denies a stay, the next step is to seek one from a state Supreme Court Justice.

4. The justice may grant the stay or refer it to the full court for decision.

WARNING: If you go ahead and publish or broadcast in the face of a court order telling you not to, you run a heavy risk. Disobedience of a court order will not be permitted, even when the order is later held to violate the First Amendment.

YOU BE THE JUDGE

In late 1983 a videotape taken by FBI agents, in which former automobile manufacturer John DeLorean was shown selling cocaine, was aired by CBS on national television. CBS had been ordered not to air the tape by the judge presiding over the DeLorean cocaine trial due to the devastating effect such apparent evidence of guilt might have on DeLorean's fair trial rights. The judge's order was overturned as a prior restraint by the Ninth Circuit Court of Appeals. After the videotaped transaction was viewed from coast to coast, the trial judge indicated his doubt that DeLorean could ever receive a fair trial anywhere in the country.

Should the tape have been aired?

If not, who had the responsibility to see that it wasn't?

I.   Television in the Courtroom

1.   Introduction

The closest many Americans ever come to attending a trial is their television set. Millions have grown up believing that "Perry Mason," "Owen Marshall" or "Peoples' Court" accurately represent what goes on in a real courtroom. Along the way, they learned that somehow justice is always served, even if this takes the murderer bursting into the courtroom dripping with guilt to confess, seconds before the station cuts to the final mouthwash commercial. And, in an ever greater distortion of the truth, they get the message that trials are never boring, always logical and over in an hour. Of course anybody who has served as a juror knows otherwise.

Given these erroneous perceptions, a real courtroom experience can come as a shock. Perhaps it's a good thing that more people will experience this reality jolt in the next few years. Why? Because, after a sixteen-year ban on electronic media in the courtroom, the Supreme Court has ruled that state courts have the authority to allow television coverage of criminal trials, even over the objection of the defendant.[11] But why the sixteen-year ban in the first place? To understand the impact of the Court's decision to permit cameras in court, we must go back a few years.

2. Historical Background — Old Technology Disrupts

Broadcast coverage of courtroom proceedings dates back to 1925, when Station WGN Chicago set up a microphone to transmit the famous Scopes Monkey Trial to a large listening audience. The ban on broadcasting can be traced to the sensational trial of Bruno Hauptmann for the kidnapping of the Lindbergh's baby[12] when 132 still and newsreel cameras vied for space and disrupted the trial. As a result, the American Bar Association adopted a rule (called a "canon" in legalese) in 1937 which effectively prohibited still and movie cameras and microphones from all courtroom proceedings. While the American Bar Association is a private group and their canons have no legal authority, they are influential; their prohibition against cameras was

---

11. *Chandler v. Florida*, 449 U.S. 560, 101 S.Ct. 802, 66 L.Ed.2d 740 (1981).
12. See discussion earlier in this chapter.

113

written into law by most states. Similarly, Rule 53 of the Federal Rules of Civil Procedure banned all cameras and microphones from criminal cases in federal courts.

The result of these restrictions was that all federal courts and all states, with the exceptions of Colorado and Texas, prohibited televising of judicial proceedings either by state statute or court rule. Meanwhile, Texas and Colorado, the two states which continued to permit cameras in the courtroom, enjoyed somewhat different experiences. In over twenty years of allowing television access to the courtroom, no Colorado case was reversed on the basis that television coverage was found to be prejudicial to the rights of the defendant. In Texas, however, the Billie Sol Estes trial resulted in a U.S. Supreme Court decision that proved to be a serious setback for television courtroom access.

3. TV Coverage Loses — the Texas Experience

Billie Sol Estes, a flamboyant Texas financier accused of swindling Texas farmers, came before a judicial hearing in Smith County, Texas, in September 1962, after a "change of venue"[13] from Reeves County, some 600 miles west. The courtroom was so packed that people were standing in the aisles. Cables and wires snaked everywhere. Even as Estes' attorney requested that the judge exclude all cameras from the courtroom, a cameraman walked behind the judge's bench to photograph the lawyer.

The judge did not grant the defense request to exclude cameras, but she did establish some limitations. The major television networks, CBS, NBC, and ABC, plus local television station KLTV, were allowed to install one television camera each (without sound recording equipment), and film was made available to other television stations on a pooled basis. Only still photographers for the Associated Press, United Press, and the local newspaper could enter the small courtroom.

Despite these limitations, the U.S. Supreme Court held that Estes had been deprived of his "due process" right to a fair trial because of the effects of live television, radio, and news photography coverage of the trial.[14] The court said:

> A defendant on trial for a specific crime is entitled to his day in court, not in a stadium or a city or nationwide arena. The heightened public clamor resulting from radio and television coverage will inevitably result in prejudice. Trial by television is, therefore, foreign to our system.

What about the First Amendment argument against barring the electronic media from the courtroom? The Court stated: "While maximum freedom must be allowed the press . . . its exercise must necessarily be subject to the maintenance of absolute fairness in the judicial process."

4. Television Makes a Comeback

More recently, rapid changes in technology have indeed resulted in profound changes in judicial attitudes. Modern electronic mini-cameras are a fraction of the size of the equipment

---

13. The trial is changed to a different court because the defendant does not think he can get a fair hearing in the original county court.
14. *Estes v. State of Texas*, 386 U.S. 532, 85 S.Ct. 1628, 14 L.Ed.2d 543 (1965).

114

used during the Estes trial and can operate under ordinary light conditions. As a result, with good planning, the filming of a trial can be done unobtrusively. Recognizing this, as many as twenty-six states permitted some television coverage of courtroom proceedings on an experimental basis in the 1970's. Most followed the approach of permitting electronic coverage only with the consent of all concerned. A few adopted a plan similar to one in effect in Florida, which permits television coverage regardless of objections from trial participants.

The Florida plan was considered by the Supreme Court in 1981. Two police officers, Noel Chandler and Robert Granger, were arrested by Miami Beach police after they allegedly burglarized a local restaurant, using police squad cars and two-way radios to assist their efforts. The case drew considerable media coverage, not only because the men were police officers, but because of their unusual capture. This occurred when an insomniac amateur radio operator inadvertently intercepted the burglars' conversations as they entered the restaurant, and alerted honest officers.

Before trial, Chandler and Granger objected to the televised coverage of both their pretrial and trial proceedings. They argued that the cameras, even if not physically disruptive, were by their very presence psychologically disruptive and thus violated their right to a fair trial and due process of law. Nevertheless, the trial was televised, the two men were convicted, and the convictions were upheld by the Florida courts.

In a unanimous decision, the U.S. Supreme Court held that television coverage had not been prejudicial.[15] The Court recognized that television cameras are now so small, and the other paraphernalia needed to film courtroom proceedings so unobtrusive, that automatically banning television no longer makes sense. The Court stated:

> An absolute constitutional ban on broadcast coverage of trials cannot be justified
> simply because there is a danger that, in some cases, prejudicial broadcast accounts of
> pretrial and trial events may impair the ability of jurors to decide on the issue of guilt
> or innocence uninfluenced by extraneous matter . . . The possibility of such prejudice
> does not warrant an absolute Constitutional ban on all broadcast coverage . . .

According to Chief Justice Burger, who wrote the decision for the Court, the "appropriate safeguard against such prejudice is the defendant's right to demonstrate that the media's coverage of a case—be it printed or broadcast—compromised the ability of the particular jury that heard the case to adjudicate it fairly." The two Miami policemen, Burger observed, "offered nothing to demonstrate that their trial was subtly tainted by broadcast coverage—let alone that all broadcast trials would be so tainted."

Accordingly, the law now allows states to experiment with different approaches toward trial coverage by television. If defendants want to exclude television from the courtroom, they must demonstrate that their rights will be prejudiced by the coverage in their specific context. This requires more than just demonstrating the jury will be aware that the trial is being televised.

Some defendants have been able to show that television coverage might jeopardize their right to a fair trial. For example, defendant Wayne Williams, when charged with the murder of a black child in Atlanta and linked to the murders of other children by press reports, was able to demonstrate the possibility of such prejudice. Requests to televise his murder trial were denied. In banning the cameras, the Georgia court also took into account the harm that could be caused to children and families affected by the case.

Thirty-seven states now allow televised news coverage of courtroom proceedings. Twenty-one have permanent programs; sixteen states have experimental programs. See the following chart. Federal courts continue to prohibit any kind of broadcast coverage of their proceedings.[16]

---

15. *Chandler v. Florida, op. cit.*
16. A coalition of 28 media organizations asked the U.S. Judicial Conference to formulate guidelines for use of cameras and recorders in federal courts in March 1983. No changes have yet been made (January 1984).

CAMERAS IN THE COURTS [17]

State-by-State Summary of Court Rules or Statutes Allowing Broadcast Coverage of Court Proceedings

State	Court Where Cameras Allowed or Proposed	Type of Plan	Consent of Defendant Required	Effective Date
Alabama	Trial, Appellate	Permanent	Yes	2/1/76
Alaska	Trial, Appellate	Permanent	Yes[1]	11/1/79
Arizona	Trial, Appellate	Experimental	No	5/31/79
Arkansas	Trial, Appellate	Experimental	Yes[8]	1/1/81
California	Trial, Appellate	Experimental	No	7/1/80
Colorado[6]	Trial, Appellate	Permanent	Yes	2/27/56
Connecticut	Trial, Appellate	Experimental	No	4/12/82
Delaware	Appellate	Experimental	N.S.	5/1/82
D.C.	Trial	Pending		Pending
Florida	Trial, Appellate	Permanent	No	5/1/79
Georgia	Trial, Appellate	Permanent	Yes[9]	5/12/77
Hawaii	Trial, Appellate	Pending	Yes	Pending
Idaho	Supreme Court	Permanent	No	8/27/79
Illinois	Trial, Appellate	Pending	N.S.	Pending
Indiana	None			
Iowa	Trial, Appellate	Permanent	No	1/1/82
Kansas	Appellate	Permanent	No	8/10/82
Kentucky	Trial, Appellate	Permanent	No	7/1/81
Louisiana[7]	Trial, Appellate	Permanent	Yes	7/13/79
Maine	Supreme Court	Experimental	No	4/2/82
Maryland	Trial, Appellate	Experimental	Yes[5]	1/1/81
Massachusetts	Trial, Appellate	Permanent	No	1/3/83
Michigan	None			
Minnesota[6]	Appellate	Experimental	No	1/27/78
Mississippi	None			
Missouri	None			
Montana	Trial, Appellate	Permanent	No	4/18/80
Nebraska	Supreme Court	Experimental	No	10/1/82
Nevada	Trial, Appellate	Experimental	No	4/7/80
New Hampshire	Trial, Appellate	Permanent	No	1/1/78
New Jersey	Trial, Appellate	Permanent	No	10/8/80
New Mexico	Trial, Appellate	Experimental	Yes	7/1/80
New York[6]	Appellate	Permanent	No	1/1/81
North Carolina	Trial, Appellate	Experimental	No	10/18/82
North Dakota	Appellate	Permanent	No	7/1/80
Ohio	Trial, Appellate	Permanent	No	1/1/82
Oklahoma	Trial, Appellate	Permanent	Yes[2]	2/22/82

17. *The News Media & the Law*, Vol.7, No.1, March-April 1983, p.42.

Oregon	Trial, Appellate	Pending	No	Pending
Pennsylvania[6]	Non-Jury Civil Trial	Experimental	Yes[1]	10/1/79
Rhode Island	Trial, Appellate	Experimental	No	9/1/81
South Carolina	None	None		
South Dakota	Trial, Supreme Court	Pending	Yes	Pending
Tennessee	Trial, Appellate	Permanent	Yes	2/22/79
Texas	None[3]			
Utah	None[4]			
Vermont[6]	None			
Virginia	None			
Washington	Trial, Appellate	Permanent	Yes[1]	9/20/76
West Virginia	Trial, Appellate	Permanent	No	5/7/81
Wisconsin	Trial, Appellate	Permanent	No	7/1/79
Wyoming[6]	Supreme Court	Experimental	No	8/14/81

1. Coverage of objecting parties is not permitted. Other coverage is allowed.
2. In civil trials, coverage of parties other than objecting defendant is allowed.
3. Audio taping of appellate proceedings is allowed.
4. Still photography is allowed.
5. Coverage in trial court is experimental; in appellate courts it is permanent. Permission is needed unless the defendant is a government official or entity.
6. Liberalization of existing coverage is being considered.
7. Statute allows coverage if all parties consent.
8. Written permission is not required, but if either party objects, coverage is not permitted.
9. Written consent is not needed in Supreme Court proceedings.
N.S.: Not Specified

5. What to Do if Your Camera or Recording Device Is Not Permitted in Court

Remember, you have no absolute right to televise court proceedings. So far, at least, "reasonable" rules governing TV in the courtroom are being upheld. This means your first job is to read and understand thoroughly the state law or federal court rule in question. Assuming that this gives the trial or appellate court judge(s) discretion as to whether you can film, it's important to understand and to be able to discuss the factors involved. By far the most important is how obtrusive your equipment will be. Be ready to present a technical expert complete with specification, diagrams, etc. Your job is to convince the judge that you'll be almost invisible in court.

Other factors the court may consider important are:
- the effect your coverage may have on the jury
- the effect your coverage will have on the physical conduct of the trial (i.e., will you be in the way?)
- the effect your coverage will have on the witnesses (e.g., children, etc.)
- the overall effect of your coverage on the course of the trial

6. Conclusion

Because of advances in technology, disruptions once caused by microphones and cameras no longer occur. Thus, the electronic media is no longer in the unique position it once held. It does, however, now share the same frustrations that have always beset the print media. The rule is that if the public has the right to attend a proceeding, then the media, both print and electronic, enjoys the same right. The one exception to this rule still involves judicial proceedings. When it comes to the courtroom, the electronic media may be excluded from public hearings if the judge believes the defendant's fair trial rights are threatened.

Unfortunately, there are still many judges who personally believe that electronic media should be banned from the courtroom. Such assumptions on the part of individual members of the judiciary will probably die a slow death, which means that many television reporters will still find themselves unwelcome in American courtrooms. There is almost sure to be more litigation on the subject.

The Journalist's Privilege

A. The Conflict

One of the most objectionable situations a journalist can face is to be ordered by a court to divulge notes, tapes or the identity of sources. Not only does revealing sources impair your ability to gather and publish the news in the future, it is very likely to violate both your personal moral code and your professional ethics.[1]

Until fairly recently, the subpoenaing of journalists and their notes rarely occurred. However, between the 1968 Democratic Convention in Chicago and the mid-Watergate period, major news media were suddenly hit with a fistful of subpoenas. The Vietnam War, a troubled economy, widespread governmental corruption, leaks of secret government information, and unflattering media coverage of public officials combined to set up a situation not unlike guerrilla warfare between the government and many journalists and media organizations. This adversary relationship was exacerbated when anti-establishment groups began supplying the media with information from classified government sources.

The government holds that reporters are subject to the same laws that affect everyone else and may therefore be subjected to subpoenas for grand jury proceedings and criminal trials. Normally, these subpoenas require journalists to come forward and tell what they know about particular criminal activities (i.e., name names). This, of course, necessarily involves disclosure of sources for news stories, which may have touched on the matter under investigation or trial.

---

1. In fact, a journalist has recently been sued by a "confidential source" because disclosure was made. How this suit will be resolved remains to be seen.

The government takes this same position whether the journalist is supposed to know the identity of the organizers of an illegal demonstration, the people who broke into a government office or persons wanted for murder.

Most journalists, on the other hand, contend that disclosure of their sources destroys the very confidential relationships necessary to report news and keep the public informed. As watchdogs over corporate and government wrongdoing, investigative journalists strongly argue that without confidential sources, they would have little to report. Some reporters are so opposed to providing information for governmental purposes they will go to jail rather than comply.

B.   Common Law Privilege

Traditionally, every person has a duty to give evidence to the government when it's required for the "administration of justice." Historically, however, there have always been some exceptions to this principle. These exceptions (termed "privileges") usually protect certain types of communications which the law considers confidential. Examples are conversations between attorneys and clients, husbands and wives, priests and penitents, and doctors and patients. When a communication is privileged, the holder of the privilege is absolved of the duty to report criminal activity to the authorities.

A doctrine known as "limited privilege" has also been applied to allow people to refuse to disclose their religious beliefs, political votes, trade secrets, state secrets, and some types of official information in certain circumstances. These exemptions are now governed by state and federal statutes.

A third type of privilege protects a person from having to testify at all, as in the case of the Fifth Amendment privilege against self-incrimination and the right of a spouse to not testify against the other spouse.

Unfortunately, the common law never accorded journalists the privilege of refusing to disclose their sources. Although many would argue that such a privilege is at least as necessary to the public welfare as many of the recognized privileges, courts in the U.S. have been generally consistent in denying it to journalists on either common law or constitutional grounds. But, as we see later, many states have enacted statutes creating the journalist's privilege on a limited basis.

In simple terms, then, if a court subpoenas your notes, photos, tapes, and the identity of your sources, there is little realistic chance you will legally prevail if you wish to withhold them, unless you work in a state with a strong press shield law. As a result, many media organizations, including the most prominent, have had to cooperate with both the courts and law enforcement agencies. Usually, this cooperation has been limited to certain restricted types of information and situations. However, it is also clear that at least a few reporters have engaged in "cooperation" that extends to the point of making them informants for government agencies such as the FBI and CIA.

On the other hand, a number of reporters have simply refused to obey subpoenas. Most were motivated by journalistic principle rather than by a lack of sympathy for the government. For example, during the period January 1981–June 1982, forty-six reporters fought subpoenas, resulting in eighteen contempt citations and thirteen jail sentences.

C.   State Shield Statutes

Since there is no common law or constitutional protection for the confidentiality of a journalist's work product, state legislatures must decide whether or not journalists should be protected, and if so, to what extent. So far, twenty-six states have enacted shield statutes of one type or another. Some of these are written in absolute terms, although they seldom provide absolute protection; others contain many conditions or qualifications. Indeed, they vary substantially with regard to whom and what they protect.

If you live in a state that has enacted a shield law, you should read the statute and be able to answer the following questions:

1. Whom does the law protect (employed reporters, free-lance reporters, other third parties)?

2. What types of media are covered (newspapers, magazines, television, radio, etc.)?

3. What type of information is protected (work project, confidential sources, etc.)?

4. In what forums and circumstances is the privilege available (judicial, legislative, executive or administrative proceedings)?

5. If there are exceptions to or conditions on the availability of the privilege, what are they?

6. Can the privilege be waived (given up) by the confidential source, and, if so, under what circumstances?

Let's take a look at a couple of fairly typical state shield laws. In 1980, California made its broad statutory shield law a part of the state constitution.[2] This constitutional privilege protects both sources and unpublished information:

A publisher, editor, reporter, or other person connected with or employed upon a newspaper, magazine, or other periodical publication or by a press association or wire service, or any person who has been so connected or employed, shall not be adjudged in contempt by a judicial, legislative, or administrative body, or any other body having the power to issue subpoenas, for refusing to disclose the source of any information procured while so connected or employed for publication in a newspaper, magazine or other periodical publication, or for refusing to disclose any unpublished information obtained or prepared in gathering, receiving or processing of information for communication to the public. Nor shall a radio or television news reporter or other person connected with or employed by a radio or television station, or any person who has been so connected or employed, be so adjudged in contempt for refusing to disclose the source of any information procured while so connected or employed for news or news commentary prupuses or radio or television, or for refusing to disclose any unpublished information obtained or prepared in gathering, receiving or processing of information for communication to the public.

As used in this subdivision, "unpublished information" includes information not disseminated to the public by the person from whom disclosure is sought, whether or not related information has been disseminated and includes, but is not limited to, all notes, outtakes, photographs, tapes or other data of whatever sort not itself disseminated to the public through a medium of communication, whether or not published information based upon or related to such material has been disseminated.

Maryland, however, is not nearly as protective of reporters. Its statutory privilege against disclosure of sources only applies to information actually published or broadcast. It provides that:

A person engaged in, connected with or employed on a newspaper or journal or for

---

2. California Constitution, Art. 1, Sec. 2.

any radio or television station may not be compelled to disclose in any legal proceeding or trial or before any committee of the legislature or elsewhere, the source of any news or information procured or obtained by him for and published in the newspaper or disseminated by the radio or television station . . .[3]

The courts have generally construed shield statutes narrowly and refused to extend protection beyond the literal meaning of their words. Further, it is possible that some courts will refuse to comply with these statutes altogether because of their possible conflict with the Sixth Amendment right of a criminal defendant to confront witnesses and produce evidence in his own behalf.[4] For example, in the *Farber* case,[5] the Supreme Court of New Jersey failed to utilize a state shield law when its application would have collided with Sixth Amendment constitutional guarantees. As the Court said, "where constitution and statute collide, the latter must yield."

In general, a reporter is most likely to be ordered to reveal information to a court if that information is centrally relevant to the issue and there are no alternative means of obtaining the information. This is particularly true where the information sought is important to a serious felony case such as a murder trial, or to a libel case against the reporter who is seeking to shield the information. At the other end of the spectrum, it is less likely a reporter will be forced to testify where his story provides just a part of the background information concerning a particular case.

D.   Proposed Federal Shield Laws

Federal shield statutes have been introduced in Congress with increasing frequency since 1929, but so far none has passed. This means that currently, journalists have absolutely no legal right to shield sources in federal court. In any case, as we've seen, the constitutionality of any federal shield law is far from assured, even if one is adopted. Further, the media community itself cannot come to a consensus as to the necessity and scope of such proposed legislation.

In one empirical study[6] concerning the opinions of journalists towards shield laws, law professor Vincent Blasi found that only eight percent of his sample of 975 newspersons thought that the overall quality of reporting had been adversely affected by the subpoena threat. Journalists did, however, have fears that without a shield law, sources might dry up; yet nearly 50 percent of the sample opposed all shield laws. If pressed, they preferred a "flexible ad hoc qualified privilege to an inflexible *per se* qualified privilege." Blasi concluded that:

> . . . reporters feel very strongly that any resolution of their conflicting ethical obligations to sources and to society should be a matter for personal rather than judicial determination, and in consonance with this belief these reporters evince a high level of asserted willingness to testify voluntarily and also a very high level of asserted willingness to go to jail if necessary to honor what they perceive to be their obligation of confidentiality . . .

Internally, news organizations have begun to face some of the same sorts of ethical issues regarding privilege. For example, should an editor or publisher have the right to know the names of everyone a reporter talked to in researching a story? This issue was much discussed

---

3. Maryland Courts and Judicial Procedure Code Annotated. Sec. 9-112.
4. One California trial court judge has so ruled, even though that state's shield law is part of the state constitution. The California Supreme Court has yet to decide the question.
5. 394 A.2d 330 (N.J. 1978). See Farber, *Somebody is Lying*, New York, 1982.
6. Blasi, "The Newsman's Privilege: An Empirical Study," 70 Mich. L. Rev. 229 (1971).

after *Washington Post* reporter Janet Cooke returned the Pulitzer Prize when it was discovered that the eight-year-old heroin addict she portrayed was fictitious. The Cooke episode pushed news organizations to clarify their own rules regarding confidential sources. Almost all the editors and publishers responding to a recent National News Council survey said that their reporters had to be prepared to divulge the name of a confidential source to an editor, or the story would not be published. [7]

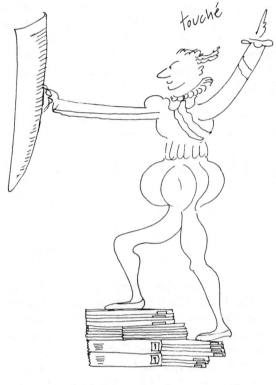

STATE SHIELD LAWS

E. Involuntary Testimony Before a Grand Jury

1. Introduction

The function of a grand jury is to decide whether or not a person should be brought to trial for having committed a crime. If the grand jury is presented with sufficient evidence to warrant a reasonable belief in a particular person's criminal guilt (called "probable cause"), it issues an indictment formally charging the individual with the offense. A grand jury is composed of between seventeen and twenty-three citizens and is usually convened by the head prosecuting attorney (e.g., district attorney) for the particular county involved.

 Grand juries were conceived in Britain as a safeguard against prosecutorial abuse. This purpose was furthered by the Fifth Amendment to the U.S. Constitution, which requires a

---

7. "'Jimmy' Hoax Backlash," *News Media and the Law*, Oct.-Nov. 1981, p.18.

grand jury indictment before a person can be brought to trial for a felony. However, in current practice, the grand jury no longer really protects the individual from oppressive prosecution. In an overwhelming number of instances, it merely rubber stamps the conclusions of the prosecutor and occasionally even assists him in his investigations. Also, the grand jury requirement only applies to federal felony prosecutions. Most state prosecutions are brought without the use of a grand jury.

Grand jury proceedings are secret. No lawyers are present (except the district attorney and occasionally a judge) in the grand jury room. The grand jurors can ask the witness any question. If he refuses to answer he can be ordered to do so by a judge. If the witness disobeys the judge's order, he can be held in contempt of court and sent to jail for the remainder of the life of the grand jury (usually about six months but sometimes longer), unless he takes the Fifth Amendment and refuses to testify on the grounds it might tend to incriminate him.

The secrecy procedures of the grand jury and the resulting abuses have led many to suggest that the grand jury system be abolished. Indeed, a number of states have already done so. At the federal level, however, abolition of the grand jury requires a constitutional amendment.

2.   The Grand Jury and the Journalist

In the late 1960's and early 1970's, the government frequently used federal grand juries to investigate political activists and counterculture dropouts. Friends, relatives, and neighbors were subpoenaed to answer prosecutorial questions on every personal aspect of the person targeted by the grand jury.

Frequently, journalists who reported on the "movement" or the "drug scene" were also unhappy visitors to grand juries. Many of these journalists willingly answered questions, but a good number refused to talk. Three of those who declined to testify ended up before the U.S. Supreme Court. They were Paul Branzburg, reporter for the *Louisville Courier-Journal*, Paul Pappas, newsman and photographer for a New Bedford, Massachusetts, television station, and Earl Caldwell, reporter for the *New York Times*. These journalists found themselves in the unfamiliar role of making rather than reporting the news.

Paul Branzburg was actually involved in two cases. The first[8] concerned his 1969 story in the *Louisville Courier-Journal* about two unidentified persons in Jefferson County, Kentucky, who synthesized hashish from marijuana. His second legal odyssey[9] began after a 1971 article describing the use of illegal drugs in Frankfort, Kentucky, for which Branzburg spent two weeks interviewing several dozen drug users. When called upon by county grand juries to identify the lawbreakers, Branzburg refused each time on grounds that the Kentucky Shield Law and the state and U.S. constitutions justified such refusals. In both cases, the Kentucky Court of Appeals held that the state shield law did not permit a reporter to refuse to testify about criminal events he personally had observed or the identities of persons he saw breaking the law. The Kentucky court, however, conceded that the law did shield the journalist from having to disclose the identity of the source of the original tip. The court rejected the reporter's claim to any First Amendment privilege.

In July 1970, Paul Pappas was permitted inside the New Bedford, Massachusetts, Black Panther headquarters on the condition that he not disclose anything except an anticipated police raid. The raid did not materialize. Pappas was later called to testify before the Bristol County grand jury and asked to disclose his experience with the Panthers. Claiming a First Amendment privilege, he refused. A lower court judge ruled that because Massachusetts had no shield law, Pappas must answer or face contempt charges. The Massachusetts Supreme Judicial

---

8. *Branzburg v. Pound* (Branzburg I), 461 S.W.2d 345 (1970).
9. *Branzburg v. Meegs* (Branzburg II), unreported.

Court affirmed the ruling and stated that the public has a right to every man's evidence except in exceptional circumstances. [10]

Earl Caldwell, a *New York Times* reporter stationed in San Francisco, was subpoenaed to appear before a federal grand jury investigating Black Panther activity in 1970. Caldwell and the *Times* resisted, claiming that such an appearance would destroy Caldwell's relationship with the Panthers and thus suppress vital First Amendment freedoms. [11]

Caldwell was cited for contempt, and appealed. The *Times* did not support the appeal, although it continued to pay Caldwell's legal expenses. "We are not joining the appeal," said Managing Editor A.M. Rosenthal in a memo to his staff, "because we feel that when a reporter refuses to authenticate his story, the *Times* must, in a formal sense, step aside. Otherwise, some doubt may be cast upon the integrity of the *Times* news stories."

Although Caldwell prevailed in the Ninth Circuit Court of Appeals[12], his case was taken to the U.S. Supreme Court and arrived there along with the appeals of Branzburg and Pappas. The joint decision on all three cases retreated significantly from the Ninth Circuit's attempt to provide the journalist with constitutional protection.

In *Branzburg v. Hayes*[13] (a 5-4 decision) the U.S. Supreme Court refused to establish either an absolute or a qualified journalist's privilege on the basis of the First Amendment. Justice White, writing for the majority, stated that the obligation of reporters, like that of other citizens, is to appear and testify before a grand jury about persons or activities deemed significant in the course of a criminal investigation.

In a concurring opinion, which weakened somewhat the effect of the White opinion, Justice Powell found a constitutional basis for First Amendment claims of privilege in some circumstances. He wrote that First Amendment claims should be judged on their precise facts "by the striking of a proper balance between freedom of the press and the obligations of all citizens to give relevant testimony with respect to criminal conduct." However, Powell believed that a reporter should at least appear before the grand jury and that his rights to confidentiality should be determined after questions have been put to him.

In a strong dissenting opinion, Justice Stewart argued that the First Amendment does protect journalists. He set forth a three-pronged test, which the government would have to meet before a journalist could be required to reveal his confidential sources at the request of a grand jury. According to Stewart, the government should have to show:

1. Probable cause to believe that the journalist has information clearly relevant to a specific probable violation of law;

2. That alternative means to obtain the needed information, less destructive of First Amendment rights, are not available; and

3. A compelling and overriding interest in the information.

Despite its official status as a dissent, this threefold test has been very influential in both civil and criminal post-Branzburg litigation involving the journalist's privilege not to disclose confidential sources.

If a reporter has witnessed a crime, the courts have generally held that the reporter may be compelled to testify. But where there are other witnesses available and the journalist's testimony is not really necessary, the dissent by Justice Stewart has been invoked successfully. For example, when a radio station refused to turn over a taped reading by fugitive Weather Underground women, a U.S. District Court upheld this decision on First Amendment grounds. The court

10. *In re Pappas*, 358 Mass. 604, 266 N.E.2d 297 (1971).
11. *Application of Caldwell*, 311 F.Supp. 358 (N.D.Cal. 1970).
12. 434 F.2d 1081 (9th Cir. 1970).
13. 408 U.S. 665, 92 S.Ct. 2646, 33 L.Ed.2d 626 (1972).

said that chances were too speculative that the tape would lead to information regarding criminal activities.[14]

F.   Subpoenas by Criminal Defendants to Testify at Trials

As we said earlier, the Sixth Amendment guarantees the right to a fair trial. This includes the right of the accused to compel testimony that might prove his innocence. A journalist's desire to protect sources sometimes collides with this constitutional guarantee. While courts generally view the defendant's Sixth Amendment interest as an extremely important one, nonetheless reporters are sometimes able to prevail in these conflicts, because the material sought is not really relevant (i.e., helpful in deciding the main issues of the case) or because the subpoena is so broad as to constitute a "fishing expedition" (i.e., a broad desire to see what's "there," if anything).

For example, in December 1978, CBS News' "60 Minutes" broadcast "From Burgers to Bankruptcy," which focused on possible fraud in the franchise operations of "Wild Bill's Family Restaurants." Nine months later, seven executives of the restaurant chain were indicted on charges of conspiracy and fraud. The defendants subpoenaed CBS News for "all notes, video tapes and audio tapes" pertaining to the preparation of the program. A judge ordered CBS to turn over the material. CBS refused and was held in contempt.

The case was appealed to the U.S. Court of Appeals for the Third Circuit. That court required CBS to turn over certain evidence as centrally relevant to the trial and unavailable from other sources. But the court also allowed CBS to withhold all other information requested by the defendants. The information was not important enough to the defense to outweigh the First Amendment right of the news organization. The Supreme Court let the Third Circuit's decision stand.[15]

In the *Abscam* investigation, federal grand juries returned indictments against a number of political figures. In Pennsylvania, the defendants claimed that government attorneys released prejudicial information to the news media in an attempt to force an indictment. A reporter named Jan Schaffer was required to take the stand to confirm that the conversations took place. The reporter refused, was held in contempt, and sentenced to six months in jail. The sentence was stayed pending an appeal.

The Third Circuit U.S. Court of Appeals reaffirmed the existence of a qualified reporter's privilege, but upheld the contempt order on the basis of Justice Stewart's threefold test in his *Branzburg* dissent that:

1. an effort was made to obtain the information from other sources,
2. the only access to the information was through the journalist, and
3. the information was crucial to the claim of the person seeking it.

---

14. *In the Matter of Larry Bensky*, Misc. 75-1800JC (D.C.Cal. April 14, 1975). On the other hand, another U.S. district court facing an identical fact situation reached the opposite conclusion. A Pacifica station had refused to deliver the original of a Patty Hearst tape recording made when she was a fugitive. On appeal the Ninth Circuit ruled that the interests of the grand jury overrode the constitutional interests of the station and the journalists were subsequently held in contempt. *In re Lewis*, 377 F.Supp. 297 (C.D.Cal. 1974), aff'd 501 F.2d 418 (1974); *cert. den.* 420 U.S. 913 (1975).
15. *Cuthbertson v. CBS*, 630 F.2d 139 (3rd Cir. 1980).

SAUTEED SUBPOENA   SQUASHED SUBPOENA   FRESH SUBPOENA PIE

THE CULINARY SUBPOENA

The Court also pointed out that disclosure of a confidential source was not involved since the source of the leak had already identified himself.

The Supreme Court refused to hear the reporter's appeal, but he was released from jail after agreeing to answer just one question from the witness stand: whether or not he had talked to a U.S. Attorney the day before his *Abscam* story. He said he had. [16]

G. Application of the Reportorial Privilege to Civil Cases

1. Libel, A Special Case

The issue of reporter's privilege is not limited to criminal cases. It also plays an important role in libel suits in which the plaintiff is a public figure or an official who is suing the media. As you will remember, for a public figure to win this sort of suit, "actual malice" must be demonstrated (see Chapter 3). The question then becomes how a plaintiff in this type of case is able to establish "actual malice", if access to how the story was researched and fact-checked is denied on the ground of First Amendment privilege. On the other hand, from a reporter's point of view, if there is an exception to the rule of journalist's privilege for libel suits, this type of suit may be commonly filed to disguise fishing expeditions for confidential sources.

These considerations have been present in a number of court cases. Where evidence was found to be indispensable to a determination of whether actual malice was present in a libel proceeding, courts have required disclosure. [17]   However, where alternative evidence of actual

---

16. *U.S. v. Criden*, 633 F.2d 346 (3rd Cir. 1980).

17. All these considerations were present in 1974 when the D.C. Court of Appeals required Britt Hume, Jack Anderson's associate, to identify witnesses to an alleged removal of records from the United Mine Workers Washington office. The evidence was indispensable, the court ruled, to the determination of whether actual malice was present in a libel proceeding involving the story. *Cary v. Hume*, 492 F.2d 631 (D.C. Cir.), *cert. den.* 471 U.S. 938 (1974).

malice is available, the reporters' privilege not to disclose confidential sources has been upheld.[18] The Supreme Court has held that inquiry into opinions, conclusions, and the bases for conclusions and intent was relevant to establishing "malice" and "reckless disregard" for the truth and that such inquiry did not violate First Amendment privilege.

The most important case in this area developed when Col. Anthony Herbert sued "60 Minutes" producer Barry Lando and CBS for $45 million. Herbert alleged that in a "60 Minutes" report and an *Atlantic Monthly* article Lando falsely depicted him as a liar for claiming to have protested war atrocities in Vietnam. Counsel for Herbert undertook massive discovery and Lando was closely questioned in twenty-six pretrial depositions as to his mental processes while engaged in preparing the report and article.

Lando refused to answer, arguing that the questions trespassed on the editorial function protected by the First Amendment. The issue subsequently reached the U.S. Supreme Court. The Court rejected Lando's constitutional argument for press immunity, holding that the inquiry into opinions, conclusions and bases for conclusions was relevant to an inquiry as to "malice" and "reckless disregard" for the truth.

At present, at least eleven out of twenty-six states with shield laws recognize the duty to balance a journalist's privilege against the need for discovery, to prove actual malice in libel suits. In New Jersey, the balance has been shifted in the journalist's favor. In amending the shield law after the Myron Farber fiasco, the New Jersey legislature provided absolute protection for the press in civil cases.

Even if the particular law in your state is very strong, however, it may not be enforced completely. For example, under the California shield law, courts have awarded judgments to libel plaintiffs when the media refused to name sources for the allegedly libelous stories. According to one such court, the shield law protects a journalist only against contempt. The journalist is not protected, however, against other court imposed sanctions, which can range all the way from economic fines against the defendant to judgment for the plaintiff.[19] In other words, if a California judge orders a journalist to disclose information to a libel plaintiff, and the journalist refuses, the journalist (and his media organization) can lose the case by default.

2. Other Civil Cases

When it comes to invoking a privilege not to testify, the media has had more success in non-libel civil cases. Why? Because these cases do not involve a criminal defendant's Sixth Amendment rights, the "law and order" interest of the state, or the journalist's state of mind. Thus in ordinary civil cases, the rule that a journalist must divulge sources only when they are necessary and material and when no alternative way to get the information exists, is applied much more frequently. Put succinctly, a qualified First Amendment-based privilege to keep sources confidential is more often recognized in litigation not involving libel or criminal prosecutions.

A good example is the civil action brought by the estate of Karen Silkwood against her former employer, Kerr-McGee, for her wrongful death from radioactive contamination caused by her employment.[20] Kerr Mc-Gee sought information from Glenn Hirsch, who made a documentary film about Silkwood's death. Hirsch refused, claiming he had promised his sources that he would not reveal their identities. The Tenth Circuit Court of Appeals first decided that a documentary film maker was a "journalist" for purposes of the statutory shield

---

18. Thus, in another somewhat similar fact situation, the attempt of St. Louis Mayor Alfonso Cervantes to compel a *Life* reporter to identify specific FBI and Department of Justice sources was denied on the ground that alternative evidence of actual malice was available. *Cervantes v. Time, Inc.*, 464 F.2d 986 (8th Cir. 1972).

19. *KSDO v. Superior Court*, 136 Cal.App.3d 375, 186 Cal.Rptr. 211 (1982).

20. *Silkwood v. Kerr-McGee*, 563 F.2d 433 (10th Cir. 1977).

privilege and then sent the case back to the District Court to balance both party's interests, keeping in mind certain standards. These were:

1. the nature of the evidence sought,
2. if there were alternative sources,
3. if the information was necessary, and
4. if it was relevant to the case.

Kerr-McGee decided it would rather drop its attempts to question Hirsch, given the stringent standard which it was forced to satisfy to get the information.

H. In-Camera Production of Evidence About Sources

Assuming a court decides to apply a qualified First Amendment privilege for a reporter to shield sources, the next question becomes, how can the court determine if the evidence is necessary, material and relevant to the issue at hand, without knowing what it is? Obviously it can't. This paradox has led many judges to require reporters to disclose the contested material to them in private ("in camera") in order to determine whether or not it is necessary to the case. Many reporters have responded to this procedure by claiming that even disclosure "in camera" compromises the First Amendment rights of the press, particularly if no preliminary showing of relevance and necessity is required.

The *in camera* question was the central issue in the celebrated *Farber* case.[21] Myron Farber, a *New York Times* journalist, investigated a number of unexplained deaths at a New Jersey hospital. Attorneys, representing a doctor accused of murder in connection with the deaths, subpoenaed Farber and *The Times* and demanded all of their notes, memoranda, tape recordings, and anything else considered relevant to the charges.

Farber moved to quash the subpoena on First Amendment grounds, because the New Jersey shield law gave absolute protection to a reporter's notes.[22] The trial judge ruled that the notes in controversy were "necessary and material" and ordered them turned over, despite a request by Farber that a hearing first be conducted into the nature of the notes.

In all, twenty-two judges were asked by Farber and *The Times* for a due process hearing on the relevancy of the subpoenas. They never got one. Ultimately, the New Jersey Supreme Court ruled that Farber and *The Times* had to obey the subpoenas before any hearing on them could be held. Shocked and dismayed, Justice Pashman wrote in an angry dissent, "I find it totally unimaginable that the majority can even consider allowing a man to be sent to jail without a full and orderly hearing at which to present his defense. Mr. Farber probably assumed, as I did, that hearings were supposed to be held and findings made before a person went to jail and not afterwards." Farber served forty days of his six month sentence and *The Times* paid $286,000 in fines.[23] In response to the Farber case, the New Jersey legislature created one of the strongest shield laws in the country.

---

21. *Matter of Farber,* 78 N.J. 259, 394 A.2d 330.

22. New Jersey's shield law had been on the books for 45 years and had been amended by the state legislature a few months before the doctor's trial to make the law one of the strongest in the country. See Richard Harris, "The (Mis)Trials of Myron Farber," *The Nation,* September 18, 1982, p. 232.

23. In January 1981, Governor Byrne of New Jersey pardoned *The Times* and Farber for their contempt convictions. The state returned $101,000.

I. To Testify or Not to Testify — That Is the Question

What advice can we give a journalist who must balance his or her own professional conscience against the demands of the state? There is, of course, no facile answer. One journalist's noble stand may look to another to be about as effective as Don Quixote charging windmills. As the decision whether to obey or resist a subpoena is, in the last analysis, an individual one, any comments by us would be presumptuous. We are, however, competent to review the available options, should a reporter receive a subpoena asking for the disclosure of sources.

Basically there are four:

1. The reporter may request a court to "quash" the subpoena (invalidate it), usually because it does not comply with technical requirements. If successful, this means the court says that the reporter does not have to appear and testify at all. Courts are reluctant to make such an order until the questions giving rise to the subpoena are actually asked in court.

2. The reporter may elect to appear but assert a First Amendment privilege on a question-by-question basis. The reporter who does this must be careful, however, to avoid the "slippery slope" of incremental waiver. This means that if a reporter answers some questions about an otherwise privileged subject, he may be considered to have given up (waived) the privilege as to the subject altogether.

For example, a California judge held reporter Glen Bunting in contempt for refusing to answer questions by defense counsel in a murder trial. Bunting had responded to prosecution questions which required only that he verify statements in his published article but not in unpublished records that involved confidential sources. The judge ruled that Bunting had waived his privilege about the unpublished material when he answered the prosecution's questions about the published article.

3. The reporter may elect to appear and testify fully, perhaps because there are no confidential sources involved or because the confidential source has consented to disclosure.

4. The reporter may refuse to appear and/or testify to anything but his name. Continued refusal after a court order to testify subjects the journalist to being held for contempt of court.

Often an important component to the question of whether or not to testify is whether a journalist has the backing of a media organization. The *New York Times* backed Myron Farber all the way and paid the state of New Jersey $286,000 in contempt fines. However, *The Times* did not join the appeal of Earl Caldwell, even though it did pay Caldwell's legal expenses.

In a decision which stunned many journalists, the *Los Angeles Daily News* ordered its reporters to reveal confidential sources in a libel suit so as to avoid a $60 million default judgment. [24]

Another important factor is the advice of competent counsel. Obviously, the law is extremely complicated in this area and the particular facts of each situation will be crucial.

In conclusion, shield laws can serve the function of educating judges and legitimizing the pursuits of the press. In the end, however, the protection the law affords the journalist is only as absolute as a judge's interpretation of that law.

---

24. *Plotkin v. Van Nuys Publishing Co.*, No. C-359227 (Cal. Super. Ct. Los Angeles, 2/82). Early in 1981 the *Los Angeles Daily News* ran a story suggesting that Iran hostage Jerry Plotkin had been involved in drug trafficking. Plotkin filed a libel action against the paper and the reporters who wrote the story. Plotkin's lawyers sought the names of the reporters' sources for the allegations in the article but the reporters refused to disclose them. The trial court initially granted a default judgment against both the reporters and the newspaper for the failure of the reporters to provide the names. Later, however, the judge allowed the paper and reporters to defend the suit but prohibited them from relying on the sources as part of their defense. In the course of this dispute, the paper itself had ordered the reporters to name the sources. When they refused to do so, the paper refused to provide any further legal representation for them, but continued to pay their legal expenses.

Newsroom Searches

A. Introduction

In the last chapter, we introduced the subject of subpoenas and whether journalists are legally required to testify about their sources. We discussed the fact that subpoenas can be challenged and quashed by a judge, and that other steps can be taken, at least to delay testifying. During this whole process, of course, a journalist could theoretically destroy the information he or she has been asked to provide. This might well be illegal and subject the journalist to criminal charges, but it would effectively accomplish one thing—the government wouldn't get the information.

How can a government determined to get information lessen the risk that it will be destroyed? One simple way is to avoid the uncertainty of the subpoena process altogether and simply grab the information in a search and seizure operation. Is this legal? We will try to deal with this question and a more fundamental one: Does the press have a constitutional protection against search and seizure based on the freedom to gather, analyze and disseminate news?

To understand this area of the law, it is first necessary to know something about search warrants. With certain exceptions, a search warrant must be obtained from a judge or magistrate to search any area in which an individual has a reasonable expectation of privacy such as his home or business office.

Under the Fourth Amendment, search warrants may be issued only if there is "probable cause." This means that the judge (or magistrate, as she is often called when issuing search warrants) must entertain a reasonable belief that the area to be searched contains either evidence of a crime, or the fruits of a crime (e.g., stolen documents). The warrant must also describe the "place" to be searched and the "things" to be seized with reasonable specificity.

In general, the police have little, if any, difficulty obtaining search warrants due to court decisions making it extremely easy to establish "probable cause." For example, "probable cause" can be established by an anonymous informant who reports to the police that photographs of a murder are hidden in a newspaper's files.

Also, the typical procedure by which warrants are issued lends to the ease by which they are secured. The process is completely one-sided. The police approach the judge with an application (often a large stack of them) and ask that a warrant be issued. There is no hearing. The judge "reviews" the papers and either signs or refuses to sign the warrant. In practice, almost all warrants are signed, due to the lack of time most judges have to give the papers a serious review. In short, if the police want a warrant, the magistrate will usually "rubber stamp" the application.

As mentioned, once the magistrate is satisfied that probable cause exists, she may issue a search warrant. Under the authority of this warrant, law enforcement officers may search the premises and take what they want (so long as it is reasonably within the scope of the items described in the warrant and located in the described area), without advance warning.

While procedures exist to challenge the legality of any particular warrant, search or seizure (e.g., the warrant was issued without probable cause, or the search exceeded the scope of the warrant), any such dispute must necessarily be resolved after the search and seizure is completed. Since the primary issue is the right of the media to keep their information *confidential*, such after-the-fact "remedies" are next to useless.

B.   The Stanford Daily Case

In 1971, a clash arose between student demonstrators and police in the Stanford University Hospital. Nine policemen were injured. Two days later, *Stanford Daily* published a special issue that included photographs of the disturbance. An investigation ensued. To obtain evidence, the police secured a warrant to search the offices of the paper on the belief that the newspaper had photographic evidence of the identity of the students involved in the violence.

Ordinarily, information of this nature is secured by a subpoena. A subpoena is far less intrusive because it gives the person or organization a chance to go into court and argue either why requested information should not be disclosed, or that it doesn't exist. This is done through a process known as a "motion to quash."

In this case, however, the offices, including the *Daily's* photographic laboratories, filing cabinets, desks, and wastepaper baskets were searched. Locked drawers and rooms were not opened, but the police had time to read notes and other matter in the course of the search.

No negatives were found, except one of a picture reproduced by the *Daily* two days after the student-police confrontation. A month later, the *Daily* brought suit in federal District Court against the municipal court judge who issued the warrant, the police who conducted the search, the chief of police, and the district attorney.

The paper claimed that its rights under the First Amendment and the Fourth Amendment (the right to be secure against unreasonable searches and seizures) had been violated. The case ultimately reached the Supreme Court. The Court's decision is still of crucial importance to understanding the rights of, and limitations on, governments in respect to news room searches.

The majority held that a search may be made of newspaper offices—or *any innocent third party's premises*—whenever there are reasonable grounds to believe that criminal evidence is located there. The warrant, however, must still meet Fourth Amendment requirements of probable cause, specificity and reasonableness. The opinion refused to concede that the possible disclosure of confidential information through searches would "chill" press activity or dry up sources.[1]

In a strong dissent, Justice Stewart described the effect that unannounced police searches of newspaper offices would have:

> ... [C]onfidential information may be exposed to the eyes of police officers who execute a search warrant by rummaging through the files, cabinets, desks and waste-baskets of a newsroom. Since the indisputable effect of such searches will thus be to prevent a newsman from being able to promise confidentiality to his potential sources, it seems obvious to me that a journalist's access to information, and thus the public's, will thereby be impaired.[2]

The reaction of most journalists to the *Stanford Daily* case was strong and bitter. *New York Times* Columnist James Reston pointed out that under the decision, President Nixon would have been able to seize the Pentagon Papers from the *Times* and block their publication. Or, Reston argued, Nixon could have sent the police into the offices of the *Washington Post* and seized the notes of Woodward and Bernstein. The media was so upset that it collectively (and with considerable clout) asked state legislatures and congress to remedy the situation.

C. The Federal Privacy Protection Act

In response, Congress enacted the Privacy Protection Act of 1980[3] which prohibits all federal, state, and local law enforcement agencies from conducting surprise warrant-searches of newsrooms, except in very limited circumstances. Under this law, in most circumstances, governmental officials may use subpoenas only to obtain information from those who have collected it "with a purpose to disseminate to the public a newspaper, book, broadcast, or other similar form of public communication." This means that the media will have an opportunity to resist the subpoena in court, as opposed to having the information seized on the spot. The law covers authors, scholars, and researchers, in addition to journalists.

The law protects two categories of materials:

---

1. *Zurcher v. Stanford Daily*, 436 U.S. 547, 98 S.Ct. 1970, 56 L.Ed.2d 525 (1978).
2. *Ibid.*
3. 42 U.S.C. Section 200 *et. seq.*

1. "Work product materials" (basically, drafts of articles prepared by the reporter or a third person, including the "mental impressions, conclusions, opinions, or theories" of the author), and

2. "Documentary materials" (basically raw materials, such as photos, audio and video-tapes and notes of interviews).

There are some exceptions, of course, which allow searches to be conducted under a search warrant in the following circumstances.

1. Work Product Exceptions

a. Where there is "probable cause to believe" that the reporter has committed or is committing a crime[4]; or

b. Where the information sought relates to national defense, classified information, or restricted data, as defined by federal statute; or

c. Where there is reason to believe "that an immediate seizure by search warrant is necessary to prevent the death of or serious bodily injury to a human being."

2. Documentary Material Exceptions

a. All of the situations listed under *Work Product*; or

b. Where there is a danger that the materials sought might be destroyed; or

c. Where the news organization has refused to obey a subpoena for the information sought, and all court appeals have been exhausted;

d. Where there would be a "delay in an investigation or trial" which would "threaten the interests of justice."

The exceptions can and probably will be turned into loopholes, particularly the "national defense" and "threaten the interests of justice" exceptions. As of this writing, however, the law has not been tested.

D. State Anti-Search Laws

In addition to the federal law, nine states — California, Connecticut, Illinois, Nebraska, New Jersey, Oregon, Texas, Washington and Wisconsin — have passed their own anti-search laws, which apply only to searches by state and local officials within their borders. Many of these are tougher than the federal law. The federal statute governs state and local, as well as federal, officials.

E. Conclusion

The subject of newsroom searches, like censorship and government secrecy, is one which will become more or less of an issue depending on who is in power and whether a "national crisis" exists. It seems clear, however, that journalists possessing confidential material which conceivably could be the subject of a newsroom search would do well to consider how best to protect against this happening. An attorney's advice may come in handy.

---

4. The "crime" the reporter is committing cannot be the receipt or possession of information unless the information is classified.

Access to News Sources

A. Introduction

Newsgathering—gaining access to the people, places and things which make up the news—is obviously the very heart of any journalistic enterprise. Any restriction of this right has the ultimate effect of directly limiting the free dissemination of ideas. Nevertheless, federal, state and local governments have, at times, all claimed a "public interest" right to withhold information about and restrict media access to their activities and operations. Unfortunately, when these restrictions have been challenged in the courts, newsgathering has been afforded very little constitutional protection. In this chapter, we discuss both court decisions and statutes (usually known as "open meeting laws") which affect the right of the press to gather news.

B. Newsgathering in the Constitutional Context

The right of journalists to government information is closely related to their right to gather information generally. The Supreme Court summed it up this way when it upheld the denial of a U.S. journalist's right to travel to Cuba: "The right to speak and publish does not carry with it the unrestrained right to gather information."[1] Seven years later, Justice White picked up the

---

1. *Zemel v. Rusk*, 408 U.S. 1, 85 S.Ct. 1271, 14 L.Ed.2d 179 (1965).

theme: "The First Amendment does not guarantee the press a constitutional right of special access to information not available to the public generally."[2]

Fortunately, the Supreme Court has also observed that "newsgathering is not without its First Amendment protections." Justice White put it this way:

> We do not question the significance of free speech, press, or assembly to the country's welfare. Nor is it suggested that newsgathering does not qualify for First Amendment protection; without some protection for seeking out the news, freedom of the press could be eviscerated.[3]

By reading the leading cases which deal with newsgathering,[4] you will discover that the Supreme Court is not about to bestow special privileges on the press. Only in one case, that of *Richmond Newspapers Inc. v. Commonwealth of Virginia*,[5] discussed in detail in Chapter 6, did a majority of the Supreme Court even hold that a First Amendment right of access to trials exists. What impact, if any, this decision will have on the constitutional right of the media of access to governmental meetings, facilities and records remains to be seen.

CONCLUSION: While this area of the law is in flux, there is presently little constitutional recognition that journalists have the right to gain access to people or places (even legislatures, governmental hearings, and the like) not open to the general public. Put another way, if you can legally exclude Joe Public, you can probably also legally exclude Josephine Journalist.

C. Rules Governing a Reporter's Access to Places

Basically, each kind of public and private location generates its own rules regarding access by journalists. So, rather than generalizing further on this subject, here are the specific rules which govern a reporter's right to get into specific places.

1. Prisons

The U.S. Supreme Court has explicitly held that the press enjoys no special right of access to prisons. Specifically, it upheld the constitutionality of a California rule that "press and other media interviews with specific inmates will not be permitted."[6] Prior to this regulation, the press had been able to broadcast or publish face-to-face interviews with prisoners. In upholding the new stricter rule, the Supreme Court claimed California was not discriminating against the press since it merely revoked a special privilege not available to the public generally.

The case of *Houchins v. KQED*[7] raised the same issues. When a San Francisco television station (KQED) reported the suicide of a prisoner, it noted the charge by a psychiatrist that

---

2. "Despite the fact that newsgathering may be hampered, the press is regularly excluded from grand jury proceedings and our own conferences . . ." *Branzburg v. Hayes*, 408 U.S. 666 at 684 (1972). See Chapter 5 for discussion of this case.
3. *Ibid.*, 408 U.S. at 681.
4. *Branzburg* (Chapter 6), *Stanford Daily* (Chapter 7), *Herbert v. Lando* (Chapters 3 and 6), and *Gannett v. DePasquale* (Chapter 5).
5. 448. U.S. 555, 100 S.Ct. 2814, 65 L.Ed.2d 973 (1980).
6. *Pell v. Procunier*, 417 U.S. 817, 94 S.Ct. 2800, 41 L.Ed.2d 495 (1974).
7. 438 U.S. 1, 98 S.Ct. 2588, 57 L.Ed.2d 533 (1978).

prison conditions caused the mental illness of his various patients there. The station requested permission to inspect and photograph the facility, was refused access, and went to court. When the case was ultimately decided by a divided U.S. Supreme Court, Justice Burger wrote in his majority opinion that "neither the First Amendment nor the Fourteenth Amendment mandates a right of access to government information or sources of information within the government's control."

Again, the court failed to take into account the function of the media as the public's surrogate. An interview, for example, is an important newsgathering tool used by a professional reporter seeking news for public dissemination. Members of the public who are not reporters, journalists or scholars might not be interested in conducting face-to-face interviews of inmates with whom they have no personal or professional relationship, but they do have a general interest as citizens to see that prisons are efficiently and humanely run.

Indeed, even Justice Burger himself conceded this point in the *Richmond Newspapers* case:

> Instead of acquiring information about trials by first-hand observation or by word of mouth from those who attended, people now acquire it chiefly through the print and electronic media. In a sense, this validates the media claim of functioning as surrogates for the public . . . [M]edia representatives "contribute to public understanding of the rule of law and to comprehension of the functioning of the entire criminal justice system."[8]

Again, it remains to be seen whether the rhetoric of *Richmond Newspapers,* or the actual results in the Supreme Court cases discussed above, will govern the question of media access to prisons.

2. Access to Federal Agency Proceedings: The Government-In-Sunshine Act

a. Introduction

Access to deliberative sessions conducted by many federal entities has been guaranteed to the public and media since 1976 by the Government-In-Sunshine Act [5 U.S.C. Section 552(b)]. Clearly, access to meetings in which federal agency decision-making occurs is of fundamental importance, if we as a society are to understand how and why our government acts. The role of the media in this regard is especially crucial, as most citizens cannot afford time out to sit through the many meetings conducted by the various agencies covered by the act. Here we provide a brief overview of how this Act operates and what the media can do if meetings supposed to be held in public are conducted behind closed doors.

b. Which Agencies Are Covered?

All federal agencies composed of two or more members (a majority of whom are appointed to such position by the President with the advice and consent of the Senate) are covered by the Government-In-Sunshine Act.[9] Thus, agencies such as the Federal Trade Commission, the Federal Communications Commission, the U.S. Civil Rights Commission, the Consumer

---

8. *Op.cit.*
9. 5 U.S.C. Section 552b(a)(1).

Products Safety Commission and the Nuclear Regulatory Commission are covered. Major Cabinet departments such as the Departments of Defense, Transportation, and Health and Human Services, however, are not (since they are headed by one Cabinet officer rather than a "collegial" body).

The following box lists most of the covered agencies along with citations to the Code of Federal Regulations (CFR), where the agency's regulations are found.

CODE OF FEDERAL REGULATIONS

Army Corps of Engineers, public observation of meetings, 33 CFR Part 209.

Civil Aeronautics Board, public observation of meetings, 14 CFR Part 310b.

Civil Rights Commission, rules on hearings, reports and meetings, 45 CFR Part 702.

Civil Service Commission, public observation of meetings, 5 CFR Part 295.

Commodity Credit Corporation, public observation of meetings, 7 CFR Part 1409.

Energy Research and Development Administration, advisory committee meetings, 10 CFR Part 707.

Environmental Quality Council, public observation of meetings, 40 CFR Part 1517.

Equal Employment Opportunity Commission, public access to information, 29 CFR Parts 1610–1612.

Export-Import Bank of the United States, public observation of meetings, 12 CFR Part 407.

Federal Communications Commission, public observation of meetings, 47 CFR Part 0.

Federal Deposit Insurance Corporation, public observation of board meetings, 12 CFR Part 311.

Federal Election Commission meetings, 11 CFR Parts 2, 3.

Federal Farm Credit Board meetings, 12 CFR Part 604.

Federal Home Loan Bank Board, public information regarding meetings, 12 CFR Part 505b.

Federal Maritime Commission, public observation of meetings, 46 CFR Part 503.

Federal Reserve Banks, public access to information, 12 CFR Part 271.

Federal Reserve System, policy as to public observation of meetings, 12 CFR Part 281.

Federal Reserve System, public observation of meetings, 12 CFR Part 261b.

Federal Trade Commission meetings practices and procedures, 16 CFR Parts 2, 3, 4.

Federal Trade Commission, nonpublic nature of hearings, 16 CFR Part 2.

Foreign Claims Settlement Commission, public observation of meetings, 45 CFR Part 504.

Harry S. Truman Scholarship Foundation, Board of Trustees, public observation of meetings, 45 CFR Part 1802.

Indian Claims Commission, public observation of meetings, 25 CFR Part 504.

International Trade Commission, public observation of meetings, 19 CFR Part 201.

Interstate Commerce Commission, public observation of meetings, 49 CFR Part 1012.

Libraries and Information Science Commission, public observation of meetings, 45 CFR Part 1703.

National Institute of Education, public observation of meetings, 45 CFR Part 1440.

National Labor Relations Board, public observation of meetings, 29 CFR Part 102.

National Mediation Board, public observation of meetings, 29 CFR Part 1209.

National Science Board, public observation of meetings, 45 CFR Part 614.

National Transportation Safety Board, public observation of meetings, 49 CFR Part 804.

Nuclear Regulatory Commission, public access to records, 10 CFR Part 9.

Occupational Safety and Health Review Commission, public observation of meetings, 29 CFR Part 2203.

Overseas Private Investment Corporation, public observation of meetings, 22 CFR Part 708.

Parole Commission, public observation of meetings, 28 CFR Part 16.

Postal Service, public observation of meetings, 39 CFR Parts 1, 7, 8.

Railroad Retirement Board, protection of privacy of individual records, 20 CFR Part 200.

Railway Association of the United States, Board of Directors, public observation of meetings, 49 CFR Part 905.

Railway Association of the United States, public observation of meetings, 49 CFR Part 903.

Renegotiation Board, public observation of meetings, 32 CFR Part 1482.

Social Security Administration, public access to official records and information, 20 CFR Part 401.

Uniform Services University of the Health Sciences, Board of Regents, public observation of meetings, 32 CFR Part 242a.

c. When and How Meetings May Be Closed

As you would expect, each agency is entitled to close portions of a meeting to the public when certain topics are being covered (see d, below). To do so, however, a majority of the entire agency membership must vote in favor of the closure. For example, if the commission in question has five members, three must vote for closure.[10] Once a vote for closure is taken, legal counsel must certify that it is legally justified under one or more of the reasons for closure listed in the Act (see discussion below). This certification must then be kept on file.[11]

Public announcements of scheduled meetings must be made a week ahead of time. The notice must include the place and subject matter of the meeting, whether any portion of it is to be closed to the public, and the name and phone number of an official designated by the agency to respond to requests for information. The time and place of the meeting may be changed under certain circumstances, but in such a case the agency must give the best possible notice under the circumstances.[12]

d. The Permitted Reasons for Closure

The closure of portions of meetings is permitted under ten conditions or exemptions.[13] Exemptions 1–4 and 6–8 are the same as the identically-numbered exemptions applicable to record gathering under the Freedom of Information Act [see Chapter 9(C)(5)]. Briefly summarized, these are matters dealing with: 1) national security, 2) government personnel, 3) matters exempted from disclosure by other federal laws, 4) information which would disclose trade secrets or damage a company's competitive position, 5) personal information maintained by the agency, 6) information compiled for the purpose of law enforcement, and 7) financial information resulting from the regulation of banks.

Exemption 5 under the Sunshine Act allows closed meetings when the agency determines that such portion or portions of its meetings or the disclosure of such information is likely to "involve accusing any person of a crime, or formally censuring any person."

Exemption 9 permits closed meetings of agencies involved in financial regulation when disclosure might cause significant financial speculation, or endanger the financial stability of an institution. The meeting can also be closed under circumstances where disclosure might frustrate implementation of a proposed agency action and such information had not been previously disclosed.

Exemption 10 allows closing meetings which concern agency participation in all types of litigation or dispute resolution.

To the extent that an agency plans to discuss any of the topics specified in these exemptions, it may exclude the public from the portion of the meeting dealing with such material. However, an entire meeting may not be closed under the Act just because a portion of it is subject to such closure.[14]

e. What to Do About Improper Closure

Many journalists entertain strong doubts about this law. After all, if an agency has ten reasons to keep you out, it can always come up with a plausible argument why one of them applies. In addition, those who haven't previously worked in this area may be wondering how you would

---

10. 5 U.S.C. Section 552b(d)(1).
11. 5 U.S.C. Section 552b(f)(1).
12. 5 U.S.C. Section 552b(e)(2).
13. 5 U.S.C. Section 552b(c)(1)–(10).
14. *Pan American World Airways Inc. v. CAB*, 684 F.2d 31 (1982).

140

ever establish an abuse of the law if the proof as to whether such an abuse happened is buried in a secret meeting. Fortunately, there are ways to keep the agencies reasonably accountable.

First, each agency must maintain a verbatim transcript of the closed portion of the meeting (in a few cases, the transcript may be replaced by detailed minutes). This transcript must then be kept for at least two years. Additionally, the part of the transcript (or minutes) covering aspects of the closed meeting which don't deal with the exempt information must promptly be made available to the public for inspection and copying (at the actual cost of making the copies). Among the information which must be included in this partial transcript (or minutes) is reference to the identities of witnesses speaking in the closed session. [15]

As a journalist, you will encounter two contexts in which you might wish to challenge the closure of a meeting—before the meeting occurs, and after.

1. **Before the Meeting:** Under the Government-In-Sunshine Act, you are permitted to go into federal court (U.S. District Court) and ask for a Temporary Restraining Order (TRO) preventing a closure from occurring. [16] If you can get to a judge before the time of the meeting, the agency will have the burden (job) of explaining why, under one of the specific exemptions, it is entitled to keep the public out. In deciding whether the agency is correct, the judge is supposed to resolve any ambiguity against the agency and rule against closure unless the agency is absolutely entitled to it under the Government-In-Sunshine Act. [17] While going to court usually involves getting a lawyer, just obtaining a TRO to open a meeting is not as expensive as many other legal endeavors. Also, there are many media organizations detailed in Chapter 9 which may provide you with legal assistance.

2. **After the Meeting:** The most common situation is where the closed meeting is held before you can get anywhere near a judge. Once the meeting is held, it may appear that you've lost by default. But although the Act does not allow an agency's action or decision to be voided just for improperly closing a meeting, [18] the media does have a remedy. An action can be filed in court challenging the closure, and if the agency fails to meet its burden of proof regarding closure under the Act, the court must order that the verbatim transcript (or minutes) of the closed portion of the meeting be made public. This has in fact happened in several cases. [19]

3. **Where the Action May Be Brought:** These court actions may be brought in the federal court nearest to where the closed meeting occurred, or in Washington D.C. [20] Thus, in most cases you will not need to travel far to obtain the help of the courts.

4. **Attorneys' Fees and Costs:** If you prevail in court, the government must pay your reasonable costs and attorneys' fees. If you lose, you do not have to pay the government anything unless the court finds your suit is "frivolous" or filed just to delay agency action. [21] As courts almost never consider a suit "frivolous" or filed just for the purposes of delay, as a practical matter you can go to court without fearing retribution if you lose.

REALITY NOTE: One of the primary purposes of the Government-In-Sunshine Act was to open up the governmental decision-making process to the public. However, agencies are often motivated to hide the true reasons for hiding their decisions. Accordingly, attempts by the media to penetrate the federal agency decision-making process by using the Act will often be met with agency attempts to get around it. Some of the ways this can be done are 1) informally conducting all important business in the "back room" and using the public meeting as a showplace, 2) misrepresenting the nature of the business being conducted in the closed portion of the meeting and 3) abusing the provisions allowing last-minute changes in the time and location of meetings.

---

15. 5 U.S.C. Section 552b(f)(1).
16. 5 U.S.C. Section 552b(h)(1); *Common Cause v. Nuclear Regulatory Commission*, 674 F.2d 921, 939 (1982).
17. 5 U.S.C. Section 552b(h)(1); *Common Cause v. Nuclear Regulatory Commission*, 674 F.2d 921 (1982).
18. 5 U.S.C. Section 552b(h)(2).
19. See e.g. *Pan American World Airways Inc. v. CAB*, 684 F.2d 31 (1982).
20. 5 U.S.C. Section 552b(h)(1).
21. 5 U.S.C. Section 552b(i).

Despite the difficulty of making agencies adhere to the letter and spirit of the Government-In-Sunshine Act, there is much in the Act to help the intrepid journalist to monitor decision-making by federal regulatory agencies, all to the great benefit of the public. Clearly, the more the Act is used, the more informed the public will be.

3. Access to State Governmental Proceedings

Almost every state has laws which require that meetings held by public entities be open to the public. If there were nothing more to it, our citizenry would be much better informed, and this paragraph would end here. However, all state open-meeting laws contain exceptions, which can be and are transformed into loopholes when the entity holding the meeting wishes to confer without the benefit of public knowledge or participation.

Of these, "executive session" is the most often used. This allows the public to be excluded from the meeting for certain kinds of issues (e.g., discussions regarding personnel and litigation). Other commonly used ruses for getting around open meeting laws are "accidentally" 1) providing inaccurate notice of the time or place of the meeting, 2) failing to place items on the agenda and 3) misstating on the agenda the true nature of items to be discussed. Last-minute scheduling changes and getting the notice out late are also popular.

Since many of your investigations will concern state or municipal government entities, it is imperative that you know the law of your state in advance and be prepared to act immediately if your legitimate request to enter into or remain at a meeting is denied. It was rumored that Justice Douglas always carried a copy of the U.S. Constitution in his back pocket. Likewise, you should carry a copy of your open-meeting law with you so that you can make immediate challenges.

In California, the California Newspaper Publishers Association[22] publishes pocket-size copies of the key portions of legislation on the state open-meeting law, open-records law, and privacy laws. Check with your state professional organization to see if they have a similar booklet.

Here are a few suggestions on how to maximize your access to public meetings and minimize the all too common headaches.

• Start by sending certified letters to every agency or other governmental body you are interested in covering. These letters should request notification of all scheduled meetings and emergency sessions. Then, make sure you actually receive such notices.

• If you are ever refused permission to attend or remain at a meeting, be sure you are dealing with the person who has authority to deny or grant access. If not, ask to see the person in charge.

• Stay cool, and quote the relevant sections of your state law authorizing access. If this doesn't work, ask to see the agency's written guidelines for accessibility, and demand a formal reason for the denial of access.

• If you are still denied access or asked to leave, obtain the name and position of the person keeping you out. Many media organizations supply reporters with a form letter ready to hand to the person in question. Others work out a procedure with their attorney in advance, so that the letter can go out on the attorney's stationery.

The important thing is, you will usually have a very short time in which to lodge your protest. Accordingly, you and your organization should have procedures worked out in advance.

Specific laws regarding what constitutes a "meeting," the kind of notice which must be provided to the public, whether an agenda must be prepared, the type of minutes which must be kept, the kinds of issues which allow the meeting to go into executive session, and the actual agencies and entities subject to the law all differ from state to state. The following chart provides the statutory source of these variables for each state.

22. 1127 11th St., Suite 1040, Sacramento CA 95814 (916) 443-5991.

STATE OPEN MEETING LAWS

State	Citation
Alabama	Title 14, Chapter 70, Sec. 393
Alaska	Alaska Statutes, Sec. 44.62.310
Arizona	Ariz. Rev. Stat. Ann. Sec. 38-43
Arkansas	Ark. Stats. Ann. Sec. 12-2801 et. seq.
California	Cal. Govt. Code Sec. 11120
Colorado	Colo. Rev. Stat. Sec. 24-6-401 et. seq.
Connecticut	Conn. Gen. Stat. Sec. 1-21
Delaware	Del. Code Ann. Tit. 29 Sec. 10001 et. seq.
Florida	Section 286.011
Georgia	Ga. Code Sec. 40-3301 et. seq.
Hawaii	Haw. Rev. Stat. Sec. 92-1 et. seq.
Idaho	Idaho Code Sec. 67-2340 et. seq.
Illinois	Ill. Rev. Stat. Ch. 102 Sec. 41 et. seq.
Indiana	Ind. Code Sec. 5-14-1, 5-1, et. seq.
Iowa	Iowa Code Sec. 28A.1 et. seq.
Kansas	Kan. Stat. Sec. 75-4318
Kentucky	Ky. Rev. Stat. 61.805 et. seq.
Louisiana	La. Rev. Stat. Ann. Sec. 42:5 et. seq.
Maine	Me. Rev. Stat. Title 1, Sec. 401 et. seq.
Maryland	Md. Ann. Code, Art. 76A, Sec. 7
Massachusetts	Mass. Gen. Laws Ann. Ch. 30A Sec. 11A
Michigan	Mich. Comp. Laws Sec. 15.261, et. seq.
Minnesota	Minn. Stat. Ann. Sec. 471.705
Mississippi	Miss. Code Ann. Sec. 25-41-1 et. seq.
Missouri	Mo. Rev. Stat. Sec. 610.010 et. seq.
Montana	Mont. Rev. Code Ann. Sec. 2-3-201
Nebraska	Neb. Rev. Stat. Sec. 84-1401 et. seq.
Nevada	Nev. Rev. Stat. Sec. 241.020 et. seq.
New Hampshire	N.H. Rev. Stat. Ann. Sec. 91-A:1 et. seq.
New Jersey	N.J. Stat. Ann. Sec. 10:4-7 et. seq.
New Mexico	N.M. Stat. Ann. Ch. 14 Sec. 10-15-1 et. seq.
New York	N.Y. Pub. Off. Law Sec. 95 et. seq.
North Carolina	N.C. Gen. Stat. Sec. 143-3181 et. seq.
North Dakota	N.D. Cent. Code Sec. 44-04-19
Ohio	Ohio Rev. Code Ann. Sec. 121-122
Oklahoma	Okla. Stat. Ann. Tit. 25, Sec. 301 et. seq.
Oregon	Or. Rev. Stat. Sec. 192.610 et. seq.
Pennsylvania	Pa. Stat. Ann. Tit. 65, Sec. 261 et. seq.
Rhode Island	R.I. Gen. Laws Sec. 42-46-1 et. seq.
South Carolina	S.C. Code Sec. 30-4-10, et. seq.
South Dakota	S.D. Compiled Laws Ann. Sec. 1-25-1
Tennessee	Tenn. Code Ann. Sec. 8-44-101 et. seq.
Texas	Tex. Govt. Code Ann., Tit. 110A, 6252-17
Utah	Utah Code Ann. Sec. 52-4-1 et. seq.

```
Vermont ....................... Vt. Stat. Ann., Tit. 1 Sec. 31 et. seq.
Virginia ........................... Va. Code Sec. 2.1-340, et. seq.
Washington ................. Wash. Rev. Code Ann. 42.30.010 et. seq.
West Virginia ...................... W.Va. Code Sec. 6-9A-1 et. seq.
Wisconsin ........................... Wis. Stat. Sec. 19.81 et. seq.
Wyoming ......................... Wyo. Stat. Sec. 9-11-101 et. seq.
```

The following are specific examples of State Open Meeting Laws. Notice the exceptions. These are usually based on employee privacy considerations, e.g., discipline or dismissal of public employees. As we mentioned, when an entity actually desires to keep the public out, there is usually a way to do it. On the other hand, it is also possible to catch them in the act. Accordingly, journalists must make sure that personnel or litigation discussions really involve these issues.

California Government Code

Sec. 11120. Public policy; legislative finding and declaration; citation of article.

It is the public policy of this state that public agencies exist to aid in the conduct of the people's business and the proceedings of public agencies be conducted openly so that the public may remain informed.

The people of this state do not yield their sovereignty to the agencies which serve them. The people, in delegating authority, do not give their public servants the right to decide what is good for the people to know and what is not good for them to know. The people insist on remaining informed so that they may retain control over the instruments they have created.

This article shall be known and may be cited as the . . . Bagley-Keene Open Meeting Act.

Sec. 11126. Closed Sessions

(a) Appointment, employment or dismissal of public employee; hearing of complaints or charges; notice of right to public hearing; exclusion of witnesses

(b) Nothing contained in this article shall be construed to prevent a state . . . body from holding closed sessions during a regular or special meeting to consider the appointment, employment or dismissal of a public employee or to hear complaints or charges brought against such employee by another person or employee unless such employee requests a public hearing. As a condition to holding a closed session on the complaints or charges to consider disciplinary action or to consider dismissal such employee shall be given written notice of his or her right to have a public hearing rather than a closed session, which notice shall be delivered to the employee personally or by mail at least 24 hours before the time for holding a regular or special meeting. If notice is not given, any disciplinary or other action taken against any employee at such closed session shall be null and void. The state . . . body also may exclude from any such public or . . . closed session, during the examination of a witness, any or all other witnesses in the matter being investigated by the state . . . body. Following the public hearing or closed session the . . . body may deliberate on the decision to be reached in a closed session.

Sec. 11A 1/2. Open meetings of governmental bodies; executive sessions; exceptions; notice; records; failure to comply; orders; nature of rights of individual.

All meetings of a governmental body shall be open to the public and any person shall be permitted to attend any meeting except as otherwise provided by this section.

No quorum of a governmental body shall meet in private for the purpose of deciding on or deliberating toward a decision on any matter except as provided by this section.

No executive session shall be held until the governmental body has first convened in an open session for which notice has been given, a majority of the members of the governmental body have voted to go into executive session and the vote of each member is recorded on a roll call vote and entered into the minutes, the presiding officer has cited the purpose for an executive session, and the presiding officer has stated before the executive session if the governmental body will reconvene after the executive session.

Nothing except the limitations contained in this section shall be construed to prevent the governmental body from holding an executive session after an open meeting has been convened and after a recorded vote has been taken to hold an executive session. Executive sessions may be held only for the following purposes:

This section shall not apply to any chance meeting or social meeting at which matters relating to official business are discussed so long as no final agreement is reached. *No chance meeting or social meeting shall be used in circumvention of the spirit or requirements of this section to discuss or act upon a matter over which the governmental body has supervision, control, jurisdiction, or advisory power.* [Emphasis added.]

Except in an emergency, a notice of every meeting of a governmental body subject to this section shall be filed with the secretary of state, and a copy thereof posted in the office of the executive office for administration and finance at least forty-eight hours, including Saturdays but not Sunday and legal holidays, prior to the time of such meeting. The notice shall be printed in easily readable type and shall include the date, time and place of such meeting. Such filing and posting shall be the responsibility of the officer calling such meetings . . .

Many times litigation is necessary to force an agency to open its meetings. For example, closed budget sessions of the Maryland State Legislature were ruled illegal by trial courts. Also, a New Jersey County Board of Freeholders' closed session was ordered opened by the trial court after *The Ocean County Times-Observer* brought suit. On the other hand, a court in Oregon ruled that the Community College District may exclude the news media from collective bargaining sessions conducted between the labor negotiator and teachers under the Oregon Public Meetings Law.

There is no way to be absolutely sure you are not covering a fake open meeting while the real meeting took place over dinner. Similarly, it is difficult to uncover a bogus reason advanced for going into "executive sessions."[23] However, executive sessions may be transcribed by a tape recorder or covered in minutes. Even if there are not, it may be possible to obtain information about the session from one of the board members. If you do succeed in unmasking the deception, generally you have recourse through the courts.

Is the right to gather news inextricably intertwined with the right to publish? Access may or may not lead the reporter to publishable information. Yet, when access is regularly denied, the

---

23. For example, over a two-year period in Emporia, Virginia, a town of 5000, the City Council, County Board of Supervisors, and School Board went into executive sessions in 80% of their meetings.

consequence is the equivalent of prior restraint. Nevertheless, so far, the courts have fairly consistently distinguished between the more limited right to gather information and the more absolute right to publish it once it is gathered. However, the fact that access to trials has taken on a constitutional dimension may help the media gain better access to other types of governmental proceedings.

HARRY'S PLACE

4. Access to Private Property

Reporters entering into private property have on occasion been convicted of criminal trespass and invasion of privacy.[24] There are exceptions, however, and occasions where the right of access has been upheld. In New Jersey, a court acknowledged that a reporter and photographer

---

24. See Chapter 4.

of the *Daily Princetonian*, the Princeton University newspaper, did have the right of access to a migrant labor camp for newsgathering purposes, even though the camp was private property. [25] In Florida, accompanying the Fire Marshal into a burned-out private home was held by the Court not to be a trespass by the reporter because it was "common usage, custom, and practice for news media." [26]

The line between private and public property is often hard to draw. Most people know that another person's home is private property, while a street corner is public. However, what about shopping centers, restaurants, theatres, "public" baths, churches, gas stations, and ice skating rinks, to name but a few types of privately-owned places where the public goes by invitation and permission.

The general rule is that the media may enter any of these types of areas for newsgathering purposes without initially being guilty of trespass, so long as they don't intrude into areas where the public is not normally expected to go (like the kitchen of a restaurant or the administrative offices of a church). However, it is also true that the press can be excluded from most of these places by specific request, since the invitation to the public is for the purpose of furthering the enterprise in question and not to produce a media event or news interview. Thus, if you walk into your neighborhood restaurant with your cameras rolling, the proprietor can properly ask you to leave but cannot successfully sue you for trespass unless you refuse to get out. See Chapter 4 (C)(3) for a discussion of newsgathering in semi-public places and the invasion of privacy tort.

D. Access to Information Under the Reagan Administration

The Reagan Administration has consistently made efforts to control access to government information. [27] It has:

* Barred entry into the country of many foreign speakers, including Hortensia Allende, widow of Chilean President Salvador Allende, because of concern about what they might say, [28]
* Prohibited certain foreign films, including Canada's Academy Award-winning "If You Love This Planet," unless they carried a propaganda stamp,
* Sought to limit the scope of the Freedom of Information Act (F.O.I.A.), [29]
* Rewritten the classification system in order to classify more materials,
* Threatened academics to prohibit them from publishing and discussing unclassified information on campus,
* Tried to require government officials to agree to a lifetime of self-censorship. [30]

Under the Reagan Administration, access to the White House has also been restricted by forbidding White House aides from making unauthorized disclosures or "leaks" to the press. In January, 1983, the White House issued a new set of "Guidelines for Press Coordination" which authorizes a small number of White House aides to answer reporters' questions on certain subjects. Undesignated Staff members must receive clearance from the Office of Communications before answering questions on those subjects. The previous standard practice was for

---

25. *Freedman v. New Jersey State Police*, 135 N.J.Super 297, 343 A.2d 148 (1975).

26. *Florida Publishing Co. v. Fletcher*, 340 So.2d 914 (Fla. 1976), *cert. den.*, 431 U.S. 930 (1977).

27. Many articles have been written discussing this control of information. See Floyd Abrams, "The New Effort to Control Information, " *The New York Times Magazine*, 9/25/83, p.22.

28. Others include the Deputy Cultural Minister of Cuba, representatives of the Cuban Women's Federation, Bernadette Devlin, a Guatemalan trade unionist, Salvadoran opposition leaders, government officials of Nicaragua, certain Italian playwrights, and many more.

29. See Chapter 9.

30. See Chapter 2.

White House aides to make comments on the condition that they not be identified.

E. Discriminatory Press Access Practices

1. Introduction

In practice, the media has access, superior to that afforded the public generally, to many places and events. However, this access can only be gained by securing press passes. The First Amendment problem in this area often has to do with controlling who gets press passes and who is left out. Specifically, the established media generally has little difficulty getting official credentials for their reporters while the alternative press is often denied them.

That press passes should be given to all legitimate news organizations, regardless of their politics is a view which has considerable institutional support under the First Amendment. If your news organization is barred from coverage while others are allowed to attend, and there is no reasonable provision for the admission of "pool" journalists to whom you have access, you should consider court action. Here are some examples of where such discrimination might be a problem.

2. The Right to a Press Pass — The Secret Service

The Secret Service sets standards for the issuance or denial of the National Press Pass and the White House Press Pass. These passes are *not* interchangeable.

a. National Press Pass

The National Press Pass is for journalists who cover events outside the White House. The purpose of the pass is to identify accredited reporters and to minimize security risks. The pass is an extension of the Master Press Index, which includes the name, sex, race, date and place of birth, social security number, telephone number, employers, specific occupation and any police record of about 62,000 journalists. All data is stored by the Secret Service in a Central Government computer. To get a National Press Pass, you must be listed on the Index and submit to the Secret Service a letter from your employer and a passport-type photo. All applicants are run through the National Criminal Information Center's computers and other FBI files.[31]

b. White House Press Pass

In recent years, courts have afforded the Secret Service complete discretion in controlling access to the White House. However, the courts have held that the constitution requires even-handedness in deciding which reporters to admit and which to exclude. Thus, when two reporters were denied White House press passes for "reasons of security," the court required the

---

31. Leslie C. Henderson, "Reporter Licensing," *Los Angeles Daily Journal.*

Secret Service to draw up a set of standards for the issuance or denial of Passes.[32] These can be found in Title 31, Code of Federal Regulations (CFR), Chapter IV, Part 409. The basic standard is "whether the applicant presents a potential source of physical danger to the President and/or the family of the President so serious as to justify his or her exclusion from White House press privileges."

c. Press Passes Issued by State and Local Governments

Commonly, a reporter might be stripped of her press pass because a story she published incurred the wrath of a public official. However, the courts have consistently looked with disfavor at this kind of governmental discrimination.

For example, the *Nashville Tennessean* was officially barred from the floor of the Tennessee Senate after one of its reporters objected to a Senate Committee voting on bills in secret session. The Court nullified the resolution as a violation of the First Amendment.[33] Similarly, the Mayor of Honolulu declared reporter Borreca of the *Honolulu Star-Bulletin* persona non grata at City Hall and instructed his staff to keep Borreca out of the Mayor's office. The Mayor felt that Borreca was irresponsible, inaccurate, biased, and malicious in reporting on city administration and that he would not talk to Borreca "until hell freezes over." The Court nevertheless ordered the Mayor to stop excluding Borreca from City Hall press conferences.[34]

One of the worst examples of discrimination involved the *Los Angeles Free Press*, a dissident weekly newspaper whose reporters were denied police passes in the early 1970's. The police department claimed to grant passes only to individuals, not to news organizations. In practice, the individuals receiving passes all worked for the regular established media (e.g., the *Los Angeles Times*, television stations, and the like). Conversely, passes could not be obtained by free-lance reporters or by those working for such "counterculture" media organizations as the *Free Press*.

A California court of appeal upheld this openly discriminatory treatment, refusing even to accept the *Free Press* as a newspaper because of questions regarding its "legitimacy" (this, despite a weekly circulation in excess of 85,000 and second-class mailing privileges). The court ruled that the *Free Press* had no First Amendment right of access to the scenes of crimes and disasters superior to that of the general public, and that police department favoritism toward media which "regularly" cover such events was not unreasonable or arbitrary.[35]

The opposite approach resulted from an Iowa case.[36] Again, access to police records was dependent on the possession of a press pass, and these were issued only to members of the "legitimate" press. But this time there were no written standards or guidelines defining "establishment" press. The federal court in Iowa ruled that the system of distributing press passes was too arbitrary. The Court also observed that the system only reinforced those media organizations that presented what the police department believed to be appropriate.

32. *Sherril v. Knight*, 569 F.2d 124 (D.C. 1978).
33. *Kovach v. Maddox*, 238 F.Supp. 835 (M.D. Tenn. 1965).
34. *Borreca v. Fasi*, 369 F.Supp. 906 (D.Haw. 1974).
35. *Los Angeles Free Press, Inc. v. City of Los Angeles*, 9 Cal.App.3d 448, 88 Cal.Rptr. 605 (1970), *cert. den.*, 401 U.S. 982 (1971).
36. *Quad-City Community News Service, Inc. v. Jebrens*, 334 F.Supp. 8 (D.C. Iowa 1971).

F. Television Coverage of Governmental Proceedings

In practice, there is no problem televising or taping any public meeting. In fact, some state open-meeting laws specifically state that any person in attendance at such meetings may record or photograph the proceedings.

However, in some places there have been attempts to prevent reporters from recording or televising certain types of legislative meetings. When settling disputes arising from decisions to ban cameras and recording devices from these meetings, courts have gone both ways.

In Chino, California, for example, the city council passed a measure which prohibited tape recorders in the council chamber. In striking down this measure, a California appellate court reasoned that since tape recorders are "silent and unobtrusive," their exclusion unreasonably deprived the reporter "of the means to make an accurate record of what transpires in a public meeting."[37]

But in another case with similar facts, a Maryland court upheld legislative rules which prevent tape recorders in Maryland Senate and House chambers without permission of the President and Speaker.[38] This case would seem to be an historical anomaly, and we believe that it means little in the march toward allowing all legislative proceedings to be televised.

The U.S. House of Representatives began television and radio coverage of its proceedings in 1979. Pressured to follow suit, the Senate has moved tentatively to allow broadcast news coverage of at least some of its proceedings.

G. Television Coverage of Executions

A television cameraman does not have a constitutional right to film an execution. In November 1976, a T.V. news reporter requested permission to film the first execution of a prisoner under Texas' new capital punishment statute, and to film interviews with death row inmates. Permission was denied. The State did allow full access to the event by news reporters, but barred photography and the recording of the event by mechanical means.

The Federal Court of Appeals (Fifth Circuit) sustained the ban, ruling that Texas had a policy against public executions and accordingly had the right to govern the means by which an execution could be covered by the media. The way the court put it, "the First Amendment does not accompany the press where the public may not go."[39]

H. Conclusion

Is the right to gather news inextricably intertwined with the right to publish? Access may or may not lead the journalist to publishable information. Yet, when access is regularly denied, the consequence is a type of de facto "prior restraint." Nevertheless, the Courts have fairly consistently distinguished between the more limited right to gather information and the more absolute right to publish information once it is gathered.

---

37. *Nevens v. City of Chino*, 223 Cal.App.2d 775, 44 Cal.Rptr. 50 (1965).
38. *Sigma Delta Chi v. Speaker, Maryland House of Delegates*, 310 A.2d 156 (1973).
39. *Garrett v. Estelle*, 556 F.2d 1274 (5th cir. 1977).

Access to Records

A.   Introduction

Needless to say, a large part of any journalist's work is reviewing information maintained in documentary or electronic form. Documents such as investigative and scientific reports, internal memoranda written by government officials, and papers filed in lawsuits provide the basis for many of the day's top news stories. The contents of computer memories and magnetic tape recordings are also increasingly being tapped for newsworthy items. Here we cover the basic laws which describe what records (whether written or electronic) are available to the public and how to gain access to them.

B.   Court Records

1. Generally

The right of access to report and gather news extends beyond the courtroom proceedings themselves (See Chapter 5). Unlike some other aspects of newsgathering, the right to inspect and copy court records is well-established in common law. Much revealing information about a case is contained in documents maintained in files open to the public in the court clerk's office. These materials may include pleadings (e.g., complaints, answers), pretrial rulings and opinions by the court on various issues, material obtained through discovery (e.g., deposition transcripts, answers to interrogatories, responses to requests for admissions), legal briefs, and any other document filed in the course of the lawsuit.

Remember, a journalist and his media organization may be subject to a libel suit if an inaccurate and negligent report on a legal proceeding is published.[1] Similarly, a journalist may face a contempt citation if a "gag order" is violated.[2] For these reasons alone, it is a good idea for the journalist covering court proceedings (especially criminal cases) to become familiar with the court's files and the types of material contained in them.

On occasion, you may encounter some hostility from a clerk when you request access to the court records. Usually this will not result in an outright refusal. Rather, you may be provided with an extremely uncomfortable place to read the material or may be charged an exorbitant rate for photocopying ($1.00 a page is not unusual). There is no easy way around these problems. Many of them can be avoided, however, if you approach court clerks the way most attorneys do—circumspectly, with courtesy and a realization that court clerks do have considerable power either to help or hinder your efforts, depending on how they feel about you.

2. Tapes

Courtroom trials, like other theatrical productions, have been transformed by electronic technology. To take but one example, juries are now able to see reenactments of automobile accidents on videotapes in personal injury trials. Also, some states are experimenting with allowing certain types of testimony to be videotaped prior to trial and presented to the jury in lieu of live testimony from the witness stand. Under common law rules, since these tapes are part of the official court records, they should be available for journalists to inspect and copy. Of course, you will have to provide your own machinery for such purposes.

Litigation over the Nixon tapes has cast some doubt on this rule, however. This occurred when Warner Communications wanted to make copies of the Nixon tapes admitted as evidence in the trial of John Mitchell and six other Nixon aides for the purpose of resale to the public. The U.S. Supreme Court ultimately denied Warner access to the tapes. Observing that Congress had prescribed the procedures for gaining direct access to the tapes in the Presidential Recordings and Materials Preservation Act, the Court held that the press did not have an independent right of access under either the First Amendment, the Sixth Amendment or common law.[3] The Court did say that journalists have a common law right to hear such tapes when played in the course of open court proceedings, and to purchase transcripts.[4]

In a situation in which presidential tapes were not involved, a U.S. Circuit Court of Appeals decision approved of direct network access to the videotapes shown at the trial of Congressman Michael Myers in the Abscam "sting" case.[5] The tapes showed the Congressman accepting $50,000 cash and demanding an additional $35,000 to help fictitious Middle Eastern businessmen immigrate to the United States. Likewise, the television networks featured excerpts from tapes in the Abscam trials of Congressmen Johanson, Schwartz, and Jenrette.

At present, therefore, the state of the law regarding access to tapes contained in official court records is a little murky. It is probably best summed up by saying that you have a broad common law right of access to electronically recorded information contained in court records *unless* this right has been curtailed or covered in some way by a specific statute, as in the case of presidential recordings.

---

1. See Chapter 3.
2. See Chapter 5.
3. *Nixon v. Warner Communications*, 435 U.S. 589, 98 S.Ct. 1306, 55 L.Ed.2d 570 (1978).
4. Ultimately, 30 of the tapes played at the trial were made available at the National Archives and Records Service in Washington, D.C.
5. *U.S. v. Myers*, 635 F.2d 945 (2nd Cir. 1980).

C.   The Freedom of Information Act

1. An Overview

The right to obtain information contained in federal government files is established by two important laws — the Freedom of Information Act[6] and the Privacy Act.[7] The Freedom of Information Act (FOIA) permits an individual to review and copy all federal government documents on a wide variety of given topics. The Privacy Act (PA) permits an individual to find out what the government has *on him* and to get the information corrected if mistakes have been made.

The FOIA and PA apply to every agency, department, regulatory commission, government controlled corporation, and "other establishment" in the executive branch of the federal government. This includes all federal agencies, Cabinet departments, commissions and boards, such as the IRS, FBI, CIA, EPA, FDA, FTS, FCC, NLRB, EEOC, DOD (Department of Defense), HHS (Department of Health and Human Services), and DOL (Department of Labor), to name but a few of the better known ones. The Act also applies to government-controlled corporations like the Post Office, AMTRAK and the Legal Services Corporation, and to the Executive Office of the President (e.g., the Office of Management and Budget). However, *neither* law covers Congress, the courts, or the President's immediate staff.

CAUTION: The Reagan Administration has proposed changes to FOIA which leave the original law on the books but restrict information disclosure in a number of contexts. As of this writing, they have not been passed, but before you use the FOIA, be sure to find out what changes, if any, have been made. A good source for this information is the FOI Service Center, a joint project of the Reporters' Committee For Freedom of The Press and The Society of Professional Journalists, Sigma Delta Chi, located at 800 18th St. N.W. Washington D.C. 20006.

2. Journalistic Uses of the FOIA

The FOIA is a wonderful tool for the investigative reporter and has done much to encourage openness and accountability in government. For example, it has been used to discover important information on the Rosenberg spy trials, FBI harassment of civil rights leaders, automobile design defects, consumer product testing, international smuggling operations, environmental impact studies, the salaries of public employees, school district compliance with anti-discrimination laws, sanitary conditions in food processing plants, and CIA spying operations on domestic political groups.[8]

In some cases, of course, the FOIA has proved to be an imperfect sword with which to slay the dragons of secrecy, non-disclosure and cover-up. Despite the FOIA, for example, the U.S. Supreme Court has allowed the government to suppress underground nuclear test information, former Secretary of State Henry Kissinger's telephone transcripts, records of government contractors suspected of overpricing, Federal Open Market Committee decisions to buy government securities, safety information on exploding television sets, witness statements before an unfair labor hearing, and other tantalizing bits of information. Still, knowing how to use the FOIA is an extremely useful skill for the working journalist.

---

6. 5 U.S.C. Section 552.

7. 5 U.S.C. Section 552a.

8. See *Former Secrets* by Evan Hendricks (May 1982), a compilation of more than 500 case studies on successful use of the FOIA, published by Campaign for Political Rights, 201 Massachusetts Ave., N.E., Washington D.C. 20002, (202) 547-4705.

3. What Is Available under the FOIA

The FOIA governs all questions (except those which arise in the context of lawsuits) regarding the availability of records under the control of the federal government. The word "records" has an extremely broad meaning, and refers to all sorts of documentary or electronic information including papers, reports, letters, films, computer tapes and printouts, photographs, video and sound recordings. About the only type of item not covered in the FOIA definition of "record" is anything which cannot be copied physically in one way or another.

4. How Information Is Made Available

a. Overview

The FOIA separates records into three groups:
- Records that must be published as a matter of course in the Federal Register,
- Records that must be maintained as a matter of course by each federal entity in an agency library available to the public, or
- Records that must be made available for inspection and copying upon request.

Each of these types of records can be of tremendous importance in understanding a particular issue or occurrence. They will be examined here in more detail.

b. Information That Must Be Published

The following information must be published in the *Federal Register* by the agency in question as a matter of course. Most of it is also contained in the *Code of Federal Regulations* volume applicable to the particular agency.
- An agency's guide to its internal organization. These guides are often helpful if you are seeking a particular piece of information. For example, if you want to find out how many

154

complaints have been filed with the Federal Communications Commission with reference to job discrimination by a particular business, you might want to ask the agency's division of civil rights. The guide will steer you to the correct person or location. If you are dissatisfied with the result, it can be useful to know to whom you should appeal. The guide will help you here, as well.

• The procedures for requesting information from the agency. Each agency is required to publish its own procedures for obtaining information held by the agency. By studying these in advance, the journalist requesting information can save himself from many false leads and dead ends.

• The procedural rules which are followed by the agency in the conduct of its business. Federal agencies have numerous functions ranging from making and enforcing regulations to hearing disputes. All agencies are required to proceed in an orderly and non-arbitrary way, and all have internal guidelines governing the manner in which they go about their business. The failure of an agency to proceed in accordance with its own internal guidelines can result in agency action being declared invalid.

• Agency regulations having a general and prospective application. These are the regulations which actually apply to the world at large. Thus, FCC regulations govern certain aspects of radio and television broadcasting policy, IRS regulations govern how we all pay (or don't pay) our taxes, and DOT regulations specify the width of interstate highways built with federal funds. Time and again we hear that the "regulations require it" or that "I would but the regulations won't let me." If there is such a regulation, it must be published in the *Federal Register* to be valid. See Appendix B for more information on finding federal regulations.

• Agency statements of general policy and interpretations of general applicability. These are expressions by the agency of what its regulations mean and how the agency plans to enforce them. For example, the Immigration and Naturalization Service (INS) has numerous regulations dealing with persons who have entered or remained in this country illegally. During the 1980 census, however, the INS issued a general policy statement claiming that it would suspend enforcement of certain of these regulations so that the census could be taken accurately. These kinds of agency policy statements and interpretations are very important in understanding how an agency views a particular situation and what they are likely to do about it. While such pronouncements might not be the "law" as such, they certainly help us predict governmental behavior and are supposed to be published in the *Federal Register* for that reason.

c. Information Available for Inspection and Copying

The FOIA requires that the following materials be made available at the agency or other public place for anybody to drop in and examine. However, the materials need not be published in the *Federal Register* or *CFR*.

• The final opinions in the adjudication of cases. If a person has been denied social security benefits, a pilot's license, or the right to conduct mining operations in the national forest, he must initially go through agency procedures — usually a hearing — before challenging the denial in court. This is called "exhaustive administrative remedies."

Agencies are required to keep records of decisions which are reached in these hearings and generally to follow such decisions in later cases presenting similar facts. These decision provide an understanding of how the agency views the law relevant to your situation. Thus, previous FCC decisions in hearings involving challenges to radio station licenses may be quite informative if you are locked in a similar struggle. Agency interpretations of the law reflected in these decisions are as important as policy declarations in being able to predict agency behavior. Each agency maintains these hearing decisions in volumes indexed by subject matter.

- Unpublished statements of policy and interpretations of law. Often times an agency is asked by an individual, a corporation, or another government agency to render an opinion about the law as it applies to a particular set of facts. For instance, suppose that two large companies want to merge. All mergers involve potential violations of the Sherman Anti-Trust Act. So, rather than merge and risk prosecution for violating the Act, these companies first request an opinion from the Justice Department about whether their merger would constitute an anti-trust violation. Similar types of interpretations and statements of policy are made by the Internal Revenue Service in response to questions by taxpayers. Because these statements of policy and interpretations are geared to individuals, they need not be published in the *Federal Register*. They are available at the agency for inspection and copying, however.

- Administrative staff manuals. Each day, an enormous number of administrative decisions are made directly affecting the property and lives of millions of people. Some of these decisions have wide-ranging consequences (such as banning a product from the market place). Other decisions affect only one individual (such as a decision on a social security claim.).

While administrative decisions must be made in compliance with the statute and with an agency's own regulations, the real operating guide for administrative decision-makers is usually an internal agency staff manual. These manuals provide guidelines for decision-making in every conceivable circumstance. For example, while an agency regulation might require that a social security disability claim be denied if the applicant can perform gainful employment, the Social Security staff manual provides much more specific guidance on what is considered the ability to perform gainful employment, what gainful employment actually is, how these factors differ with respect to different age groups, what weight to give what type of evidence in support of disability, and so on.

All agencies have staff manuals, all decision-makers use them, and a journalist who wants to know either the reason for a particular decision or the manner in which an agency's decision might be made in the future should become familiar with the agency's staff manuals and the methods for obtaining access to them.

INDEX NOTE: Fortunately, the FOIA also requires agencies to maintain a current index of all the materials required to be made available under this section. If you are not sure of exactly what you are looking for and want to see what's available, this index should be of great help. You should also remember that most federal agencies maintain regional and district offices, and therefore you don't have to travel to Washington, D.C. every time you want to take advantage of this section of the FOIA.

d. Information Available Upon Request

In addition to requiring some information to be published and other information to be made available as a matter of course, the FOIA requires all covered federal agencies to disclose any record possessed by them to any person who requests it, *except* where the record requested is specifically exempted from disclosure by Congress or by the FOIA itself.

This means that if you happen to know of a government report, letter, computer tape, file, or whatever, and you want to see it and/or receive a copy of it in the mail, all you have to do is file a request with the appropriate agency.

Of course, there are certain types of records which agencies are entitled to withhold under the Act. In recognizing the need for a certain amount of confidentiality, however, Congress expressly tipped the scales in favor of disclosure by requiring an agency to justify the withholding of any document under a particular exemption. Further, in reviewing an agency denial, the courts must interpret each statutory exemption strictly and against the agency. This means that unless the exemption clearly exempts the requested record, it must be disclosed.

IMPORTANT: You should always ask for what you want without regard to the exemptions. Agencies will often disclose exempt material through inadvertence or because they don't care. Further, if a particular record is withheld, it is up to the agency to cite chapter and verse justifying its action.

5. The Nine FOIA Disclosure Exemptions

The FOIA includes nine exemptions or reasons allowing the government to refuse to disclose information. Broadly speaking, these exemptions cover documents relating to: national security, personal privacy, law enforcement investigations and investigatory strategies, the confidentiality of proprietary or business data, and the candid internal deliberations of governmental advisers and policy makers.

Eight of the nine exemptions are not mandatory, which means that even if records fall within these categories, they can still be released at the government's discretion. This is particularly true if you can show that disclosure would be "in the public interest."

Furthermore, even though requested material contains some words, sentences, or paragraphs which are covered by an exemption, the FOIA requires the government agency to release the remainder of the material with the exempt part edited out.

Exemption One: National Security

(A) Matters that are authorized under criteria established by an Executive Order to be kept secret in the interest of national defense or foreign policy and
(B) in fact properly classified pursuant to such Executive Order.

When the agency refuses to disclose a document under this exemption, an immediate question arises. Who determines whether the document is really within the exemption? It is easy for the government to claim that particular material is classified and therefore non-disclosable. Thus, there is a real need for an impartial person to review the material and decide on the propriety of the claim. With all the other exemptions, a judge will examine the material privately (i.e., "in camera") and decide accordingly, assuming a lawsuit has been filed challenging the agency denial. However, in national security matters, the executive branch has traditionally been reluctant to let even the judge see the items in question.

In 1974, Congress expressly authorized judges to conduct an "in camera" inspection of materials withheld under this exemption, but few do so. Rather, when a national security claim is made, courts routinely give great weight to the expertise of the government agency involved, especially when such expertise is buttressed by affidavits (sworn written statements) and testimony. The courts generally presume that the government is telling the truth unless otherwise indicated.

For example, the author Studs Terkel requested from the FBI information about himself. He was denied substantial portions on the ground that the material would endanger national security or compromise pending law enforcement investigations. Refusing to examine the material in camera, the Court found that the FBI's affidavits "generally provided adequate information to establish the specific and identifiable portions of the challenged documents" fell within the national security exemption. Accordingly, the Court upheld the FBI's denial of Terkel's request.[9]

NOTE: Executive Order (E.O.) 12356, discussed below, makes it easier to classify national security information. Thus, more and more information is being covered under Exemption 1, with a resulting increase in secrecy.

---

9. *Terkel v. Kelley,* 559 F.2d 214 (7th Cir. 1979).

Exemption Two: Internal Agency Rules

Matters related solely to the internal personnel rules and practices of an agency.

This exemption covers materials such as manuals that relate only to internal management and organization of an agency (e.g., employee parking rules and agency cafeteria regulations). It does not exempt staff manuals instructing federal employees on how to perform their jobs or containing descriptions of these jobs. If such materials are clearly in the public interest, then the government should disclose them despite this exemption unless such disclosure would risk circumvention of agency regulation or disclose the agency's investigation strategies. [10]

Exemption Three: The Catch-All Exemption

Information "specifically exempted from disclosure by (another federal) statute . . . provided that such statute (A) (clearly) requires that the matters be withheld from the public, or (B) establishes particular criteria for (discretionary) withholding (of the information sought) or (narrowly specifies) particular types of (information) matters to be withheld.

There are more than 100 federal statutes prohibiting disclosure of one type of material or another. Most have not been tested in court to determine whether or not they actually fall under the "catch-all" exemption. About the only way to handle this exemption is not to worry about it unless or until it is raised by the agency. Then, you can examine the statute referred to by the agency and decide whether it does, in fact, authorize or require the withholding of the requested documents. As a general matter, the courts will interpret such statutes in favor of disclosure.

For example, in one case the *Washington Post* requested data from the State Department concerning expenditures from the department's emergency fund. The State Department claimed that the statute authorizing the fund allowed the Secretary of State to maintain secrecy in respect to expenditures of "such amounts as may be specifically appropriated . . . for unforeseen emergencies arising in the diplomatic and consular service." Upon review, the Court of Appeals held that Exemption Three did not apply, because the FOIA required exemptions to be drawn narrowly, and the emergency fund statute was too vague. The court ordered the information released. [11]

Exemption Four: Trade Secrets

Matters which are "trade secrets and commercial or financial information obtained from a person and privileged or confidential."

Business concerns commonly attempt to use the FOIA to obtain information provided to the federal government by competitors. Thus, if a large pharmaceutical house files a request with the FDA for approval of a new product, the information contained in the application might be of great use to other drug manufacturers. Because companies are often required to file information with the federal government, Congress felt that such information should be protected from disclosure if it is "privileged and confidential." What do these terms mean?

---

10. *Department of the Air Force v. Rose,* 425 U.S. 352, 96 S.Ct. 1592, 48 L.Ed.2d 11 (1976).
11. *U.S. Dept. of State v. Washington Post,* 456 U.S. 595, 102 S.Ct. 1957, 72 L.Ed.2d 358 (1982). The Supreme Court reversed the Court of Appeals and held that the citizenship information sought by the *Washington Post* was within Exemption 6 of the FOIA as "similar files" which is to have a broad rather than narrow meaning. Thus, the records in this case could be withheld.

Courts have said information is "confidential" only if its disclosure would be likely:

1. "to impair the government's ability to obtain necessary information in the future," or

2. "to cause substantial harm to the competitive position" of the person or entity from whom the information was obtained. The mere possibility of competitive harm is insufficient.

On the ground they would suffer competititve disadvantage if certain materials were disclosed, several private firms sued the agency in question to block disclosure. These "reverse FOIA suits" caused the U.S. Supreme Court to rule that federal agencies have the sole responsibility for deciding whether or not business information submitted to them is releasable or not, and private companies have no right to intervene in that process. [12]

Exemption Five: Executive Privilege

Matters that are inter-agency or intra-agency memoranda or letters which would not be available by law to a party other than an agency in litigation with the agency.

This exemption is widely used by the government. The courts allow nondisclosure when the requested records carry preliminary views and recommendations of federal officials on policy or legal matters, i.e., when they are part of the "deliberative process." Thus, if the information sought is pre-decisional or deliberative, it is exempted from disclosure. If it is post-decisional or explanatory, on the other hand, then it must be released. [13]

The primary reason behind this exemption has to do with the practical realities of governmental decision making. Typically, dozens or even hundreds of people will have direct input into major government decisions. Often vigorous debates will occur over a number of possible courses of action. Congress felt that the disclosure of materials reflecting this debate might interrupt the ongoing process and discourage agency personnel from engaging in open and frank debate, if their preliminary views were exposed to potential disclosure.

On the other hand, once the debate is over and a decision made or a policy formed, the disclosure of materials reflecting the actual decision or policy would not operate to interrupt the decisional process and accordingly is not covered by this exemption. For example, the FBI

---

12. *Chyrsler Corp. v. Brown*, 441 U.S. 281, 995 S.Ct. 1705, 60 L.Ed.2d 208 (1979).

13. *NLRB v. Sears Roebuck Co.*, 421 U.S. 132, 95 S.Ct. 1504, 44 L.Ed.2d 29 (1975).

refused a *Playboy Magazine* request for a 302-page report investigating allegations that informant Gary Thomas Rave was involved in the Ku Klux Klan shooting death of Viola Luizzo in Alabama in 1965. The FBI cited FOIA Exemption Five as a justification, since, in its opinion, disclosure of the report would have revealed the deliberative process of the agency. Categorizing the report as post-decisional in nature (i.e., the report represented the results of the investigation), the D.C. Court of Appeals ordered the FBI to release most of it. [14]

Specific documents or memoranda protected by Exemption Five often contain some factual material or expert opinion which is not exempt. If the issue is raised in court, a federal judge may conduct an in camera inspection to decide which parts of a particular document fall within the exemption and which do not. If the judge finds that some parts of the material should be disclosed, he will order the agency to excise the exempt portions and produce the rest for inspection and copying. This occasionally results in virtually illegible documents, due to heavy blackout marks over every other word or sentence.

Exemption Six: Personal Privacy

Matters that deal with personnel and medical files and similar files the disclosure of which would constitute clearly unwarranted invasion of personal privacy.

This exemption does for individuals what Exemption Four attempts to do for businesses. However, not all invasions of privacy are unlawful under FOIA. The question of which ones are and which are not has been the subject of considerable litigation. Courts have usually tried to decide this issue by balancing the public interests which would be served by disclosure against the private interest involved in non-disclosure.

The "similar files" component of the exemption's "personnel, medical, or similar files" coverage was previously thought to embrace only those records containing information as intimate as that normally found in personnel or medical records. In one case, for example, journalists were trying to find out whether or not certain Iranian nationals held valid United States passports or were U.S. citizens. The Court of Appeals viewed citizenship as not being an intimate personal detail and ordered appropriate disclosure.

However, the U.S. Supreme Court has rejected this interpretation and construed Exemption Six to cover any information that applies to a particular individual, the disclosure of which would constitute a clearly unwarranted invasion of that person's privacy. [15] This interpretation makes it unnecessary to focus on the type of record or file in which the information is contained, and instead requires the balancing test discussed above.

Exemption Seven: Law Enforcement

Matters which are investigatory records compiled for law enforcement purposes, but only to the extent that the production of such records would:
    a) interfere with enforcement proceedings,
    b) deprive a person of a right to a fair trial or an impartial adjudication,
    c) constitute an unwarranted invasion of personal privacy,
    d) disclose the identity of a confidential source (in a criminal or national security investigation),
    e) disclose investigative techniques and procedures, or
    f) endanger the life or physical safety of law enforcement personnel.

---

14. *Playboy v. Dept. of Justice,* 677 F.2d 932 (D.C. Cir. 1982).
15. *U.S. Dept. of State v. Washington Post,* 456 U.S. 595, 102 S.Ct. 1957, 72 L.Ed.2d 358 (1982).

Clause (a) of Exemption Seven is the one most often cited by the agencies when they deny FOIA requests. Clause (c) is also commonly relied on by the government and reviewed by the courts. For the most part, the U.S. Supreme Court has upheld the agencies on these.

For example, in a 5-4 decision, the U.S. Supreme Court ruled that information originally collected for law enforcement purposes remains exempt, even if it is later used for another purpose.[16] In this case a freelance journalist had asked the FBI for a list of the "name check summaries" (requested by then President Nixon) of persons who had signed a *New York Times* ad protesting the Administration's Vietnam policy. The FBI claimed the information consisted of "investigatory records compiled for law enforcement purposes." The journalist, on the other hand, argued that the records were not investigative files, but rather, internal documents compiled to monitor the activities of White House opponents.

The Court upheld the FBI on its first claim. Thus, under the authority of this case, once information has been compiled for law enforcement purposes, it seemingly has found permanent shelter under Exemption Seven. The Court's holding unquestionably expands the scope of the exemption and violates the general rule requiring strict interpretation against the agency. However, for now it constitutes the law of the land.

Following the Supreme Court's lead in supporting non-disclosure by law enforcement agencies, some courts have even held that FBI records are *per se* "investigatory records compiled for law enforcement purposes," despite the illegality or non-law enforcement purposes of the underlying investigation.

Exemption Eight: Bank Reports

Matters contained in or related to examination, operating, or condition reports prepared by, on behalf of, or for the use of an agency responsible for the regulation or supervision of financial institutions.

This refers to reports prepared by or for an agency responsible for the supervision of financial institutions, like the Securities and Exchange Commission. Its purpose is to prevent disclosure of sensitive financial reports or audits that, if made public, might undermine public confidence in the banking system. Enough said.

Exemption Nine: Oil and Gas Wells

Matters involving geological and geophysical information and data, including maps, concerning wells.

This provision is infrequently used. However, the Federal Power Commission used it to deny Ralph Nader access to FDC and American Gas Association estimates of natural gas reserves, even though Nader claimed that Exemption Nine applied only to geological data that would benefit a competitor.

THE IRS EXEMPTION: A rider to the Economic Recovery Tax Act of 1981 permits the IRS to withhold information used for "the selection of returns for examination of the data used or to be used for determining such standards, if the (agency) determines that such disclosure would seriously impair assessment, collection or enforcement under the internal revenue laws." Although this is not an amendment to the FOIA, it is a direct legislative reponse to an FOIA case ordering the IRS to disclose computer tapes containing information from the IRS's Taxpayer Compliance Measurement Program.

While we have provided you with a summary of the nine FOIA exemptions, we have

---

16. *FBI v. Abramson*, 102 S.Ct. 2054 (1982).

foregone describing the gory details of the many court decisions applying them to specific cases. That is because of our strong belief that you should just ask for what you want without worrying why the agency might deny your request. Since a denial of a FOIA request must be accompanied by chapter and verse, you will have a later opportunity to research your case if you don't get what you're after. For that purpose, we suggest that you consult *Legal Research: How to Find and Understand the Law*, by Stephen R. Elias, Nolo Press (order information at the back of this book) and the other resources on the Freedom of Information Act listed later in this section.

6. How to Use the FOIA

a. The Informal Request (or, It Never Hurts to Use the Back Door)

Sooner or later you will encounter a public servant who, out of ignorance, obstinance, or fear will improperly deny you access to documents which you are seeking by way of a formal FOIA request. Knowing this, common sense dictates that you should first *informally* attempt to obtain the information you need. This generally means contacting the individual who has direct control over the records (if you know who this is) instead of going through channels.

In the case of the FOIA, these channels involve the agency's FOIA officer who is made responsible for handling all FOIA requests from the public (and media). Because that officer may take it upon himself to deny as many requests as possible (notwithstanding the spirit of the act), you might do well to avoid him in the first instance. By first going directly to the custodian of the records, as we suggest, you may save an enormous amount of time and hassle.

For example, a Nolo Press editor once asked a regional Federal Highway Administration official to let him see any information the official happened to have on the administration of a new rural transportation program. The official responded, "Sure, come on in and take a look at what we've got." When the editor arrived, the official genially conducted him to a large file cabinet, opened two drawers, and said, "That's it, and you can use that desk over there to read it. Let me know if you want to copy anything." The material obtained through this process provided great insights into how the rural program actually worked (and didn't work) and proved to be extremely valuable for the editor's project.

In connection with the same project, an attorney in Washington D.C. sent a formal FOIA request to the central office of the same agency and received an enormous amount of obfuscatory flak. He never got what he had asked for.

However, even if informality does not get you the actual records you desire, it is often possible at least to ascertain how they are labelled (e.g., The "Evans Report" or the "Clearcreek Memorandum"), if you don't already know. This information can be valuable later if you make a formal request, since the law requires that you "reasonably describe" the records you want.

b. The Formal FOIA Request

Here are some general principles on how to request information under the Freedom of Information Act:

- Any person may request any record from a federal agency for any purpose.
- Requests must be reasonably specific (so that an agency official has a good idea of where to look).
- Each agency has its own set of rules for how to request materials from that agency.

These rules are published in the *Federal Register* and in the *Code of Federal Regulations* (CFR) title and section applicable to that agency, or may be obtained by contacting the agency.

- A list of citations to the CFR section for each agency is located in the *U.S. Code Service Lawyers Edition* directly after the FOIA (5 U.S.C. Sec. 552) *and* in the CFR Index under "Freedom of Information."

- Agency procedures for requesting documents should be followed as closely as possible, although many agencies will be reasonably accommodating if you make a mistake.

- All information not otherwise required to be published or maintained for the public by the agency as a matter of course must be disclosed to the public upon request, unless exempted.

- The burden is on the agency either to disclose *or* justify non-disclosure by referring to one of the nine FOIA exemptions.

- The agency may charge reasonable fees for locating requested items and copying them.

- These fees may be waived if disclosure will benefit the public, as determined by the agency.

- The agency must respond to a request for material within ten working days, either by disclosing or specifying the exemption, except that this period can be extended by the agency for an additional ten working days for good cause.

- You have a right to appeal to a bureaucrat in a higher supervisorial position in the agency upon a refusal to disclose. Procedures for appeal are contained in the CFR.

- A decision on your appeal must be handed down within twenty working days, except that this period may be extended for ten working days for certain reasons of good cause.

- Failure by the agency to comply with these time limits constitutes a denial of your request, which can be challenged in court. However, we recommend that you give the agency a certain amount of latitude before running off to seek a court order.

Here are some specific procedures for making FOIA requests:

- Determine which agency has the records. If you don't know, make an educated guess. If you send it to the wrong agency, they will often forward it to the correct place.

- Read that agency's rules for making requests.

- Address your request to the person, office, or location indicated in the rules.

- State that your request is being made pursuant to the FOIA and the agency's rules.

- Describe the material being requested in as many ways as possible and as specifically as possible. For example, if you want a copy of a specific letter sent by your employer to a government agency about some matter, refer to the letter by date, by subject matter, by the sender's name, by the recipient's name, by number of pages, and so on.

- Do not discuss or argue the exemptions in your request. It is better to ask for what you want and let the agency determine whether the material is exempted and if so, why. However, it is advisable to ask for specific exemptions to be cited if the agency denies all or part of your request so that you can better argue your case on appeal.

- Ask for a waiver of fees on the ground that the disclosure being sought by you will benefit the public. Although you don't have to, it may help your chances of getting a waiver, if you tell the agency why you want the materials. On the other hand, if your real goal is to file a lawsuit, and you don't want them to know, come up with a more general reason.

- Request that time limitations on the agency be complied with.

- Make sure that your address and telephone number are prominently displayed in your letter.

- Keep a copy!

Here is a sample FOIA Request:

```
                                              May 29, 1984


FOIA Officer
Environmental Protection Agency
401 M Street, S.W.
Washington, D.C. 20460

Dear Officer:

    This is a request under the Freedom of Information Act and under your
regulations published in 40 CFR Division 2.  I am requesting copies of docu-
ments, reports, memoranda, notes, letters and computer files which your
agency has regarding chemical dump sites in the state of Oregon.  I am
particularly interested in the location of these sites and what chemicals
were, and are, dumped.  I have been reading in the paper that this type of
information is being collected by your department and I have enclosed copies
of the article so that you will know what I am asking for.

    If, in fact, the article is wrong and the information is being collected
by another federal agency, I would appreciate your either informing me of
the fact or forwarding this request to that agency.

    I believe that the disclosure of the information contained in this re-
quest would clearly benefit the public and am therefore asking that you
waive any fees which arise from the location and copying of the materials
which I'm requesting.

    If there is any confusion concerning this request, or you have any
questions, please telephone or write me a note as soon as possible.  My
address and phone number are provided below.

    If you deny any part of this request, please advise me of the specific
exemption on which you're relying for the part denied and forward the part
which you determine not to be exempt.

    I look forward to hearing from you within the ten working days provided
by law.


                                    Sincerely,


                                    John A. Johnstone
                                    2468 Justice Road
                                    Portland, Oregon 97800
                                    (503) 987-6543
```

A SPECIAL NOTE ON FEES: Government agencies are permitted to charge requesters only for the cost of searching for and duplicating requested documents. These fees vary, depending on the agency involved. Fee schedules can be obtained from each agency.

Agencies are required by the FOIA to waive or reduce fees when releasing the information that would primarily benefit the general public. This rule has not been working well during the early 1980s. Agencies that don't want to release materials routinely demand high fees. In one case, a freelance writer asked the CIA for its documents on the underground press. A year after the initial request, the CIA estimated it would cost $61,501 to search—not to copy—its files, with no guarantee of ultimate disclosure. A down payment of $30,000 was demanded by the agency before it began the search. The writer sued and then reached an agreement with the CIA that he would not be charged for documents relating to thirty-eight of the newspapers listed in his original request.[17]

Another example concerned a researcher who was writing a book on U.S.-Israeli relations. His request to the Defense Intelligence Agency for documents on the 1973 Arab-Israeli war was met with a bill of $208,000. A lawsuit is pending.

In January 1983, the Reagan Administration issued new guidelines concerning this provision of the FOIA. Under them, the following five criteria will be applied to determine whether or not fees should be waived:

1. Is there a genuine public interest in the subject matter?
2. Will the disclosable contents of the records in fact be of interest to the public?
3. Is the information "already available in the public domain?"
4. Does the requester have adequate "qualifications" to understand the material and disseminate it?
5. Does the benefit to the public outweigh "any personal interest of the requester?"

As a reporter, you should argue that these five criteria fit you like a glove and that your request is in the public interest. See the sample letter above. Since the guidelines are new, we cannot determine how liberally they will be interpreted.

17. Angus MacKenzie, "The Operational Files Exemption," *The Nation*, 9/24/83, p.233.

7. Appealing a Denial

In the event that any part of your request is formally denied by the FOIA officer, or the agency unreasonably delays its response, or you disagree with the fees being charged, you are entitled to appeal to the head of the agency. This is not a difficult procedure. Although each agency maintains its own regulations for how and when to do this (these can be found in the CFR applicable to each agency), the general idea is to summarize briefly the history of your request and of your reasons for disagreeing with the excuse given for the initial denial. It is a good idea to attach copies of all previous correspondence in this matter, although it is probable that the agency file will contain them anyway.

Although it may seem fruitless to appeal (i.e., you have requested the FBI file on Ronald Reagan and you somehow feel deep down in your bones your request will be denied on all levels), you need to go through this step if you later wish to seek judicial review of the agency denial. This is known as the requirement that you "exhaust your administrative remedies" before going to court.

8. Challenging a FOIA Decision in Court

If your appeal is denied, or if the agency fails to respond to your appeal within twenty working days, you may file a FOIA lawsuit in the United States District Court most convenient to you. Although there is a six-year statute of limitations period, you should try to file the suit as soon as possible. Even though you are entitled to file the suit if the agency has not complied with the proper time limits, the court is entitled to give the agency some additional time to meet your request, if good cause is shown for the delay. However, in at least one case involving the FBI, four years was ruled to be a lack of "due diligence."

The FOIA 1) requires that the court give FOIA suits "expedited" treatment, 2) gives the government the burden of proving the existence of a justification for withholding information under any of the nine exemptions, and 3) awards attorneys fees to the prevailing party. Federal courts allow non-lawyers to file for themselves (pro se). If you think that your case is more or less routine, you might wish to do so. However, if the Justice Department is not willing to negotiate with you, and your request is other than routine, you may find yourself involved in a complicated lawsuit and want the help of a lawyer.

There is much about the FOIA which is still a matter of conjecture. Substantial amendments may be imminent, and pending cases will probably result in new legal interpretations. In sum, there will certainly be times when the help of a lawyer thoroughly conversant with the area will be advisable. Such advice is available through the FOI Service Center (see Section 9 below).

9. Further Sources of Information on the FOIA

The FOI Service Center, a joint project of The Reporters Committee for Freedom of the Press and the Society of Professional Journalists, Sigma Delta Chi, has prepared a booklet, "How To Use the Federal FOIA." The booklet contains detailed instructions and comes complete with sample letters, forms, and directories of names, addresses and telephone numbers of major federal agencies. In addition, the Service Center provides hot-line telephone help, legal advice, research memos, representation assistance, a complete state-federal FOI research library, and other written materials. This valuable resource can be reached in care of The Reporters Committee, 1125 15th St., N.W., Washington, D.C. 20005, (202) 466-6312. The booklet is

166

available at 50 cents per copy.

Another resource is the Campaign for Political Rights, which published a compilation of more than 500 case studies on successful use of the FOIA by consumers, labor unions, researchers, reporters and others. Their "Organizing Notes" keep track of decisions and legislation on access to information about government policies and actions. A number of other organizations as well are working to preserve the Freedom of Information Act and can provide advice and materials about filing FOIA and PA requests.

Campaign for Political Rights
201 Massachusetts Avenue, N.E.
Washington, DC 20002
(202) 547-4705

Fund for Open Information and
  Accountability, Inc.
339 Lafayette Street
New York, NY 10012

Center for National Security Studies
122 Maryland Avenue, N.E.
Washington, DC 20002

Reporters Committee for Freedom of the Press
1125 15th Street, N.W.
Washington, DC 20005

Freedom of Information Clearinghouse
c/o Public Citizen Litigation Group
2000 P Street, N.W.
Washington, DC 20036

MATERIALS FOR FILING FOIA REQUESTS:

"Are You Now or Have You Ever Been in the FBI Files," Anne Marie Buitrago and Andrew Immerman. Fund for Open Information and Accountability, Inc.

"How to Use the Federal FOI Act," Reporters' Committee for Freedom of the Press.

"Litigation Under the Federal Freedom of Information Act and Privacy Act," edited by Morton Halperin and Allan Adler, Center for National Security Studies.

"Using the FOIA: A Step by Step Guide," Center for National Security Studies.

D. The Federal Privacy Act

In 1974, Congress passed a comprehensive Federal Privacy Act, 5 U.S.C. Sec. 552(a). It was enacted to protect individuals against misuse of personal data gathered by the federal government. It permits American citizens and permanent residents to discover what kinds of files and record systems are being kept on them, and provides access to those files so that the people in question can correct erroneous data if necessary.

The Privacy Act states that:

• Agencies must publish the existence of all record systems maintained on individuals in the *Federal Register*.

• Information contained in these record systems must be accurate, complete, relevant, and up-to-date.

• Procedures must be established so that individuals can inspect and correct inaccuracies in almost all federal files.

• Information about an individual gathered for one purpose must not be used for another without the individual's consent.

• Agencies must keep accurate accounting of the disclosure of records and, with certain exceptions, give notice to the subject of the records.

The Privacy Act applies only to personal records maintained by the executive branch of the Federal Government concerning individual citizens or permanent residents. It does not apply to records held by state and local governments.

Like the FOIA, the Privacy Act is relatively simple to use. You can make your request by telephone or in person, but a certified letter is your best bet. Include enough information about yourself so that the agency can be sure of your identity and know which files to search.

CAUTION: You need only provide sufficient information for a records search. You do not have to provide information the agency did not have already. For example, you may not want to give the FBI enough information to start a file on you if you didn't have one before.

The letter should be addressed to the head of the agency or to the Privacy Act Officer. Indicate on the envelope "Privacy Act Request/Do Not Delay."

```
                                        Address
                                        Daytime telephone number
                                        Date

Agency Address
To the FOI Officer

    This is a request under the Freedom of Information Act, as amended (5
U.S.C. Sec. 552), in conjunction with the Privacy Act (5 U.S.C. Sec 552a).

    I wish to obtain a copy of all documents retrievable in a search for
files listed under my name. [If you are requesting files from the FBI, add
the following:  Please advise me if my name is contained in other "See
Reference" files as well, so that I can make a decision about whether or
not to have any such files searched.]

    I also ask that you check for additional records in your field offices
in the following cities:

[If requesting records from the FBI, you must file a separate request with
each relevant field office.]

    If all or any part of my request is denied, please list the specific
exemption(s) which is (are) being claimed to withhold information.

    If you determine that some portions of the requested material are
exempt, I will expect, as the Act provides, that you will provide me with
the remaining, non-exempt portions.  I, of course, reserve the right to
appeal any decision to withhold information and expect that you will list
the address and office to which such an appeal can be sent.

    If you have any questions concerning this request, please telephone me
at the above number.  As provided in the Privacy Act, I expect to receive
an acknowledgment of this request within ten working days, and the mate-
rials within thirty working days.

                                        Sincerely,


                                        Your full name
                                        Social Security number
                                        Date and place of birth
```

[Your signature must be notarized. Mark clearly on envelope: "Attention: Freedom of Information/Privacy Act Unit"]

Most agencies require proof of identity before they will release records. Although the requirements differ, you are generally in compliance if you include your full name, social security number, date and place of birth, and a notarized signature.

NOTE: Anyone who "knowingly and willingly" requests or receives access to a record about an individual "under false pretenses" is subject to criminal penalties. This means that you can be prosecuted for deliberately attempting to obtain someone else's records.

Under the Privacy Act, agencies are permitted to charge fees to cover the actual costs of copying records, which usually come to ten cents a page. In addition, unlike the FOIA, the Privacy Act does not require agencies to process your request within ten business days, although the request "should" be acknowledged by the agency within that time, and the records themselves "should" be produced within thirty working days.

Unlike the FOIA, the Privacy Act provides no standard procedure for appealing denials. However, many agencies have their own regulations, and, if your request is denied, the agency should advise you of its appeal procedure and tell you to whom to address your appeal.

It is inevitable that the principle of governmental openness and the desire to maintain personal privacy will collide at some points. Thus, the FOIA and the Privacy Act may be in conflict when certain information is sought. What happens? The Privacy Protection Study Commission says,

> When the two Acts are read together any disclosure of a record about an individual in a system of records as defined by the Privacy Act to any member of the public other than the individual to whom the record pertains is forbidden if the disclosure would constitute a "clearly unwarranted invasion of personal privacy." The reverse obligation also holds: even though a record is about an individual, it cannot be withheld from any member of the public who requests it if the disclosure would not constitute a clearly unwarranted invasion of personal privacy. [18]

Ultimately, it is a question of balancing interests and attempts by the courts to define what is a "clearly unwarranted invasion of privacy."

E. Federal Legislation Which Blocks Access to Records

1. Executive Order on Classification

In 1982, President Reagan issued Executive Order 12356 on the subject of classification. This order reversed an earlier trend toward reducing the number of documents ordered classified. In effect, the new Order directs government officials to resolve any doubts about the need for classification in favor of secrecy. It also eliminates the FOIA requirement that records be reviewed for declassification after twenty years.

The legality of the order is debatable. There is no statute which specifically authorizes the President to issue it. Like executive privilege, the claim is that the President has this power under authority of the U.S. Constitution as part of his role as Commander-in-Chief and in respect to his responsibility to conduct foreign affairs.

Before Reagan's Order, records were to be classified only if publication would cause

---

18. *Report of the Privacy Protection Study Commission*, p.25.

"identifiable" harm to the national security. Now, however, there need only be an expectation of unspecified "damage" in order to classify a document. Likewise, there no longer need be a balancing of the need for secrecy against "the public interest in access to the document in question. The most unusual provision of this order permits reclassification of information that had been previously disclosed if such information is again deemed sensitive and can "reasonably be recovered." Because the FOIA permits officials to withhold information if it is properly classified under an Executive Order, this Order may weaken dramatically the Freedom of Information Act.

F. Intelligence Identities Protection Act

Any writer exposing the identity of an intelligence agent with "reason to believe" that so doing would "impair or impede foreign intelligence activities of the United States" is subject to imprisonment for up to four years and fines of $15,000, under the Intelligence Identities Protection Act.[19]

Although the Act was ostensibly designed to silence publications like *Counterspy* and the *Covert Action Information Bulletin* from "naming names," this law has more wide-reaching implications. For example, under the Act, reporters are guilty of a crime if they reveal information on U.S. intelligence activities *even if the information is obtained from public records.*

It is easy to predict long debates in editorial rooms as to whether or not to inform the American public of past or present abuses by the U.S. intelligence agencies. It is less easy to predict the outcomes of such debates but it is probable that in some instances, if not many, the public's right to know will lose out.

G. State Open Records Laws

All of the states now have open records laws, although there are many variations. As a general rule, state laws are less liberal than the federal FOIA, but this is not invariably true. For example, unlike the FOIA, some states decree fines and/or jail terms for violators. For example, anyone who violates Michigan's open records law could be fined a maximum of $500 and/or jailed for not more than one year. As with open meeting laws, it is a good idea to know your state public records law inside-out. Thus, we have also provided you with a citation to your state's law. Refer to Appendix B for suggestions on how to look this up for yourself.

STATE PUBLIC RECORDS LAWS

State	Citation
Alabama	Ala. Code, Tit. 36 Sec. 36-12-40
Alaska	Alaska Stat. Sec. 09.25.100
Arizona	Ariz. Rev. Stat. Ann. Sec. 39-121

---

19. See Chapter 2.

Arkansas . . . . Ark. Stats. Ann. Sec.12-2801
California . . . . Cal. Govt. Code Sec. 6250 et. seq.
Colorado . . . . Colo. Rev. Stat. Sec. 24-72-201 et. seq.
Connecticut . . . . Conn. Gen. Stat. Sec. 1-18a
Delaware . . . . Del. Code Ann. Art. 29 Sec. 10111
Florida . . . . Fla. Stat. Section 119.01
Georgia . . . . Ga. Code Sec. 50-18-90
Hawaii . . . . Haw. Rev. Stat. Sec. 92-50
Idaho . . . . Idaho Code Sec. 9-301
Illinois . . . . Ill. Rev. Stat. Ch. 116 Sec. 43.4
Indiana . . . . Ind. Code Sec. 15-14-1-1
Iowa . . . . Iowa Code Sec. 68A.1
Kansas . . . . Kan. Stat. Sec. 45-201
Kentucky . . . . Ky. Rev. Stat. 61.870
Louisiana . . . . La. Rev. Stat. Ann. Vol. 24, Tit. 44 Sec. 1
Maine . . . . Me. Rev. Stat. Tit. 1 Sec. 401
Maryland . . . . Md. Ann. Code, Art. 76A, Sec. 1
Massachusetts . . . . Mass. Gen. Laws Ann. Ch. 66 Sec. 10
Michigan . . . . Mich. Comp. Laws Sec. 15.231
Minnesota . . . . Minn. Stat. Ann. Sec. 15.17
Mississippi . . . . Miss. Code Ann. Sec. 25-51-1
Missouri . . . . Mo. Rev. Stat. Sec. 109.180
Montana . . . . Mont. Rev. Code Ann. Sec. 2-6-101
Nebraska . . . . Neb. Rev. Stat. Sec. 84-712
Nevada . . . . Nev. Rev. Stat. Sec. 239.010
New Hampshire . . . . N.H. Rev. Stat. Ann. Sec. 91-A:1
New Jersey . . . . N.J. Stat. Ann. Sec. 47:1A-1
New Mexico . . . . N.M. Stat. Ann. Sec. 14-2-1
New York . . . . N.Y. Pub. Off. Law Sec. 84 et. seq.
North Carolina . . . . N.C. Gen. Stat. Sec. 132-1
North Dakota . . . . N.D. Cent. Code Sec. 44-04-18
Ohio . . . . Ohio Rev. Code Ann. Sec. 149.43
Oklahoma . . . . Okla. Stat. Ann. Tit. 51, Sec. 24
Oregon . . . . Or. Rev. Stat. Sec. 192.410
Pennsylvania . . . . Pa. Stat. Ann. Tit. 65, Sec. 66.1
Rhode Island . . . . R.I. Gen. Laws Sec. 38-2-1
South Carolina . . . . S.C. Code Sec. 30-4-10
South Dakota . . . . S.D. Compiled Laws Ann. Sec. 1-27-1
Tennessee . . . . Tenn. Code Ann. Sec. 10-7-503
Texas . . . . Tex. Govt. Code Ann., Tit. 110A, 6252-17a
Utah . . . . Utah Code Ann. Sec. 63-2-59
Vermont . . . . Vt. Stat. Ann., Tit. 1 Sec. 315
Virginia . . . . Va. Code Sec. 2.1-340
Washington . . . . Wash. Rev. Code Ann. 42.17.260
West Virginia . . . . W.Va. Code Sec. 29B-1-1
Wisconsin . . . . Wis. Stat. Sec. 19.21
Wyoming . . . . Wyo. Stat. Sec. 16-4-201

H. Conclusion

In the last generation, journalists and scholars have repeatedly confirmed the age-old suspicion that it is the tendency of government, including the U.S. Government, to conceal information. One of the most important functions of a free press is to dig out this information and put it into general circulation. Unless this is done, the public's right to know cannot be protected.

Not surprisingly, our government has not made it easy for the press to gather news freely. The executive branch has attempted to weaken the FOIA in recent years, and the courts, as evidenced by many of the decisions discussed in this and other chapters, have not always been willing to provide constitutional protection to journalists. As former U.S. Supreme Court Justice, Potter Stewart, stated in his 1974 address at Yale Law School:

> The press is free to do battle against secrecy and deception in government. But the press cannot expect from the Constitution any guarantee that it will succeed. There is no constitutional right to have access to particular government information or to require openness from bureaucracy. The public's interest in knowing about its government is protected by the guarantee of a Free Press, but the protection is indirect. The Constitution itself is neither a Freedom of Information Act nor an Official Secrets Act. [20]

In our discussion of prior restraints on publication in Chapter 2, we noted that there was a "heavy presumption against the constitutional validity of such government action." There are less restrictive rules governing subsequent punishment for publishing unpopular or "dangerous" ideas. This is because freedom from prior restraints at least allows the information to be disseminated in the first place.

It should be obvious that consistent denial of access to newsgathering produces the same result as prior restraint—the information is not disseminated; the public doesn't know what the government is doing.

As Justice William O. Douglas stated in the Pentagon Papers case (*U.S. v. New York Times*)[21]:

> The dominant purpose of the First Amendment was to prohibit the widespread practice of governmental suppression of embarrassing information . . . Secrecy in government is fundamentally anti-democratic, perpetuating bureaucratic errors. Open debate and discussion of public issues are vital to our national health. On public questions there should be "open and robust debate."

---

20. Stewart, "Or of the Press," 26 *Hastings L.Rev.* 631, 636 (1975).
21. See Chapter 2.

Government Regulation of the Electronic Media

A. Introduction

The electronic media, which has been regulated by the federal government for many years (fifty to be exact) is facing the definite possibility that its existing regulatory structure may be dismantled. Our task in this chapter is therefore problematic. Do we emphasize the existing structure or its collapse? Regulation or deregulation?

To accommodate this problem, we present a concise overview of the major doctrines associated with regulation and the main areas of current conflict. We emphasize those aspects of regulation which affect the content of programming. We do not offer practical advice for how to cope with regulation, however. This should come from attorneys hired by the media organizations in question. We also will not dwell on current efforts to deregulate the electronic media, due to our inability to forecast the ultimate results.

B. Rationale for Regulation

Why can the government regulate the electronic media without violating the First Amendment, when regulation of the print media would be ruled unconstitutional?

When first presented with these questions back in 1943, the Supreme Court upheld regulation (the Communications Act of 1934) as being necessary because the air waves were a scarce public resource which should be used in the public interest.[1] In the last fifteen years, the Court has justified regulation of the broadcast media for two reasons:

1. The public needs a government guarantee of access to a broad range of social and political ideas;[2] and

2. Radio and television enjoy a "uniquely pervasive presence" in our lives.[3]

Although the second reason still exists, the first no longer makes sense. When the Communications Act of 1934[4] passed the Congress, there were thousands of newspapers, but only a relative handful of frequencies available for broadcast by the then infant radio industry. When television emerged after World War II, there were similarly only a few channels which could be used. Today, however, the situation has been reversed. The electronic media offers the average citizen a much greater variety of news and other programming than in the past. There are well over 9,000 AM and FM radio stations, 1,000 VHF and UHF television stations, and a seemingly unlimited profusion of cable outlets. In contrast, there are only some 1600 daily newspapers still being published in the U.S. In other words, some of the reasons previously advanced for government regulation of the electronic media appear now to be obsolete. For this reason, broadcasters are arguing for deregulation. Since full deregulation will take some time to occur, however, it is useful to explore the high points of regulation as it exists today.

C.   An Overview of What Regulation Does

In the Communications Act of 1934, Congress decided to treat the radio spectrum as a scarce natural resource belonging to the public as a whole. Because those using such a publicly-owned frequency would be exercising exclusive control over it, the act formulated what has become known as the "public interest standard." This standard, the cornerstone of broadcast regulation, requires a broadcaster to operate a station "in the public interest, convenience, and necessity." The act also created the Federal Communications Commission (FCC) to oversee and implement the act's public interest principle.

The act prohibited a radio station from broadcasting unless a license was first obtained from the FCC. The FCC, in turn, was prohibited from granting, renewing, or modifying a permit unless it first found that the station would serve the "public interest, convenience and necessity." Defining what this standard actually meant was left to the FCC. In language almost as vague as that of the act, the FCC determined that the public interest standard encompassed an "affirmative responsibility on the part of broadcast licensees to provide a reasonable amount of time for the presentation over their facilities of programs devoted to the discussion and consideration of public issues. . . ."[5]

Under this test, the FCC has, over the past 50 years, approved over 100,000 licenses, while rejecting less than 50. The bias of the FCC has always been to allow the free market, rather than itself, to channel programming in the direction of the public interest, even though history has proven that marketplace forces rarely have produced programming that is truly in the public interest.

---

1. *National Broadcasting Co. v. United States*, 319 U.S. 190, 213, 63 S.Ct. 997, 1008, 87 L.Ed. 1344, 1361 (1943).

2. *Red Lion Broadcasting Co., Inc. v. FCC*, 395, U.S. 367, 89 S.Ct. 1794, 23 L.Ed.2d 371 (1969).

3. *FCC v. Pacifica Foundation*, 438 U.S. 726, 98 S.Ct. 3026, 57 L.Ed.2d 1073 (1978).

4. 47 U.S.C., Section 301.

5. *Report on Editorializing by Broadcasting Licensees*, 13 FCC 1246 (1940).

D.   The Federal Communications Commission

To understand the history of government regulation of the electronic media, it is important to understand a few basics about the FCC. First and foremost, it is a typical regulatory agency. Created by Congress, its members (seven commissioners) are appointed by the President of the United States with the advice and consent of the Senate. The President designates the chairman. Not more than four of the seven commissioners can be members of the same political party. Commissioners are appointed for a term of seven years on a staggered basis, so that each year one commissioner's appointment expires. What this means, of course, is that each newly-elected President is able to appoint the chairperson of his choosing. Further, over a four-year period, the political leanings of the agency can be significantly molded.

As a regulatory agency, the FCC's powers are defined by the Communications Act of 1934, including the broad discretion to define and shape the public interest doctrine. But, because of its changing membership and its broad discretion to interpret the act, the FCC has on occasion shifted its perception of what is and is not in the public interest and what standards a particular broadcaster must maintain. It is important to remember that today's rule may be tomorrow's history.

E.   Licensing by the FCC

A primary function of the FCC under the act is licensing. The Commission grants television stations licenses for five-year periods, renewable each subsequent five years. The period is seven years for radio stations. In order to obtain and/or renew a license, the applicant must first meet several qualifications. Applicants must be U.S. citizens or U.S. corporations essentially controlled by citizens. A second criterion is character. An application may be denied if there is evidence of bad character which would interfere with the responsible operation of the station. The applicant must have sufficient funds to construct the station and operate it for three months following construction without relying on advertising revenues. All applicants must demonstrate that they will meet all of the technical requirements necessary to broadcast.

Television applicants are required to submit detailed descriptions of 1) their proposed programming based on the needs of the community to be served by the station (called ascertainment surveys) and 2) the percentages of program time which will be devoted to meeting those needs. Applications for radio licenses, however, need only be accompanied by a general assurance that programming "relevant to issues facing the licensee's community" will be provided.[6]

F.   Specific Licensing Activities Affecting Program Content

1. Competing Applicants

When there are competing applicants for a radio or television frequency, the FCC must decide between them. This decision is based in substantial part on the type of programming being

---

6. *FCC v. WNCN Listener's Guide*, 450 U.S. 582 (1981).

offered by the applicants. Thus, if one applicant proposes twenty-four hours of music, while the other offers a balanced menu of music, news, talk shows, and sports, the latter applicant may receive more favorable treatment. On the other hand, if the latter applicant is of a political persuasion very different from the views of the majority of the FCC, while the all-music proposal comes from people who are politically "correct," you may well be listening to a steady diet of the "Top 40." In other words, politics plays a part in deciding who gets media licenses, just as it does in deciding who gets airline routes and national park concessions.

Wouldn't such favoritism on the basis of an applicant's politics violate the First Amendment? Probably. However, when the FCC chooses one applicant over another, it considers a variety of criteria in deciding which applicant would best serve the public interest. These are:

- Local residence of station owners;
- Direct management of the station by its owners;
- Participation by owners in civic affairs;
- Proposed station programming;
- Broadcast experience of owners;
- Prior broadcast record of owners;
- "Character" of owners (i.e., law violations, etc.);
- Diversification of control;
- Differences in areas and populations to be served.

Because the FCC's decision is based on a consideration of all these factors, it is usually impossible to tell the real reason for its decision in any particular case. Thus, even if it favors one station over another for political reasons, the FCC can usually base its decision on one of the politically neutral factors listed above.

2. License Renewal Proceedings

Every five years, the FCC reviews the performance of a television licensee (every seven years for a radio license). This provides an opportunity for the FCC and public interest groups to exert pressure on the licensee in question to increase diversity and local responsiveness in their programming. A public group may participate in the licensing process if it can show the application sought would have an effect on it.[7] For example, a group of black citizens might protest a renewal grant to a licensee who had repeatedly manifested insensitivity to the needs of the black community.

In recent years, citizen's groups have participated in hundreds of licensing hearings. To do so, the group must file a "Petition to Deny" the application. Under Section 309(d)(2) of the Act, the FCC must either grant the petition (i.e., deny the license) or deny the petition with an accompanying concise statement of the reasons for denial. Despite these challenges, stations rarely lose their licenses, particularly for reasons of program content.

Renewal proceedings also provide an aspiring competitor an opportunity to take over the license by convincing the FCC that the existing licensee has failed to serve the public interest. A widely-publicized example of this involves WVCA-FM, a one-man, all classical music radio station run by Simon Geller of Gloucester, Massachusetts from his basement. Geller plays classical music for fourteen hours a day without interruption, except for four public affairs segments a month dealing with social security, a weekly update of United Nations activities, and announcements of upcoming local events. He sometimes shuts off the station to go to a movie.

In May 1982, the FCC refused to renew Geller's license to operate his station and instead awarded it to a competing applicant who promised to devote 28.7 percent of its programming to news, public affairs, and other non-entertainment features. With listener support, Geller has appealed the FCC decision to the D.C. Circuit Court of Appeals. A decision is pending.

G. Objectionable Material and the Criminal Law

Obscenity has never been considered "speech" within the definition of the First Amendment guarantee of freedom of speech. Thus, if "speech" as such (whether actual or symbolic) can be characterized as obscene, it can also be censored and punished. The big question, of course, has been to define what is and is not obscene. For the purposes of this chapter, obscene language is that which expressly refers to sexual acts for the purpose of pandering to the audience's sexual tastes. (See Chapter 2 for more discussion of obscenity.)

To complicate matters a little more, it is a federal criminal offense to broadcast any material over the radio which is obscene or indecent. Thus, radio broadcasters must not only watch out for "obscene" speech, but must also curtail "indecent" speech, that is, speech which is patently offensive to the mores of the community. For the most part, any language which you would hesitate to put in print or use in polite company runs the risk of being considered obscene or indecent. Specifically, such words as "shit," "fuck," "cunt," "cock," "motherfucker," and their derivative phrases should be considered out-of-bounds.

Although the radio broadcasting of obscene or indecent language is a crime under the Criminal Code, it is not prohibited by the Communications Act of 1934. In fact, there is an apparent contradiction between the U.S. Criminal Code and the Communications Act. The two acts read, in part, as follows:

> Section 326 of the Federal Communications Act states:
>
> Nothing in this chapter shall be understood or construed to give the commission the power of censorship over the radio communications or signals transmitted by any radio station, and no regulation or condition shall be promulgated or fixed by the Commission which shall interfere with the right of free speech by means of radio communication.

---

7. *Office of Communications of the United Church of Christ v. FCC*, 359 F.2d 994 (1966).

The U.S. Criminal Code, 18 U.S.C. Section 1464 provides as follows:

> Whoever utters any obscene, indecent, or profane language by means of radio communication shall be fined not more than $10,000 or imprisoned not more than two years, or both.

The Communications Act prohibits censorship and the Criminal Code prohibits the broadcasting of obscene or indecent language. In order to "harmonize" this conflict (and thus give effect to both provisions), the courts have ruled that the Communications Act bar on censorship does not apply to the language prohibited by the Criminal Code. Consequently, the FCC may prohibit the broadcasting of obscene, indecent or profane language[8] and impose fines in the event such a broadcast is made.

Such punishment occurred in the *WUHY* case.[9] On January 4, 1970, WUHY-FM in Philadelphia broadcast an interview with Jerry Garcia, leader of The Grateful Dead. In the course of the interview, Garcia expressed his views on a variety of subjects and frequently used the words "fuck" and "shit" as an integral part of his speech (i.e., as adjectives, introductory expletives, and substitutes for et cetera, as in "shit, man," ". . . and shit like that," and "900 fuckin' times"). Because the interview was taped ahead of time (which had provided the management the opportunity to self-censor), the FCC imposed a fine of $100 on the station and focused on the word "indecent." Thus, programming which would not be considered "obscene" under the Constitution could be prohibited for merely being indecent.

In a later case, the FCC determined that a station broadcasting a mid-day "topless radio" show involving personal topics, usually sexual, was both "indecent" and "obscene" because it intended to titillate, pander, and exploit sexual materials, and was without redeeming social value. The FCC levied a $2,000 fine, which the Circuit Court of Appeals upheld, in part, on the ground that there were significant numbers of children who might be exposed to the broadcast, due to its mid-day timing.[10]

This same rationale was subsequently adopted by the U.S. Supreme Court in *FCC v. Pacifica Foundation*, a case involving an afternoon broadcast of a monologue by the comedian George Carlin which contained a number of "forbidden words." The Court squarely ruled that the FCC could constitutionally prohibit indecent language from being broadcast over radio even though such language would not constitute obscenity as such. The reason advanced by the Court for its ruling was, in part, the same as it used to justify government regulation generally — the "uniquely pervasive presence of the broadcast media." The Court also emphasized the fact that the interview in question was "uniquely accessible to children," but stressed that its ruling was narrow:

> The Commission's decision rested entirely on a nuisance rationale under which context is all important . . . As Mr. Justice Sutherland wrote, a "nuisance may be merely a right thing in the wrong place — like a pig in the parlor instead of the barnyard." We simply hold that when the Commission finds that a pig has entered the parlor, the exercise of its regulatory power does not depend on proof that the pig is obscene.

Presumably, the Court would have viewed the case differently had the Carlin monologue been broadcast late at night when fewer children would be listening. In fact, the *Pacifica* case may not necessarily signal a drastic expansion of powers of the FCC in censoring content of

---

8. *FCC v. Pacifica*, 438 U.S. 726 (1978).
9. *In Re WUHY-FM Eastern Education Radio*, 24 FCC 2d 408 (1970).
10. *Illinois Citizens Committee for Broadcasting v. FCC*, 15 F.2d 397 (D.C. Cir., 1975).

programs. In 1978, Morality in Media of Massachusetts petitioned the FCC to deny the license renewal application of WGBH, a PBS station in Boston.

Morality in Media charged WGBH with having failed its responsibility to the community by consistently broadcasting material which was "offensive, vulgar" and . . . "otherwise harmful to children" without adequate warning of the need for parental supervision. The group cited segments of *Masterpiece Theater, The Thin Edge, Monty Python's Flying Circus* and *Rock Follies*.

The FCC disagreed with Morality in Media and renewed WGBH's license. It cautioned that the *Pacifica* ruling was very narrow (i.e., involved a broadcast at a time when children might be expected to be part of the audience) and that the Communications Act prohibition against censorship prevented punishing a station for the language used in a broadcast except in such limited circumstances.[11]

Where does all this leave us? Basically, the FCC may punish broadcasts involving language definable as obscene (generally that which is expressly descriptive of sexual behavior) or indecent ("nasty" words) if the broadcast is made under circumstances where children can be anticipated to be part of the audience.

H.   The Equal Time and Fairness Doctrines

1. Introduction

To fulfill the Communications Act mandate that licensees conduct their business in the public interest, the FCC has imposed on them an "affirmative responsibility" to devote some air time to issues of great public concern. To implement this requirement, the FCC has relied on provisions in the Communications Act to fashion two doctrines immediately recognizable by most readers — the Equal Time Doctrine and the Fairness Doctrine. Over the years, each has been subject to attack by all parts of the political spectrum. Currently, they are being seriously eroded by those who wish to totally deregulate the broadcast industry.

2. Equal Time Doctrine

The "equal time" or "equal opportunities" doctrine affects candidates for political office and

---

11. *In re Application of WGBH Educational Foundation*, FCC 78-522, 7/31/78.

arises from Section 315 of the Communications Act of 1934. That provision states that if a station provides time for one political candidate, it must do so for his or her opponents. Of course, this requirement is riddled with exceptions. Thus, if a "legally qualified" candidate appears on 1) "a bona fide newscast," 2) a "bona fide news interview," 3) a "bona fide news documentary" where the appearance is incidental to the main subject matter, or 4) an "on-the-spot coverage of bona fide news events," the station is under no obligation to offer time to other candidates.

Those of you familiar with the law will immediately recognize the many opportunities for legalistic quibbling which Section 315 presents. What is a "legally qualified candidate?" What is a "bona fide" newscast? Because of the importance that the electronic media has assumed in our political life, these issues have been the subject of fierce judicial battles which continue to the present. Further, because of the move toward deregulation, the law in this area is changing even more rapidly than might otherwise be the case. Here is a concise overview.

a. Who Is a "Legally Qualified" Candidate?

On December 19, 1967, the three commercial television networks carried a joint hour-long interview with President Lyndon Johnson. Eugene McCarthy, who had announced his own candidacy for the Democratic Party's presidential nomination before the broadcast, requested "equal time" on the ground that President Johnson was a legally qualified candidate for the same nomination. The station denied the request and McCarthy complained to the FCC. Because Johnson had not publicly announced his intention to run for re-election, the FCC decided he was not a "candidate" and accordingly denied McCarthy's appeal. The Court of Appeals upheld the FCC's interpretation.[12] Despite this strict interpretation of the term "candidate," however, the FCC clearly extends the Equal Time Doctrine to all "legally qualified candidates," no matter how minor the office.

b. Interpreting the Exemptions

The exemptions from the Equal Time Doctrine were enacted so that, for example, a newscast featuring an incumbent at a routine affair such as a ribbon cutting ceremony, or greeting visiting dignitaries, wouldn't trigger demand for equal time by other candidates for the office. Certainly, these exemptions help free the media to inform the citizenry about political issues. On the other hand, free publicity for the elected representatives of dominant parties diminishes the prospects of third party candidates.

PRESIDENTIAL DEBATE EXCEPTION: Since November 1983, the FCC has allowed debates to be considered "bona fide news events" and accordingly has exempted them from the Equal Time Doctrine. Under the old rule, giving one candidate access to air time outside of news programs required the broadcaster to provide equal time to all other candidates no matter how minor. To get around this, the debates themselves would be sponsored by a third party, for example, the League of Women Voters. The broadcasters, then, would be seen as simply covering a news event. Now, however, the event itself can be staged in the network studios without the need for third party sponsorship. Although the FCC has urged broadcasters not to "favor" or "disfavor" any particular candidate, there is no requirement that all candidates be included in the debate. Thus, such favoring or disfavoring seems inevitable.

c. Is Initial Access Required?

Except for the debates discussed above, the Equal Time Doctrine requires a broadcaster to allow

---

12. *McCarthy v. FCC*, 390 F.2d 471 (D.C. Cir., 1968).

all legally qualified candidates for a particular office to appear on its airwaves at a reasonable cost once one "legally qualified candidate" for that office has appeared. This raises the question as to whether the Communications Act of 1934 requires the broadcaster to grant any candidate access in the first place. The answer is that there is no such requirement. However, the Federal Election Campaign Act of 1971 (Campaign Act) independently requires access be given to candidates for federal office.[13]

Initial access was tested in 1979, when the Carter-Mondale Presidential Committee requested each of the three major television networks to provide a paid half-hour slot. Each network refused, arguing that Carter was trying to start his campaign too early and that they were not obligated by the Campaign Act to sell him air time until a date closer to the 1980 primary races. The FCC, and ultimately the U.S. Supreme Court,[14] decided that the networks had violated the Election Act, ruling that "it is the right of viewers and listeners, not the right of the broadcasters, which is paramount." At present, therefore, the electronic media must allow federal candidates reasonable access to their airwaves.

d. Access for Supporters of Candidates

Neither Section 315 of the Communications Act nor the Campaign Act applies to appearances made on behalf of candidates, that is, by the candidates' supporters or allies. However, in 1970, the FCC adopted the *Zapple* rule[15] which applies to supporters of spokespersons for a candidate. Basically, this rule requires broadcasters to provide some "comparable" (but not necessarily equal) access for one candidate's supporters if the supporters of another candidate have appeared.

e. Access for State and Local Candidates

There is no access requirement in the case of state or local candidates or their supporters. This means that broadcasters can technically avoid equal time problems by denying access to all candidates. However, this would certainly not be in the public interest and might land the broadcaster in trouble with the FCC on grounds discussed earlier in this chapter. Once a candidate is given access, however, others must be treated fairly under the Equal Time Doctrine.

f. What Is a Reasonable Charge?

The essence of Section 315 of the Communications Act is really in the words "equal opportunities," not "equal time." If one candidate is sold time, and his opponent cannot afford time, the station is not required to allow the poor candidate to speak for free. But when a station does sell time to a candidate, it must do so at comparable price and time. Whether a candidate is running for federal or state office, he or she cannot be charged a greater amount than for a comparable commercial. During a specific election period (45 days preceding the date of a primary election and 60 days preceding the date of a federal or special election), a station may charge a political candidate no more than the lowest unit charge for the same class and time period.

---

13. 47 U.S.C., Section 312(a)(7).
14. *CBS Inc. v. FCC*, 453 U.S. 367, 101 S.Ct. 2813 (1981).
15. Letter to Nicholas Zapple, 23 FCC 2d 707; reaffirmed in *In re: Complaint to Committee for the Fair Broadcasting of Controversial Issues*, 25 FCC 2d 283 (1970).

3. The Fairness Doctrine

a. Overview

The Fairness Doctrine is the second major means by which the FCC has attempted to further the public interest. It refers to the affirmative obligation of a broadcaster "to operate in the public interest and to afford reasonable opportunity for the discussion of conflicting views on issues of public importance." In other words, a broadcaster must devote some time to controversial issues of public importance and permit opposing views to be heard.

Most broadcasters meet their Fairness Doctrine obligations when their news divisions cover "controversial issues" and solicit views and comments from "both sides of the fence." However, when only one position has been broadcast, there must be an opportunity for opposing views to be heard. The Fairness Doctrine is always in operation by affirmative obligation.

Unfortunately, the details of this doctrine have been developed over time by Congress, the FCC, and the courts, and are not set down in one particular document. Rather, they are contained in statutes, court opinions and a series of agency decisions and special reports going back to 1927.[16] Here are a few of the high points.

b. Complaints to FCC

The FCC does not constantly monitor licensees to assure compliance with the Fairness Doctrine. Instead, enforcement only occurs when a member of the public files a complaint. The FCC has specific requirements for what information must be in the complaint and will act only if the complaint is adequate. Basically, a complaint must accurately describe the controversy, the facts supporting the claim of one-sidedness, and a statement of whether the station plans to afford any time for contrasting views.

The most common error in filing complaints is a mis-identification of the controversial

---

16. The FCC's 1964 report is formally titled *Applicability of the Fairness Doctrine in the Handling of Controversial Issues of Public Importance.* It is often referred to as the *Fairness Primer* (40 FCC 598). The FCC's 1974 report is formally titled *Fairness Doctrine and Public Interest Standards, Fairness Report Regarding Handling a Public Issue.* It is often referred to as the *Fairness Report* (48 FCC 2d 1).

issue. Under FCC rules, the Fairness Doctrine only operates in regard to the specific issue or issues raised in a particular program. Thus, a program dealing with whether our military procurement program is fiscally sound does not have to extend an opportunity to every business and supplier who might be implicated in some way. In such a case, the issue would be whether the military is spending tax money wisely, not whether individual military suppliers are over-charging for their products.

In one case, a private pilots' association complained that its members were treated unfairly by a program dealing with air safety. The FCC ruled that the association's petition describing the fairness issue as "whether private pilots are a major safety hazard" must be denied as being too narrow. According to the FCC, the program was actually concerned with the issue of "congestion over large airports."

In another case, the FCC considered a complainant's statement of a controversy as involving "national security" and "humanism" as too broad for consideration under the Fairness Doctrine. If you think this demonstrates that the FCC often uses technicalities to avoid issues, you are right.

c. What is a Controversial Issue under the Fairness Doctrine?

If complaints which raise narrow issues and broad issues don't require a FCC response under the Fairness Doctrine, what does? The answer is: complaints which allege that well-defined controversial issues of public importance have been treated in a one-sided way. This means that an issue must be both controversial and of "public importance." Remember, whether or not a particular matter meets these two criteria is initially left up to the licensee. The FCC only gets involved if there is a complaint by a member of the public.

According to the 1974 Fairness Report issued by the FCC, an issue is controversial if it "is the subject of vigorous debate with substantial elements of the community in opposition to one another" at the time the program was broadcast. A major factor in determining the controversiality of an issue is "the degree of attention paid to the issue by government officials, community leaders, and the media." Thus, a clear example of a controversial issue is any question raised on a ballot (e.g., initiative, referendum, bond issue, candidacy for public office).

In one case, the FCC determined that an NBC program called *Pensions: The Broken Promise* involved a controversial issue of public importance and was therefore subject to a Fairness Doctrine complaint. However, a reviewing court ruled that while the pension issue was of public importance, it was not controversial. This conclusion was based on the court's finding that the program's criticism of some private plans was balanced by positive comments about many others. The court went on to say that although the specific content of remedial legislation might be controversial, the program's general assertion of the necessity for the legislation was not. [17]

d. What Constitutes Public Importance?

The public importance requirement is primarily to ensure that the Fairness Doctrine is triggered only by those issues having a real impact on the community, and not by purely private disputes. In other words, issues that are only of academic or historical interest, or which have an impact in a foreign country but not in the local community, are not subject to Fairness Doctrine review. For example, the FCC has found that the firing of a station employee and the outcome of a criminal trial, while possibly controversial, were not of public importance.

17. *NBC v. FCC*, 516 F.2d 1101 (D.C. Cir., 1974).

Determining what is and is not "of public importance" is at least as tricky as determining "controversiality." Thus, the FCC has said that if the issue involves a social or political choice, the broadcaster is to consider "whether the outcome of that choice will have a significant impact on society or its institutions." However, the FCC has made it clear that this is not the only method of determining an issue's public importance and that "judgments can be made only on a case-by-case basis."

REMEMBER: The "subjective" evaluation of whether an issue is controversial and of public importance is to be made, at least initially, by the broadcaster rather than the FCC or potential complainant.

e. Applying the Fairness Doctrine to Programming

By simply viewing a typical network newscast, it is easy to get a good idea of what "fairness" in broadcasting actually means. When any issue appears to be controversial, the journalist will usually interview a number of people to obtain a variety of viewpoints. For example, when the U.S. role in the Middle East is discussed, a full panoply of opinions may be presented for the viewer's consideration. At the end of the Middle East segment, you should not be left with the feeling that you've only received one side to an issue.

However, the Fairness Doctrine does not require that each program be balanced. Most of the segments in the CBS production *60 Minutes*, for example, take a definite position on the controversial issues which are under investigation. Yet, CBS does not necessarily violate the Fairness Doctrine, even if it is "unfair" in an individual program. So long as CBS finds time in its overall programming for the presentation of opposing views, even if it does so at a different time and in a different format, the Fairness Doctrine is not violated. Thus, if a guest on the CBS evening news show (aired at 11:00 pm) speaks in opposition to an investigative piece done by Mike Wallace on *60 Minutes*, CBS may have satisfied its obligation under the Fairness Doctrine.

Over the years, the FCC has developed criteria for deciding whether a reasonable opportunity for reply has been afforded under the circumstances. The total amount of time afforded to each side, the frequency with which each side is presented, and the size of the listening audience during the various broadcasts, are all taken into account. In addition, the FCC views some times (e.g., prime time television and "drive-time" radio) as being more influential than others.[18]

f. The Broadcaster's Responsibilities under the Fairness Doctrine

If a broadcaster presents a controversial issue of public importance, it should diligently search out opposing views. It is not enough to simply respond to complaints after the broadcast. Similarly, if an unbalanced program is broadcast, the broadcaster should make a good-faith effort to communicate to potential spokespersons the station's willingness to present their views. Unbalanced discussions of major issues require an even more diligent effort to seek such persons.

Suppose that a broadcast involving a controversial issue of public importance is paid for rather than aired as part of a newscast. Does the broadcaster have to find someone willing to pay to present the opposing views? The answer is no. Under the *Cullman Doctrine*,[19] a broadcaster

---

18. *Public Media Center v. FCC*, 587 F.2d 1322 (D.C. Cir., 1978).
19. *Cullman Broadcasting Co.*, 40 FCC 576 (1963).

must provide sufficient contrasting viewpoints, even if no contrasting spokespersons are willing to pay for the opportunity. In such cases, contrasting spokespersons must be given sufficient balancing time without charge.

Broadcasters should be sensitive to the possibility that a particular issue may involve a spectrum of views. If so, the FCC requires efforts to present a fair sampling of them. But the FCC has also indicated that in most cases it may be possible for the broadcaster to determine that only two or a few viewpoints are significant enough to warrant coverage. Unfortunately, this aspect of the Fairness Doctrine is vague because it has never been officially enforced by the FCC.

In addition, the broadcaster must attempt to select genuine partisans of the opposing views rather than neutral spokespersons. Therefore, while presentation by a news reporter or other impartial commentator may partially fulfill Fairness Doctrine requirements, such representations are not fully adequate to provide balance. In the final analysis, however, if no partisan of a viewpoint can be found after a diligent search, the broadcaster is off the hook. This will seldom happen.

g. Documentaries and the Fairness Doctrine

There are certain inherent difficulties in the Fairness Doctrine. For example, suppose a television station airs a two-hour documentary on child molestation which recommends stricter enforcement of the law. Does that station have a Fairness Doctrine obligation to a group which believes in encouraging sexual relations between adults and children? Probably not.

Although there is little definitive law on the subject, the Fairness Doctrine is most likely to be successfully invoked when the program in question chooses sides between two powerful social interests (e.g., pro and anti-nuclear disarmament) and less likely to be applied where most citizens would agree with the position advanced (e.g., corruption in government should be rooted out).

h. Entertainment and the Fairness Doctrine

Likewise, the question of whether the Fairness Doctrine applies to dramatic presentations has not yet been fully answered. One effort was made to do so in a complaint filed by anti-abortion groups regarding two segments of the CBS situation comedy show, *Maude*. The groups charged that Maude's decision to have an abortion presented only the pro-abortion argument. Here is one of the allegedly unfair segments:

Walter: Maude, I think it would be wrong to have a child at our age.
Maude: Oh, so do I, Walter. Oh Walter, so do I.
Walter: We'd make awful parents.
Maude: Oh, impatient, irascible. For other people it might be fine, but for us. I don't think it would be fair to anybody.
Walter: Are you frightened about the operation, I mean . . .
Maude: Honey, it's all right. Just tell me. Walter, I'm doing the right thing not having the baby.
Walter: For you, Maude, for me, and for the privacy of our own lives, you're doing the right thing.

The anti-abortion groups requested that two anti-abortion shows be presented on successive Tuesday evenings at 8 pm (when *Maude* was usually aired). CBS responded that *Maude* was dramatic entertainment and therefore not covered by the Fairness Doctrine. The FCC ruled for CBS, but in doing so really didn't decide whether the Fairness Doctrine applied to entertainment or not. Instead, it dismissed the complaint because the groups had failed to prove that CBS had only presented one side of the abortion issue in its overall programming.[20]

REVIEW OF THE FAIRNESS DOCTRINE

- The presentation of points of view on any controversial subject of public importance *must* be balanced in the context of the station's or network's overall programming.
- The Fairness Doctrine extends to all programming and not just to editorials.
- A reasonable opportunity for the presentation of any contrasting viewpoints must be provided.
- If the station or network cannot find sponsors willing to pay for the expression of opposing views, it must sponsor such expression itself.
- The format for program balance is left to the broadcaster's discretion.

NOTE: Do not confuse "balanced" programming with equal time. Equal time and equal opportunity apply only to political broadcasts.

---

i. The Personal Attack Rule and the Fairness Doctrine

Another aspect of the Fairness Doctrine involves the Personal Attack Rule. This rule allows a person who has been personally attacked over the air free access to the broadcast facilities to defend herself. Unlike other aspects of the Fairness Doctrine, this rule is very precise. If any attack is made upon the honesty, character, integrity or like personal qualities of an identified person or group during the presentation of views on a controversial issue of public importance, the brodcaster must promptly notify the target of the attack and furnish her with a transcript, tape or summary of the attack along with an offer of time to reply. The rule does not apply to:

- attacks on foreign groups or foreign public figures;
- personal attacks made by legally qualified candidates, their authorized spokespeople, or persons associated with them, or
- attacks arising in the course of bona fide newscasts, news-interviews, or on-the-spot coverage of news events.

The most famous case dealing with the Personal Attack Rule is *Red Lion Broadcasting Co. v. FCC*.[21] In 1964, the Red Lion Broadcasting Co. carried a program series entitled *The Christian Crusade*. One of the programs included an attack by Rev. Billy James Hargis on an investigative reporter who had authored a highly critical biography of Barry Goldwater, entitled *Goldwater—Extremist of the Right*. Cook asked the radio station for an opportunity to reply to Hargis. The station demanded payment or proof of indigence. Cook refused. This dispute, as well as another involving the constitutionality of the notice provision, ultimately found their way to the U.S. Supreme Court.

---

20. *Diocesan Union of Holy Name Societies of Rockville Centre and Long Island Coalition for Life,* 41 FCC 2d 497 (1973).
21. 395 U.S. 367, 89 S.Ct. 1794, 23 L.Ed.2d 271. For a good discussion of this case see *The Good Guys, the Bad Guys and the First Amendment,* by Fred Friendly, Random House, 1975.

Deciding the two cases together, the Supreme Court unanimously endorsed the right to defend oneself as set out in the Personal Attack Rule. In the course of doing so, the Court flatly declared that the central First Amendment interest in free speech resides in the public and not in the broadcaster. Overall, the case emphasized the importance of the public's access to ideas and, over time, has served to strengthen the First Amendment arguments that the media must protect freedom of speech and, by extension, the public's right to be fairly informed.

But the people as a whole retain their interest in free speech by radio and their collective right to have the media function consistently with the ends and purposes of the First Amendment. It is the right of the viewers and listeners, not the right of the broadcasters, which is paramount . . . It is the purpose of the First Amendment to preserve an uninhibited marketplace of ideas in which truth will ultimately prevail, rather than to countenance monopolization of that market, whether it be by the Government itself or by a private licensee . . . It is the right of the public to receive suitable access to social, political, esthetic, moral, and other ideas and experiences which is crucial here.

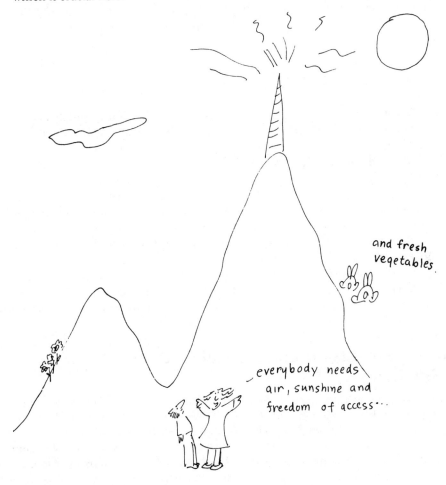

j. Editorials and the Fairness Doctrine

The FCC has stated that it is not contrary to the public interest for stations to overtly editorialize "within reasonable limits and subject to the general requirements of fairness . . . ." What does this mean in real life? If a station broadcasts an editorial endorsing or opposing a political candidate, the opposing candidates are supposed to be notified within twenty-four hours after the editorial, and furnished with the transcript and an offer of time.

Stations funded by the Corporation for Public Broadcasting, however, are prohibited from editorializing by The Public Broadcasting Act of 1967. Litigation over the constitutionality of such prohibition is pending.[22]

When a candidate is endorsed on radio or television, the other candidate must be given:
1. notice as to the date and time of the editorial,
2. a script or tape of the editorial, and
3. an offer of a reasonable and free opportunity to respond.

When a candidate is opposed on radio or television, where a station editorially opposes a legally qualified candidate for public office, it is required to send the notice and offer to the candidate opposed. The notice and offer must be sent within twenty-four hours after the broadcast. If the editorial is to be broadcast within seventy-two hours of election day, the station must transmit the notice and offer "sufficiently far in advance of the broadcast to enable the candidate or candidates to have a reasonable opportunity to prepare a response and to present it in timely fashion."

k. Editorial Advertising

The FCC does not require stations to provide time for editorial advertising, commonly known as Public Service Announcements (PSA). But since stations have an affirmative obligation to broadcast in the public interest, PSAs are a good way to satisfy their obligations, since they're easily scheduled in one-minute segments. They are often aired in unsold air time—late at night or early Sunday mornings.

A different question, however, is posed once the station has accepted advocacy ads. The FCC said that for purposes of the Fairness Doctrine, those advertisements that "consist of direct and substantial commentary on important public issues should be recognized for what they are—editorials paid for by the sponsor" and as such are subject to the Fairness Doctrine.

Editorial advertising can come under many guises. Advertising designed to present a favorable public image of a particular corporation or industry rather than to sell a product may in fact be editorializing. One example is the old ESSO commercials advocating the development of the Alaskan pipeline. More recent examples are public utility ads lauding the benefits of nuclear power.

l. Advertisements for Commercial Products or Services

Until 1967, the Fairness Doctrine was applied only to the airing of major social and political issues. Then John Banzhaf III appeared on the scene. Banzhaf, a young lawyer, asked WCBS-TV in New York for reply time to respond to cigarette commercials. Banzhaf claimed that the "portrayal of youthful and virile looking or sophisticated persons enjoying cigarettes in interesting and exciting situations deliberately seeks to create the impression . . . that smoking is socially acceptable and desirable, manly, and the necessary part of a rich, full life." WCBS-TV refused Banzhaf's request. The FCC, however, ruled that time should have been provided for reply to the cigarette advertisements because, among other reasons, the question of whether or not cigarettes were a threat to health was a controversial issue. The Court of Appeals for the

---

22. *League of Women Voters v. FCC*, 489 F.Supp. 517 (1982); *cert granted* 51 U.S.L.W. (2/28/83).

Washington D.C. Circuit affirmed the FCC decision ordering reply time to counter cigarette advertising.[23]

More recently, the FCC has reversed its policy on "counter-commercials." Currently, unless the advertisement very explicitly addresses an issue, the FCC will not accept a Fairness complaint. But, what is substantial and obvious to you may not appear so to the FCC. For example, gasoline, auto, snowmobile and toothpaste commercials have all been attacked for raising issues about health and environment. Yet, the FCC has rejected all such complaints.

m. Conclusion

A broadcaster has never lost a license for failure to comply with the Fairness Doctrine requirements. Nevertheless, the Communications Act does establish that the broadcaster is a trustee of the community and must see that the public is presented with a wide variety of viewpoints. The rationale is that by virtue of their franchise, the media have a special duty to speak and communicate ideas the community needs to hear.

At the time of this writing, the Fairness Doctrine is under attack. The Chairman of the FCC, the Administration, and several members of Congress are all advocating its abolition. They assert, as do many broadcasters, that it is undesirable for the government to be involved in any way in their free speech. But however attractive the broadcasters' argument is, the courts have established that the public has the greater claim.

And finally, if we may be permitted a little editorial of our own, here is our view. The Fairness Doctrine is not perfect, but it's the best mechanism we have to balance the competing First Amendment claims of broadcast journalists and the public. After all, the First Amendment was conceived to foster "uninhibited, robust, wide-open" debate on public issues. The Fairness Doctrine protects the "paramount right of the public . . . to be informed . . . and to have presented to it . . . different . . . viewpoints concerning those vital and often controversial issues. . . ." As such, we believe it should be retained.

---

23. *Banzhaf v. FCC*, 405 F.2d 1082 (D.C. Cir., 1968).

APPENDIX A

An Overview
of the
Legal System

A. Introduction

Journalists are forever grappling with our judicial system. Whether reporting on day-to-day courtroom dramas or being on the receiving end of a lawsuit, the journalist needs a good understanding of the law itself and how it is implemented by the courts. This is no easy task. To adequately explain media law, we necessarily and frequently refer to legislative enactments, judicial opinions, and court procedures. Although some of you will have a better grasp of all this than others, we think a brief review of how our legal system works (or doesn't work, depending on your point of view) is in order.

It's neither our goal to duplicate information you learned in government classes nor to go into great detail on the "how to's" of legal research. Other good sources are available to help you with these topics. Instead, this chapter primarily emphasizes how the layers of our state and federal legal systems work and mesh with one another. We hope this will help you better understand the workings of the courts and what we mean by the phrase "media law."

B. An Overview

The U.S. Constitution plays center stage in the law of mass communications. This is because the First Amendment guarantees free press and free speech. Virtually every law or procedure that has to do with journalists, no matter how arcane or tangential, must sooner or later pass consitutional muster. Even areas such as defamation and privacy, which by and large are covered by state laws, are subjects which must also be scrutinized through consitutional glasses.

In accord with pertinent decisions by the U.S. Supreme Court, our lower federal and state courts determine what is and is not constitutional. To understand media law, however, it will not do to simply read Supreme Court pronouncements. Simplicity and law, it seems, are mutually exclusive concepts. Instead of the U.S. Supreme Court deciding a legal question first (e.g., the constitutionality of a certain type of gag order), with the lower courts then falling in line, the issues are initially presented to a wide range of lower state and federal courts, oftentimes with just as wide a range of results. In addition to Supreme Court decisions on media law issues, therefore, there exist influential rulings by a great number of other courts on a wide variety of issues.

The plethora of courts, judges and legal procedures so dear to the lawyer can be a nightmare to the journalist. To put it mildly, it isn't easy to understand how or why a particular case moves through our courts, or exactly how one legal decision will influence the next. But, given a little perseverance on your part, the information provided here will help you understand the law as it affects the media.

C.   A Working Understanding of "Law"

Most countries in Western Europe as well as former European colonies operate under a system known as "civil law." In these countries, the law consists of "codes" or "statutes" (collections of written laws) which are usually enacted by a legislature (e.g., Parliament, Congress, Chamber of Deputies). Courts in these "civil law" countries resolve disputes by applying the appropriate code or statute to the specific factual situation. The primary source of the law in these countries, therefore, are collections of written rules which prescribe acceptable, and prohibit unacceptable, behavior.

In England and her former colonies, however, the primary legal system is known as "common law." Common law has evolved over time and consists of court decisions in specific cases which delineate legal principles. These principles serve as guides for the resolution of future disputes. In the common law system, therefore, courts become the primary creators of the law by applying these principles to particular situations.

While the United States inherited the common law, many areas of the law have also been heavily influenced by statutes and administrative regulations. In the U.S. today, then, the "law" is a combination of statutes, regulations and court decisions. Finding the answer to a particular legal question often involves analyzing all three of these primary sources.

When the United States Constitution was ratified in 1789, all U.S. law, common and statutory, became subject to constitutional constraints. No matter what statute is passed by the legislature, or what court decision is handed down as guidance for future cases, the requirements of the U.S. Constitution must be met for the law or case to be upheld. Still, to fundamentally understand what the law is, you have to consult legislative enactments, court decisions, and relevant administrative regulations, and then determine whether they pass constitutional muster.

As you will see throughout this book, our analysis of media law follows this system. On most important questions, our concentration is divided between existing federal and state court opinions and statutory law on the one hand, and the dictates of the U.S. Constitution on the other.

First, we will review how the court system in the United States is structured. Then, we will examine the different types of cases which normally appear in the courts, and how the courts decide them. Finally, we will briefly explain how cases are "litigated" and provide some guidance on where to locate legal sources in the law library.

D. The American Court System—An Overview

1. Federal and State Courts

In the United States, we have two parallel court systems—state and federal. In general, cases based on state law are brought in the state courts whereas cases involving federal statutes or regulations are brought in the federal courts. Libel and slander are good examples of subjects based on state law, as are divorce, drunk driving, wills, personal injuries, or landlord–tenant cases. Examples of issues based on federal law are bankruptcy, federal income tax, admiralty (the law of the sea), and anti-trust.

Frequently, areas of the law involve both federal and state law and are therefore brought in both state and federal courts, depending on a variety of considerations. These include civil rights, environmental protection, consumer protection, veteran's benefits, health law, welfare law, occupational safety, subsidized housing, transportation, and discrimination. As a general rule, where federal funds pass to the states under a grant-in-aid, reimbursement or cost-sharing program, both federal and state law is involved.

Although federal courts generally handle cases involving federal law and state courts handle state law, there are many exceptions. State courts often handle certain types of federal law claims. Conversely, federal courts handle state law actions when they are related to federal claims or when the plaintiff and defendant are residents of different states. When there is a choice between the state and federal courts, lawyers choose the court system in which they are most likely to get a favorable decision (this is called "forum shopping").

What about cases involving the U.S. Constitution? Where are these heard? They may be initially raised in any court. If the dispute persists, however, the U.S. Supreme Court has the ultimate authority to decide the question. Likewise, the state supreme courts are the final arbiters of the meanings of their own state constitutions and statutes. When there is a conflict between state and federal law, however, the U.S. Supreme Court decides.

For example, suppose Alabama has a law requiring labor unions to obtain a license before publishing a newsletter. Assume a union challenges this law in court on the ground it conflicts with the First Amendment to the U.S. Constitution. If either side is dissatisfied with the result in the trial court (where the case is first filed and decided), the issue might ultimately reach the Alabama Supreme Court through the appeal process.

The Alabama Supreme Court is the final authority on the meaning and construction of the statute in question (state law). Thus, that court might interpret the statute to not require the license and such decision would be final. If, however, the court confirms that unions must obtain a license before publishing their newsletters, it will then proceed to decide whether the statute violates the First Amendment.

The decision on the constitutional issue, however, will not necessarily be final. Since the U.S. Constitution is involved, either side can ask the U.S. Supreme Court to consider the case and make a final determination. However, even if that court agrees to hear and decide the constitutional issue, it cannot review the Alabama Supreme Court's decision in respect to the meaning of the Alabama statute. Put briefly, the state supreme courts have final say over state law questions, while the U.S. Supreme Court calls the ultimate shots on federal and constitutional questions. The following diagram puts these relationships in visual perspective.

RELATIONSHIP BETWEEN FEDERAL AND STATE COURTS CONCERNING MEDIA LAW

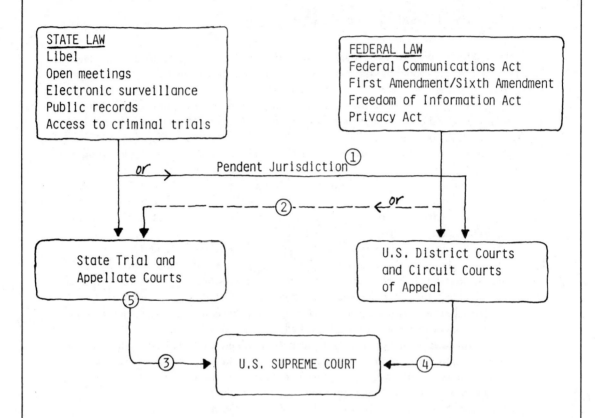

STATE LAW
Libel
Open meetings
Electronic surveillance
Public records
Access to criminal trials

FEDERAL LAW
Federal Communications Act
First Amendment/Sixth Amendment
Freedom of Information Act
Privacy Act

or → Pendent Jurisdiction ①

② *or* ←

State Trial and Appellate Courts ⑤

U.S. District Courts and Circuit Courts of Appeal

③ → U.S. SUPREME COURT ← ④

1. Federal courts can determine state law issues incidental or "pendent" to federal law issues. They must act as if they were a court of the state in question when they do so.

2. State courts can consider federal law issues raised by the parties in a state court action if the state issues are more significant. In addition, all state law issues are subject to the Federal Constitution.

3. State court decisions on federal law or U.S. Constitutional issues may be reviewed by the U.S. Supreme Court.

4. U.S. Supreme Court mostly reviews federal court decisions on federal law and U.S. Constitutional issues

5. State court determination of state law issues which do not raise legal questions under the U.S. Constitution are final.

2. Trial and Appellate Courts

In both the state and federal court systems there are three basic types of courts. These are trial courts, intermediate appellate courts and supreme courts.

The trial court is where almost all cases begin — where the complaint and answer are filed, where the parties discover information about each other's cases, where evidence is heard and considered, and where the first judgment about the legal and factual issues in a case is made. The formal name for these courts varies from court system to court system. For example, the main trial court in the federal system is called the "U.S. District Court." Other federal trial courts which handle special types of cases are known as the "U.S. Court of Claims," the "U.S. Tax Court," and the "U.S. Patent Court."

In most states, the trial courts are given different responsibilities and names. For example, the courts which handle injunctions, large money damages cases, and felonies might be called the "superior court" or "county court" whereas courts which handle small money matters and minor crimes might be termed "district," "municipal" or "justice" courts. Some courts are known as "Court of Common Pleas" and "Surrogate's Court" while others may be referred to by their specialty (e.g., "Family Court" and "Probate Court"). All these courts, however, qualify as "trial courts" in that disputes are presented to them for resolution in the first instance.

As mentioned, if a party to a case in the trial court is unhappy about the outcome (whether by jury verdict or court ruling), he or she can appeal the case to a higher, or "appellate" court for review. However, since in most cases there is even a higher court, usually called the "Supreme Court," these middle-level courts are often referred to as "intermediate appellate courts." These courts also have a wide variety of names, but usually contain a variant of the word "appeal," such as "appellate," as in "appellate department" or "appeals," as in "Court of Civil Appeals" or "Circuit Court of Appeals." In the federal system, the intermediate appellate court is divided into geographical circuits, as in "Ninth Circuit Court of Appeal," "Second Circuit Court of Appeal," and so on. Each circuit covers the U.S. district courts for a particular part of the country.

The top and most influential court in each state, and in the federal court system, is called the "Supreme Court" (except in New York, where the top court is termed the "Court of Appeals" and the trial court termed the "Supreme Court"). The following section examines how these different levels of court actually operate, both within their own judicial system and in connection with others.

E. The Judicial Process

1. Trials

After a case ("dispute") is first filed in a trial court, a ritual legal dance ensues. Cases may be decided by 1) a judge at the very outset if a complaint or petition does not make sufficient allegations to support a lawsuit (through devices called motions to dismiss and demurrers), 2) a judge without a trial (called "summary judgment") if there does not appear to be a substantial

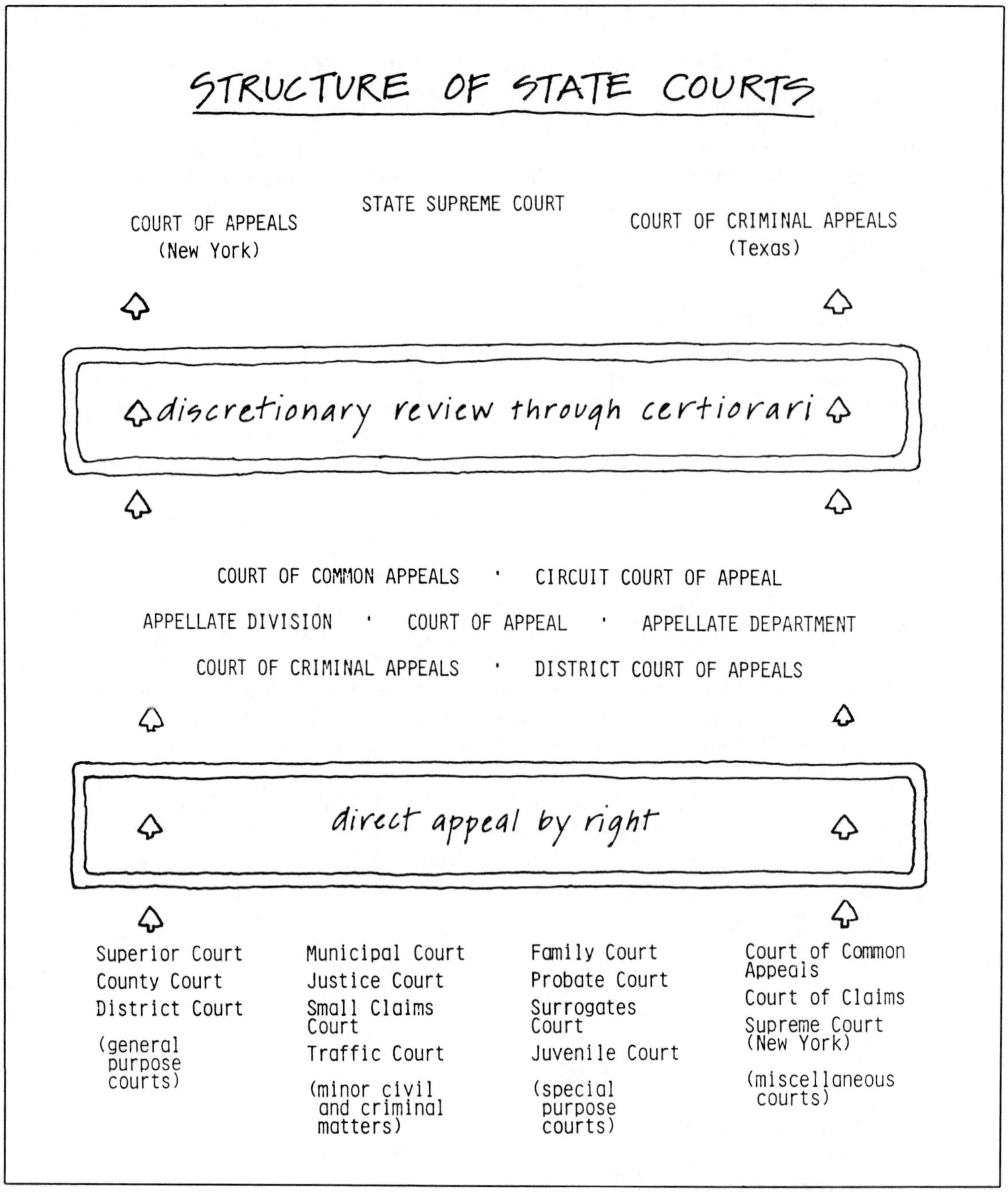

STRUCTURE OF STATE COURTS

STATE SUPREME COURT

COURT OF APPEALS
(New York)

COURT OF CRIMINAL APPEALS
(Texas)

⇧ ⇧

⇧ *discretionary review through certiorari* ⇧

⇧ ⇧

COURT OF COMMON APPEALS · CIRCUIT COURT OF APPEAL

APPELLATE DIVISION · COURT OF APPEAL · APPELLATE DEPARTMENT

COURT OF CRIMINAL APPEALS · DISTRICT COURT OF APPEALS

⇧ ⇧

⇧ *direct appeal by right* ⇧

⇧ ⇧

Superior Court
County Court
District Court

(general
purpose
courts)

Municipal Court
Justice Court
Small Claims
Court
Traffic Court

(minor civil
and criminal
matters)

Family Court
Probate Court
Surrogates
Court
Juvenile Court

(special
purpose
courts)

Court of Common
Appeals
Court of Claims
Supreme Court
(New York)

(miscellaneous
courts)

argument about the facts, 3) a judge or jury after a full trial, or 4) the parties themselves in a
settlement conference (the way most cases end).

If either side thinks the judge or jury made a mistake, or simply wants to delay the effect of
the judgment, an appeal can be filed and an intermediate appellate court can be asked to review
the trial court proceedings.[1] Most of what we know as media law results from decisions made by
either these courts or by the state or U.S. supreme courts.

---

1. During the appeal process (which may take a long time), one of the parties may ask for a "stay," i.e., an order
preserving the *status quo*.

KEY EVENTS IN A TRIAL

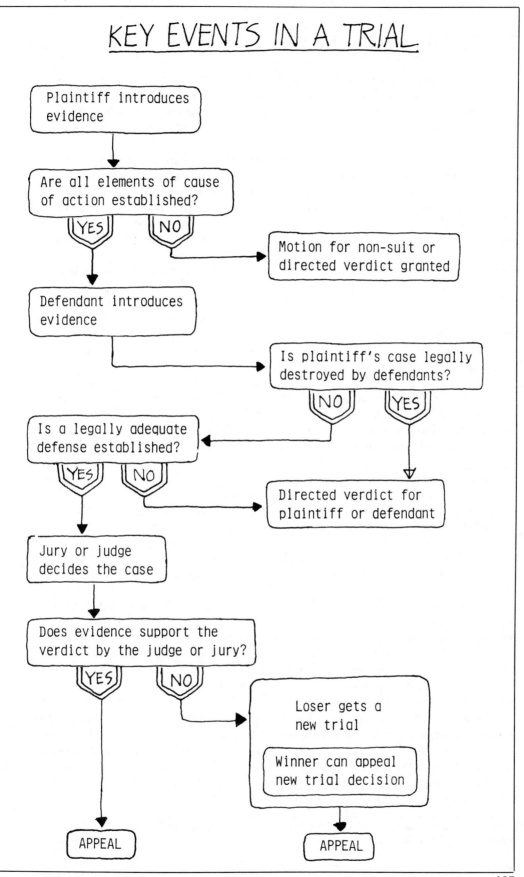

Plaintiff introduces evidence

Are all elements of cause of action established?

YES NO

Motion for non-suit or directed verdict granted

Defendant introduces evidence

Is plaintiff's case legally destroyed by defendants?

NO YES

Is a legally adequate defense established?

YES NO

Directed verdict for plaintiff or defendant

Jury or judge decides the case

Does evidence support the verdict by the judge or jury?

YES NO

Loser gets a new trial

Winner can appeal new trial decision

APPEAL

APPEAL

2. The Appellate Process

In most of the cases discussed in this book, and most First Amendment cases generally, the crucial questions that determine the outcome do not depend on disputes about the facts. Rather, the parties disagree over what legal rule applies to an accepted set of facts. In other words, the question is often not what happened, but rather, assuming it happened, so what? This is almost certainly the situation when a case "goes up" on appeal.

When an appeal is taken, "briefs" (written arguments of each party's view of this case) are submitted. The appellate court also has a copy of the entire written "record" of the trial court, which typically includes the papers filed by the parties, evidence submitted, and transcripts of any hearings (including the trial) which are relevant to the issues on appeal.

The appellate court considers the briefs, the trial court record, and usually hears oral arguments from the attorneys. After the oral argument, the judges (between three and nine, depending on the court) discuss the case among themselves and arrive at a decision. A judge representing the majority is assigned to write the opinion. It is this opinion which will be examined for guidance on legal principles in future cases.

Throughout this book, we use terms such as "unanimous court," "divided court," "close split," "in a 5-4 (or 2-1) vote." These phrases refer to the degree of agreement or disagreement among the justices (appellate court judges) deciding the case and give some indication of whether a particular legal principle contained in an opinion is firmly entrenched or is subject to change in the event a minor change occurs in the court's personnel.

Most opinions are written by only one justice, whose name appears at the beginning of the opinion. This single opinion has the support of the majority of the participating justices and is called the "opinion of the Court." As such, it becomes binding on the court, establishing a precedent for subsequent decisions. If there is no additional court opinion or notation as to a conflicting view, the other judges are said to "concur" with this opinion and it is considered "unanimous."

The other justices who are deciding the case may, however, disagree with the first opinion or agree with its conclusion but not necessarily all the reasoning necessary to arrive at it. If they disagree with any part of the decision, they "dissent" as to that part. If they agree with the decision but use a different reasoning process than that used by the opinion's author, they write a separate "concurring" opinion. A majority of the court members deciding the case must concur with the decision in order for any decision to issue; however, a majority need not agree with the opinion's reasoning. In the event the latter occurs, the result is known as a "plurality" opinion.

When the majority of the court concur in the reasoning of the "court opinion," the case is entitled to respect as a guideline for future cases. This is called "precedent."[2] If the opinion is only backed by a plurality, however, then it is not as persuasive in subsequent cases. A five-to-four decision of the U.S. Supreme Court (or a two-to-one decision of a federal circuit court or state court) is technically just as binding on future cases as is a nine-to-zero decision. However, as we mentioned, when the court is "sharply split" in a particular case, the decision has far less precedential value in practice.

REMEMBER: The actual decision in a case is the most important aspect since it serves as precedent for other courts. Other discussion in the case may be helpful in understanding it, but is not binding for future cases. The court's decision and its reasoning is called the "holding." The rest of the decision is called "dicta." It is the holding which provides guidance for the future. Concurring and dissenting opinions, on the other hand, are not authority or precedent, but can be helpful in understanding what was at stake in the case.

---

2. Precedents are important because they establish predictability of how courts will interpret future cases and act, therefore, as guides for behavior.

3.   A Closer Look at Federal Courts

Almost all the cases in this book have been decided by an appellate court—the majority, but by no means all, in the federal system. Let's take a closer look at how this specific system works.

The federal judicial system rests on a network of trial courts called U.S. district courts, located primarily in the larger cities of each state. Each state has at least one. Appeals of the decisions from these district courts are taken to the appropriate circuit courts of appeal. These courts of appeal are divided into eleven circuits covering groups of states and territories; the twelfth is limited to the District of Columbia, and the thirteenth applies to the Court of Claims and Court of Customs and Patent Appeals. For example, appeals from the federal district courts in Massachusetts, Rhode Island, New Hampshire, Maine and Puerto Rico are taken to the United States Court of Appeals for the First Circuit, while appeals from Texas, Louisiana and Mississippi are taken to the Fifth Circuit Court of Appeals, and so on.

A decision by one of these thirteen courts of appeal may be reviewed by the Supreme Court of the United States whether or not it involves a federal constitutional question. In this context, the Supreme Court is simply the last step in the federal court system. However, the Supreme Court more often than not declines to hear disputes arising out of the federal lower court system. Instead, it commonly limits its attention to those cases involving important questions about the U.S. Constitution and federal statutes.

As we mentioned in our Alabama example, constitutional questions can also reach the Supreme Court through the state courts. Many of the famous criminal law cases (e.g., *Miranda v. Arizona* and *Gideon v. Wainwright*, arrived at the U.S. Supreme Court through this route.

In most instances, the Supreme Court has the discretion to choose what cases it will hear. Of the many thousands of cases that are brought each year, the Court only accepts about 200 for hearing and decisions. To seek review by the Supreme Court, the litigant who lost the case in the lower court files a "Petition for a Writ of Certiorari," which describes the nature of the dispute, the decision in the lower court, and the reasons why the Court should review this case.

The Supreme Court usually chooses those cases which present interesting or important questions of law. The Court is also likely to accept a case if it appears the federal courts of appeal for one or more circuits disagree about an important issue, since in such a case the constitution or federal law might be applied differently in different parts of the country.

In deciding whether or not to grant a petition for certiorari (or "cert"), all the Supreme Court justices meet in conference and vote. If four out of the nine justices believe the case should be heard, the petition for certiorari will be granted. If there are not enough votes to hear the case, the court will usually not state its reasons and will issue an order that says simply, "The petition for certiorari is denied," [3] abbreviated to "cert. den." in case citations.

Although the denial of cert. favors the party who won in the lower court, the legal effect is different than when the Supreme Court hears and decides the case. A denial of cert. only means that the Court did not think the case worthy of review. It is thus incorrect to report "Joe Schmoe's appeal was thrown out," or "The Supreme Court upheld the decision in the court below."

As with other appellate courts, if the Supreme Court takes the case, it studies the briefs submitted by the parties and hears oral arguments. The Court then decides the case and issues an opinion.

On occasion, cases are filed in the Supreme Court in the first instance under constitutional provisions giving that court original jurisdiction over certain types of cases. Most commonly, this happens when one state sues another.

---

3. A revealing discussion of this process is contained in Woodward and Armstrong, *The Brethren*, Simon & Schuster, 1979.

4. How Opinions Are Structured

Normally, every written opinion ("case") contains four basic elements:

    a.   The opinion usually presents a detailed listing of the facts which are accepted by the court as true. These facts are taken from the lower court's determination of the facts, except in the very unusual situation when the lower court's factual conclusions were not logically justified ("clearly erroneous," in legal lingo).

    b.   The opinion formulates the "legal issue" or "issues" which are presented to the appellate court by the parties for decision. For example, whether or not a judge's order barring reporters from covering a criminal trial is unconstitutional.

    c.   The opinion describes the actual decision of the court (its "holding"), and its legal basis. A part of the holding involves what it is the appellate court actually orders. It is this part of the opinion which actually forms the precedent.

    d.   The opinion contains an extended discussion of why the holding was made (the "reasoning" or "rationale"). This reasoning is important in future cases, but it is not considered as precedent or therefore binding on future courts unless it is absolutely necessary to explain and justify the actual holding or decision in the case.

There are six possible actions the court can take:

1.   It can agree with the lower court's disposition of the case. This is called "affirming."

2.   It can disagree with or "reverse" the lower court opinion.

3.   It can agree with some parts of the lower court decision and disagree with other parts. This is called "affirming in part" and "reversing in part."

4.   If the appellate court agrees substantially with the lower court, but disagrees with some particular point, it may "modify" or "amend" the decision to reflect the minor disagreement.

5.   If a lower appellate court has written and published an opinion in a case which is reversed by the higher appellate court, the opinion will be ordered "vacated" as part of reversal. In many circumstances, this happens automatically.

6.   When the court reverses a decision, it will "remand" the case (send it back) to the lower court to take further action consistent with the appellate court's opinion.

F.   Types of Media Law Cases

1.   Criminal

The kinds of cases discussed in this book generally fall into three categories. The first category is "criminal." In a criminal case, one of the parties is always the government. The government is trying to punish a party for a certain type of behavior, either by fine or imprisonment or both.

These cases are usually brought in and appealed through the state court system. Most end at the state intermediate appellate or supreme court level. A few which raise important claims under the U.S. Constitution go on to the U.S. Supreme Court. This occurs when the defense claims that the law which was violated is invalid because it conflicts with the First Amendment or other part of the U.S. Constitution. If it accepts the case, the Supreme Court must decide whether the particular criminal statute is constitutional, unless on closer examination the decision can be disposed of in some other way.[4]

For example, assume a Boston ordinance prohibits distribution of printed matter in a

---

4. All courts, including the Supreme Court, generally like to take the path of least resistance and decide cases on the narrow factual issues before them or on the basis of legal technicalities.

subway car because it causes litter. If members of an anti-nuclear weapons group are arrested for violating the ordinance, their defense will surely be that the law violates the First Amendment.

If the "Republicans for Peace Through Strength" were also handing out flyers and the authorities arrested only the nuclear disarmament members, another defense will be that the ordinance *as applied* is in violation of the Fourteenth Amendment equal protection clause. The U.S. Supreme Court might potentially be the final arbiter of these two constitutional defenses.

2.   Declaratory Relief

The second and third types of media law cases found in this book do not usually involve imprisonment or fines. The second type seeks judicial relief in the form of "declaratory judgments" and "injunctions," both of which are commonly awarded in legal disputes of constitutional dimension. Take our Boston example. Instead of passing out the leaflets, getting arrested, and challenging their convictions in appeals, the disarmament group members might first seek a judgment from the court declaring the ordinance unconstitutional and unenforceable.

Alternatively, they can seek an "injunction" (an order requiring or forbidding some activity) prohibiting city officials from enforcing the ordinance — again on the ground that to do so would violate their constitutional rights. Either way, instead of distributing the pamphlets and risking criminal prosecution, the disarmament group would initiate suit first so that they could pass out leaflets in the subway without fear of arrest.

3.   Tort Law

The third type of case we discuss involves a subcategory of civil litigation known as "tort law." The tort suit is filed when the "plaintiff" (the party who sues) thinks the "defendant" (the party who is sued) engaged in careless or intentional acts directly resulting in harm to the plaintiff. The objective of the tort suit is to obtain judicial relief in the form of money judgments (called "damages") to compensate for the injury.

Unlike the prior two categories of actions discussed earlier, tort suits usually involve private parties rather than governments, although governments may be sued for tort damages. Since the U.S. and state constitutions operate as restraints on governments rather than private parties, these sources of law are not usually relevant in the normal tort case. However, if the state libel or privacy law itself is challenged as violative of the First Amendment, a court may well end up passing on constitutional issues, even though governmental action as such is not an issue in the action.

Tort law has developed primarily in the courts, but today numerous statutes exist which affect this area of civil law. The torts of most concern to the media are those involving defamation (libel and slander) and invasion of privacy. For example, when William Westmoreland sued CBS, claiming he was defamed in a "Sixty Minutes" segment about his conduct in the Vietnam War, he filed a "tort suit."

G.   How Does a Court Case Work?

All cases in the state and federal courts are handled by procedures and rules which are substantially similar. This is true even though the details of different state rules vary and similar procedures are often referred to by different names. For example, an eviction action in California is called "unlawful detainer" and in Massachusetts, "summary process."

Obviously procedural and lingo differences can cause real problems for the unwary journalist. To make sense of local legal procedures and terms, check to see if your state publishers' association, bar association or judges' association publishes an explanatory guide. In California, the California Judges Association issues *The Courts and The News Media*.[5] Nolo Press publishes an extremely helpful guide called the *Nolo Press Law Dictionary* by Stephen Elias, which translates legal gobbledygook into English.

Let's look at how a typical case develops and proceeds through the courts.

1.   The Plaintiff's Complaint

A case begins when a "complaint is filed by the plaintiff. This document tells what happened and what the plaintiff wants done about it (i.e., money damages, injunctive relief, etc.).

2.   The Defendant's Response

After the defendant is actually provided (served) with a copy of the complaint, he or she is given a certain time period to "respond" in writing (usually 30 days). If no such response is made, a "default" judgment may be obtained by the plaintiff, which means that the plaintiff wins without a fight. This rarely happens if the defendant wants to oppose the lawsuit, as the prevailing philosophy is that everyone should have his or her day in court.

As with all things legal, labels are put on this written response. A common type of initial response is called a "motion to dismiss" or "demurrer" (the defendant "demurs" to the complaint). Assuming the case is not dismissed, the defendant will be required to serve and file an "answer" to the complaint (i.e., make a written statement setting out which allegations in the complaint she wishes to contest). These two responses are briefly explored below.

a.   Motions to Dismiss and Demurrers

Before actually answering a complaint, the defendant commonly asks (moves) the court to dismiss the suit on the ground the complaint is legally inadequate. Commonly, the basis for this request boils down to this — even if the facts in the plaintiff's complaint are true, so what? Or to put the same thing a little more formally, the defendant is alleging the complaint has stated no legal theory on which a lawsuit may be based, or that the plaintiff has not complied with some important legal technicality which allows him to file a lawsuit in the first place. In essence, the defendant is requesting the court to stop wasting everyone's time, and to end the matter pronto.

The Court will not decide any facts as part of a hearing on a motion to dismiss or demurrer. Just for the purpose of deciding whether the defendant is correct, the court will assume the factual statements in the complaint to be true and then rule whether the law supports the claim for relief.

A dramatic example of this point recently appeared in a major metropolitan newspaper. A woman had brought a tort action against a lawyer for getting her pregnant after misrepresenting he had obtained a vasectomy. For the sole purpose of ruling on the lawyer's demurrer, the court accepted the woman's allegations as true and ruled she could proceed with her case. One

---

5. Available from the California Judges Association, Fox Plaza, Suite 416, 1390 Market St., San Francisco, CA 94102 (415) 552-7660.

newspaper prominently reported the court's decision as concluding the lawyer had in fact behaved as alleged. Several days later an equally prominent retraction appeared.

If the judge grants the motion or demurrer "without prejudice," the plaintiff can prepare another complaint (called "amending") and try again. If the motion or demurrer is granted "with prejudice," the case is ended unless the plaintiff successfully appeals the decision. If the judge denies the motion or demurrer, the defendant must either file an answer or appeal the denial.

b.   The Answer

This is the defendant's main court paper ("pleading," in legalese). Here she admits and/or denies[6] each charge or allegation that the plaintiff has made in his complaint. Under the procedural rules of most states, the defendant can also raise affirmative defenses (i.e., factual statements of the reasons or excuses for why the defendant did what was done) and counter-claims (i.e., claims that the plaintiff did something and in fact owes the defendant money), or can state that she does not have enough information about the allegations and therefore denies the complaint on that basis.

3.   Summary Judgment

Once the complaint and answer are on file, either side is entitled to seek a judgment without trial if the party can show there is no real dispute about any facts important to deciding the case (called "triable issues of material fact") and that the law clearly supports the person making the motion. Each side presents its evidence to the court in the form of written statements under oath ("declarations" or "affidavits"). The court then examines the documents and decides whether any significant issues can be resolved solely on a legal basis because of the absence of any real dispute as to the facts.

For example, to successfully sue a newspaper for libel a public official must allege a published defamatory statement was false and made with actual malice (knowing or reckless disregard of the truth). Newspaper defendants in libel cases commonly move for a summary judgment on the ground that even if the plaintiff's allegations are true, they do not legally amount to "actual malice" and the plaintiff cannot therefore prevail. (See Chapter 4 for an in-depth discussion of these concepts.)

4.   Discovery

After the Complaint has been filed and served on the defendant, each party may engage in the pre-trial information gathering activity known as "discovery." Under discovery statutes, parties to a case may use a variety of devices to collect information necessary to prepare and bolster their cases and to prevent the other side from springing Perry Mason types of surprises at trial.

It is the discovery stage of a case which often adds considerably to the delays and expense associated with major litigation. Why? Because each side usually attempts to avoid giving up information to the other. Thus, disputes are constantly arising between parties to a lawsuit over what information must be turned over to the other side and what can be kept from disclosure. These disputes are resolved by the trial court in "discovery motion" proceedings. If a party does not like the judge's resolution of the dispute, it is usually possible to immediately take the matter

---

6. It is common practice for the defendant to deny everything he can.

to a higher court. During disputes over discovery, the underlying lawsuit usually goes into a "holding pattern."

Discovery commonly consists of the following devices:

a.   Depositions

Witnesses are required to go to the office of an attorney and answer questions in the presence of a stenographer who records the testimony. Usually the attorney for the side of the case on which the witness will testify is also present. Media reporters are not allowed to attend depositions.

b.   Interrogatories

Written questions are sent by one party to another to be answered under oath within a specified period of time. Interrogatories are also used to request documents. A typical question in a media libel case interrogatory would ask the defendant to list the name, address, and phone number of every person who was consulted in respect to the story in issue.

c.   Requests for Admissions of Fact

A series of factual statements are set out in a document and mailed to the other party. These must either be admitted or denied. If the other side does neither, the statements are considered as admissions. This device helps narrow down the actual facts and issues still in dispute during the different stages of preparation for trial.

d.   Production of Documents

Requests are made by one party to another for the production of specified documents. In a complex case, one side may ask the other for file cabinets full of material. Arguments often occur about how much "fishing" one side can do in the other's records.

5.   Motions

Any time after the complaint and answer have been filed but before trial, one side may ask the court to order the other side to do something or to refrain from doing something. Sometimes these requests (called "motions") are used to preserve the status quo until the case can come to trial on the actual issues presented for resolution (the "merits"). For example, if the circumstances are truly urgent, a party may obtain a "temporary restraining order" (TRO) which immediately stops the defendant from acting (e.g., publishing an article) pending further hearing on the matter.

The TRO is usually only good for 10 or 15 days. To extend this "injunctive relief" until the actual trial, the plaintiff must make a motion for a "preliminary injunction." To be successful in this motion, the plaintiff must establish that he or she will probably prevail in the end and that serious and immediate harm is likely to occur in the absence of such interim relief.

As we will see, because our legal system has a traditional and long-standing dislike of "prior

YOUR COURT OR MINE?

RITUAL LEGAL DANCE

restraint," TROs and preliminary injunctions are rarely, if ever, granted to stop publication of a disputed story. (See Chapter 3 for more details.)

Motions can also be brought to enforce discovery (i.e., to require a party to answer questions or produce documents when appropriate), to protect a party against abusive discovery (i.e., requiring attendance at a week-long deposition), or to request any other type of court order which seems necessary at the time.

6. Trial

The trial is the formal setting for resolving all important factual differences between the parties. If the trial is by jury, the jury is instructed by the judge on what law applies in the case and is then asked, in light of these legal principles, to decide who should win. In court trials, the judge performs the role of the jury in finding facts to be true or false. Whether a case is tried before judge or jury depends on the state, the type of case, and the wishes of the parties. Fortunately for the taxpayer and most civil litigants, few civil cases actually go to trial. Most are settled somewhere along the way or dismissed for lack of prosecution.

HOW A CASE MOVES THROUGH THE COURTS

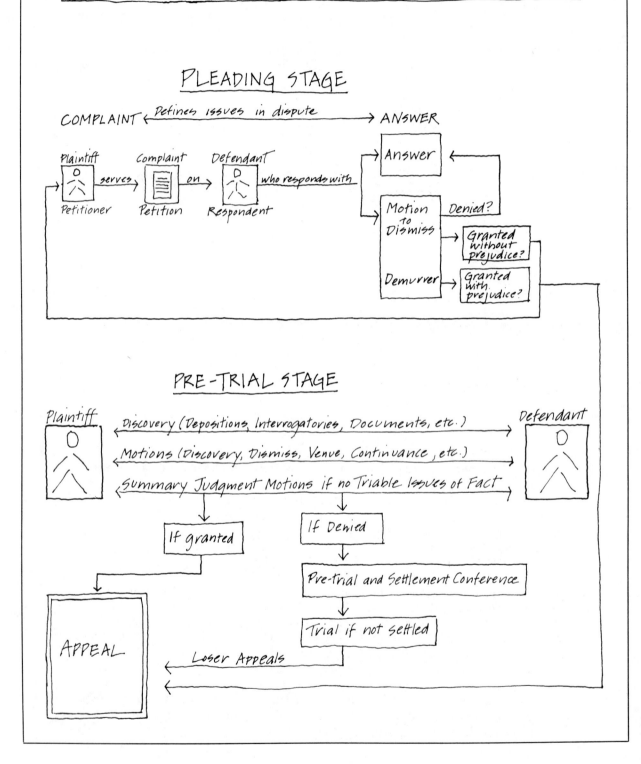

PLEADING STAGE

COMPLAINT ← Defines issues in dispute → ANSWER

Plaintiff — serves → Complaint — on → Defendant — who responds with →

Petitioner / Petition / Respondent

Answer

Motion to Dismiss — Denied?

Demurrer → Granted without prejudice?

Granted with prejudice?

PRE-TRIAL STAGE

Plaintiff — Discovery (Depositions, Interrogatories, Documents, etc.) → Defendant

Motions (Discovery, Dismiss, Venue, Continuance, etc.)

Summary Judgment Motions if no Triable Issues of Fact

If granted

If Denied

Pre-trial and Settlement Conference

Trial if not settled

APPEAL ← Loser Appeals

APPENDIX B

Legal Research

A.   Introduction

Cases, statutes and constitutions are the primary stuff of the law. If you cannot retrieve and read them, you are forever doomed to secondary sources — that is, you will be stuck with someone else's interpretation. Stephen Elias' book, *Legal Research: How to Find and Understand the Law* (Nolo Press, 1982) is the best guide to both primary and secondary sources and we believe it to be a necessary part of every journalist's library. Armed with this book, you should be able to handle almost any legal research problem which comes your way.

B.   Case Citations — An Overview

Throughout this book, we give you the names of cases and their "citations." The citation is the code which will tell you where to find the full text of the opinions in the law library. It consists of the case name, the volume number of the book where the case can be found and read, the name or title of the book, and the page number on which the first page of the case is located. Some additional detail on these points should prove helpful.

   A case name is made up of one plaintiff's name and one defendant's name (e.g., *Sullivan v. N.Y. Times*). The plaintiff's name goes first. However, if the case is appealed (say the *N.Y. Times* loses at trial), the party appealing is called the "appellant" and the person (Sullivan) who responds to the appeal is the "respondent." Appellant's names tend to go first. Thus, a case which starts out in the trial court as *Sullivan v. N.Y. Times*, may be changed to *N.Y. Times v. Sullivan* (this in fact happened).

HINT: If you are looking up a case under one name and cannot find it, switch the names and try again.

Books containing written court opinions are called "reports" or "reporters." For example, the full citation for *New York Times v. Sullivan* is 376 U.S. 254; 84 S.Ct. 710, 11 L.Ed. 2d 686 (1964). The "U.S." is an abbreviation for "United States Reports." The same case can also be found in the book abbreviated as "S.Ct.," which is short for "Supreme Court Reporter." A third publication contains this same case in "Supreme Court Reports, Lawyers' Edition," abbreviated to "L.Ed."

When the same case appears in more than one series of reports, the citations are called "parallel." Supreme Court opinions appear in all three of the reports just covered.

Let's look at the citation again:

New York Times v. Sullivan, 376 U.S. 254; 84 S.Ct. 710, 11 L.Ed. 2d 686 (1964)

If you wanted to read that case, you would simply locate any one of the three reports in your local law library, find the appropriate volume, and turn to the indicated page.

Current decisions of the United States Court of Appeals are found in the *Federal Reporter Second Series* (F.2d). For example, the citation to *Public Media Center v. Federal Communications Commission*, an important case having to do with the fairness doctrine, is 587 F.2d 1322. This means the case can be found on page 1322 of volume 587 of the second edition of the report known as the *Federal Reporter*.

Decisions of the United States District Courts are found in the *Federal Supplement* (F.Supp.) and may be located in the same manner described above.

NOTE: Some law libraries have all three of the reports containing the Supreme Court opinions while others have only one or two of the three. All law libraries have the *Federal Supplement* and *Federal Reporter*.

C.   State Case Citations

State cases are also found in reports. Each state has its own report and, in addition, a national system of reports contains state court cases by region. The following chart shows the usual form of the regional citation, the full name of the report, and the state courts which it covers.

CITE	FULL NAME OF REPORT	NAME OF COURT
100 A.2d 100	Atlantic Reporter, Second Series	Appellate courts in D.C., Conn., Del., Maine, Md., N.H., N.J., Pa., R.I., Vt.
100 N.E.2d 100	Northeastern Reporter, Second Series	Appellate Courts in N.Y. (Court of Appeals only), Ill., Ind., Mass., Ohio.
100 N.W.2d 100	Northwestern Reporter, Second Series	Appellate Courts in Iowa, Mich., Minn., Nebr., N.Dak., S.Dak., Wis.

100 P.2d 100	Pacific Reporter, Second Series	Appellate Courts in Alaska, Arizona, Calif. (Supreme Court only), Colo., Hawaii, Idaho, Kansas, Mont., Nev., N.M., Okla., Oreg., Utah, Wash., Wyo.
100 S.E.2d	Southeastern Reporter, Second Series	Appellate Courts in Ga., N.C., S.C., Va., W.Va.
100 So.2d 100	Southern Reporter, Second Series	Appellate Courts in Ala., Fla., La., Miss.
100 S.W.2d 100	Southwestern Reporter, Second Series	Appellate Courts in Ark., Ky., Mo., Tenn., Tex.
100 N.Y.S. 100	New York Supplement	All New York Appellate Courts
100 Cal. Rptr. 100	California Reporter	All California Appellate Courts.

COMMENT: In addition to these series of books, some states have "official reports" which contain cases for only the state designated in the report title. Thus, *California Reports* only contains California cases. Official reports are generally no more accurate than the regional reporters listed above but some libraries only carry the official reports. If there are no regional reporters, ask your librarian what the official state report is for your state.

D. Advance Sheets

Very recent cases are not found in bound volumes. To locate these decisions, you must go to paperbound books called "advance sheets." These are commonly kept on the library shelf following the last bound volumes of the particular series and are usually several months behind. Thus, if you wanted a fairly recent case decided by the U.S. Court of Appeals, you would look in the advance sheets following the last bound volume of the *Federal Reporter*.

But, what if you need an opinion in a case that was decided more recently? Normally, you would have to go to the clerk of the court where the decision was made and obtain a copy of the case (called a "slip opinion"). Very important cases appear in a service known as *U.S. Law Week*, which comes out weekly and can be found in most law libraries and major law firms. Also, the legal newspapers in some metropolitan areas reprint verbatim recent United States Supreme Court opinions as well as other opinions of general interest.

E. Statutes

1. An Overview

Statutes are enactments by legislative bodies. Because of our federal system, we are always operating under both federal and state statutes. Sometimes there is no overlap, but increasingly there is. As we mentioned earlier, this is partly due to the widespread use of federal funds by state governments. Since federal money is always followed by federal supervisory statutes, there are numerous areas such as welfare, education, environment, consumer protection, and health, to name a few, which require a study of both federal and state legislation for a full legal understanding of what's going on.

For the purpose of media law, you will mainly look at state statutes when the subjects are defamation (Chapter 4), privacy invasion (Chapter 5), journalist access to the courtroom (Chapter 6), journalist privilege and shield laws (Chapter 7), and open meeting laws (Chapter 10). On the other hand, access to federal records and meetings, and the ins and outs of government regulation of the electronic media, both involve federal statutes and regulations. Also of course, the media have a real interest in being able to locate any statute of interest for the sheer purpose of reporting on items of public interest.

2. Reading and Understanding Statutes

It is relatively easy to find statutes, as we show you below. Understanding them is another question altogether. Statutes are usually the product of legislative compromise and are often amended by various special interests who are adversely affected. Thus, by the time you look at a statute, there are so many conditional clauses and oblique references to other statutes and abstruse legal principles that the normal person would despair of ever understanding it. Still, there are several basic rules which will help you in this task.

- The first rule is to read the statute at least three times.
- The second rule is to make sure you understand the results of the commas, "ands," and "ors." Whether a clause is disjunctive or conjunctive can make a world of difference. For example, if a statute allows a judge to close a criminal hearing if she finds "there is substantial danger of prejudice to the defendant" *and* "no overriding social reason for allowing journalists in," the judge must make *both* findings. If the statute contained an "or" instead of the "and," however, the judge could close the trial if she made *either* of the two findings.
- The third rule is to assign some meaning to every word in the statute. Although statutes often appear to be filled with redundancies, the courts struggle to assign a separate meaning to each word when asked to interpret them. You should do likewise when trying to understand them. A corollary to this rule is to interpret the statute so that it is internally consistent and makes sense. No matter how nonsensical a statute may seem on its face, the courts are duty-bound to assume that the legislature is sane and actually intends to be meaningful and consistent.
- The fourth rule is to interpret statutes so they are consistent with other statutes. The legislature is not supposed to contradict itself, and the courts will indulge in this fantasy when searching for the true meaning of any given statute. Thus, if your interpretation appears to make the statute in question inconsistent with others, strain for another interpretation where consistency will prevail.

For example, assume one statute located in your state *Code of Civil Procedure* appears to give you the absolute privilege of refusing to disclose your notes at a criminal trial. Another statute located in your state's criminal code provides that reporters in a criminal case may be compelled to come forward and give testimony about their sources if the information is relevant to the proceeding. The statutes would appear to be in conflict, right?

Your job will be to read them both so they are in harmony, if this is humanly possible and does not mangle the language too much. If you cannot reconcile them, then you may have a true conflict. On occasion, the courts are willing to recognize that the legislature screws up from time to time. Consider this expression of frustration from an appellate court justice:

> As to the appeal itself, I concur in the opinion of the majority because its construction of Code of Civil Procedure section 660 seems plausible and hence probably correct, although — given the cosmic incomprehensibility of the section — one can never be absolutely sure.
>
> It occurs to me that section 660 illustrates poignantly the maxim so useful in statutory construction — that if the Legislature had known what it meant, it would have said so.
>
> It seems to me shameful, however, that large sums of money should change hands depending upon one's view of what this dismal, opaque statute means.
> — an excerpt from the decision *Bunton v. Arizona Pacific Tanklines*
> (141 Cal. App. 3d 210)

- The fifth rule is that civil statutes passed to benefit a class of people should be interpreted liberally in favor of the benefit intended, whereas criminal statutes should be interpreted strictly against the state and in favor of the criminal defendant. If, for example, the legislature passes a statute intended to protect journalists from a judge's contempt power, the courts will interpret the statute to place a restriction on the judge rather than on the journalist, if at all possible. Conversely, if a statute makes the disclosure of certain classified information a crime, the courts will scrutinize the statute very carefully to see whether any reasonable interpretation would render the behavior in question innocent rather than violative of the law.

For a more detailed, but quite readable, guide to understanding statutes, read *Legislative Analysis: How To Use Statutes and Regulations*, by William Statsky, (1976) West Publishing Co.

3.   Statutory Citations

As we mentioned, statutes are one of the three primary sources of the law. There are many occasions when the working journalist will desire to see this law firsthand. Whether the journalist desires to study a new shield law or better understand a new controversial enactment, there is no substitute for going to the horse's mouth.

Fortunately, enacted statutes are ultimately compiled and published according to their subject matter and can therefore be readily accessed. However, if the journalist wishes to read a bill prior to or immediately after its final passage, it is important to understand how statutes are labeled prior to such subject matter compilation.

As statutes are introduced to legislatures, they are assigned a number corresponding to the date of their introduction and the branch of the legislature involved. Thus "HR 242" is "House of Representatives Bill Number 242," "SB 1" is the first bill introduced in the Senate for that legislative session, and "AB 576" is the five hundred and seventy-sixth bill introduced in the Assembly (a common name for one of two state legislative branches, the other usually being "Senate.").

These numbers stay with the bill up until the time it becomes law or is not passed, whichever the case may be. However, once a statute passes the legislature and is signed by the chief executive (president or governor), a new label is attached. In the case of Congress, this label consists of the title "Public Law" (P.L.), the number of the Congress and the order in which the bill became law that session. Thus, if HR 242 is passed and signed by the President during the 99th Congress, and is the first bill to do so during that session, it would earn the new label of P.L. 99-1. Likewise, the last bill to be passed that year would be something like P.L. 99-2046.

In the case of state statutes, the normal label to be applied is "Chapter" and the number which represents the order of passage. Thus, AB 576 might end up as Chapter 1.

At the end of any given legislative session, then, there are a series of bills which have passed the legislature, been signed by the chief executive, and therefore constitute the law of the jurisdiction.

At this point, the titles and numbers of these statutes do not reflect their subject matter content. As mentioned earlier, however, these statutes are due to be compiled according to their subject matter. They will thus receive yet another label to accomplish this purpose.

Compilations of statutes by subject matter are usually referred to either as "codes" or as "collected statutes." Thus, the laws regarding health and hospitals would typically be found in a "health code." In the case of states with "collected statutes," a health law might be collected in a particular volume known as "Title 12."

One more example. If a state legislature passes hypothetical AB 689, which absolutely prevents libel suits from being based on journalistic accounts of political rallies, this statute would be grouped with the state's other statutes governing libel and placed in the "Title" or code dealing with such general subject matter (e.g., "Torts").

Because of this organization of statutes by subject matter, it is easy to find them by using subject matter indexes attached to the code or "collected statutes" volumes. Once a pertinent statute is located, the chances are good the other statutes in the immediate vicinity of the first one will also relate to your issue. Thus, when doing statutory research, it is a good idea to browse backwards and forwards from the statute you were initially referred to.

With this overview in mind, a closer look at how federal and state statutes are found and understood is warranted.

4. Federal Statutes

Even if you employ the general rules of statutory interpretation discussed earlier, it is often difficult to understand a statute without knowing a little about its history and how it's been interpreted by the courts. To help you do this, the U.S. Code has been published in two sets of annotated collections. Both the *United States Code Annotated* (U.S.C.A.) and the *United States Code Service Lawyers Edition* provide notes about the statute's history, cross-references to other statutes, library references which might be helpful in understanding the statute, research guides, and, most important, one paragraph summaries of case decisions which have interpreted the specific clauses contained in the statute.

As mentioned, these codes are generally organized according to the subject matter covered by the statutes. Thus, the statutes dealing with the income tax are found in one set of volumes, collectively known as Title 10, while the federal statutes relating to education are found in Title 20. In all, the U.S. Code is made up of fifty titles. Some titles only take up one volume, while others take up many. Thus, even though there are fifty titles, there are many more volumes.

The last volume of each title contains an index to that title. In addition, the entire code has a general index. If you know what title you're looking for, then it helps to start out with the index to that title. If you don't know what title your statute is in, then it is usually appropriate to turn to the volumes that contain an index to the entire code. For example, if you were looking for restrictions on the use of federal education funds by state schools, you could turn directly to the index for Title 20 and look under "federal funds," "restrictions," or whatever. If you didn't happen to know that Title 20 contains the education statutes, however, you would use the general index at the end of the entire code.

Many times, you may be dealing with a statute which you know by a name (e.g., The Civil Rights Act) but don't have a reference or citation to where it's located. Fortunately, the U.S.C.A. has a special index called a "Popular Names Index" which will route you to the correct title and section for a wide variety of federal statutes. This can be especially useful for journalists who often hear the popular names of federal laws bandied about like magic words.

Like cases, statutes are referred to, or cited, in a particular way. Whenever you see something like 42 U.S.C.A., §1983, the first number is the title, the letters refer to the publication, and the final number refers to the section number in the particular title. The symbol directly preceding the last number is legalese for "section."

Because Congress is forever messing with federal statutes, it is important to get the most up-to-date version. The U.S. Codes are published in hardcover volumes and also contain annual paper update supplements which are usually stuck into the back of each volume (aptly referred to as "pocket parts"). When researching a statute, always make sure to check the pocket part for possible amendments or even repeals. Occasionally, so many changes have been made since the hardcover volume was published that they won't fit in the pocket part. In that case, paper supplements are published separately and are included on the shelves along with the hardcover volumes.

Finally, if you want to read a statute which has just become law and is not yet incorporated in the *U.S. Code*, a publication called the *U.S. Code Congressional and Administrative News* will help you do this. Each month, this service publishes a pamphlet which contains the text of all new federal statutes. Here, the statutes are organized by the congressional session label (e.g., P.L. 99-2430), but each pamphlet also has a subject matter index. Thus, if you know the number of the statute, you can turn right to it. Otherwise, a few minutes of searching in the subject matter index should pay off.

5. State Statutes

As with federal statutes, it is possible to keep abreast of state statutes through annotated "codes" or "collected statutes." Some examples of how these statutory compilations are referred to are "Vermont Statutes Annotated" (V.S.A.), "California Penal Code" (P.C.) and "Massachusetts General Laws Annotated" (M.G.L.A.). A citation to statutes in these resources would look like this: 12 V.S.A. Sec. 3405 [Title 12 Vermont Statutes Annotated Section 3405]; P.C. Sec. 1538.5 [Penal Code Section 1538.5]; and M.G.L.A. 239 Sec. 8A [Massachusetts General Laws Annotated Chapter 239, Section 8A].

Also, as with the federal statutes, each state has an update service allowing you to read statutes shortly after they become law. These are generally referred to as "legislative update services." In fact, the law libraries of most states maintain copies of bills which have been introduced into the legislatures but which have not yet become law. This is extremely helpful to those who are keeping track of a particular bill's progress.

F.   Law Libraries and Librarians

Just about every county in the country maintains some type of law library open to the public.

These are usually found in the county courthouse and are maintained with public funds (often taken from filing fees). Many law schools also open their doors to the public, at least during certain hours. Although many non-lawyers feel a bit out of place in these seemingly sacred preserves of lawyers and judges, there is really no reason to. Most law librarians are eager to help people learn how to use their library and can be relied on to help you find what you're looking for. While they won't, usually, do your research for you, they will tell you where to find the codes and reports and other materials which we discuss here and in the next section.

G.   Legal Research for Journalists

There are a few publications of special interest to the journalist which are not usually mentioned in general legal research books. An invaluable resource is the Bureau of National Affairs *Media Law Reporter (Med.L.Rptr.)*. On an almost weekly basis, it reports all cases that have a bearing on journalism and communication law. Typical issues include recent court decisions and regulations, occasional bibliographies, Supreme Court schedules or dockets, and special reports. An important feature is its presentation of complete decisions covering the broadest spectrum of mass communication law, saving you the trouble of looking them up. Unfortunately, subscriptions are expensive. The *Media Law Reporter* is not generally available in county law libraries, but can be found in most large law school libraries.

Another good resource which is easily affordable is *The News, Media, and the Law*, put out by the Reporters Committee for Freedom of the Press. Issues come out every two months and highlight the most important cases in different categories of media law.

An alternative which is more general and available in law libraries is *United States Law Week (USLW)*. It comes in two parts. One contains Supreme Court opinions shortly after they are issued. The other concentrates on new federal statutes, administrative agency rulings, and significant lower court decisions. The latter part has subsections for "Media Law" and "Freedom of Information Act."

To see what others have written about a legal topic in which you are interested, you can check the *Index to Legal Periodicals*. Look under the category, "Freedom of the Press," which refers to articles on the topics in this book.

Finally, virtually every periodical devoted to activities of the media, such as *Editor & Publisher, Broadcasting, The Quill, Access, More, Publishers Weekly* (emphasis on books) and the *Columbia Journalism Review*, faithfully reports legal developments of interest to the media.

Index

self-help law books

BUSINESS & FINANCE

How To Form Your Own California Corporation

By attorney Anthony Mancuso. Provides you with all the forms, Bylaws, Articles, minutes of meeting, stock certificates and instructions necessary to form your small profit corporation in California. It includes a thorough discussion of the practical and legal aspects of incorporation, including the tax consequences.
California Edition. $21.95

The Non-Profit Corporation Handbook

By attorney Anthony Mancuso. Completely updated to reflect all the new law changes effective January 1980. Includes all the forms, Bylaws, Articles, minutes of meeting, and instructions you need to form a nonprofit corporation in California. Step-by-step instructions on how to choose a name, draft Articles and Bylaws, attain favorable tax status. Thorough information on federal tax exemptions which groups outside of California will find particularly useful.
California Edition $21.95

The California Professional Corporation Handbook

By attorneys Mancuso and Honigsberg. In California there are a number of professions which must fulfill special requirements when forming a corporation. Among them are lawyers, dentists, doctors and other health professionals, accountants, certain social workers. This book contains detailed information on the special requirements of every profession and all the forms and instructions necessary to form a professional corporation. $21.95

Billpayers' Rights

By attorneys Honigsberg & Warner. Complete information on bankruptcy, student loans, wage attachments, dealing with bill collectors and collection agencies, credit cards, car repossessions, homesteads, child support and much more.
California Edition $10.95

The Partnership Book

By attorneys Clifford & Warner. When two or more people join to start a small business, one of the most basic needs is to establish a solid, legal partnership agreement. This book supplies a number of sample agreements with the information you will need to use them as is or to modify them to fit your needs. Buy-out clauses, unequal sharing of assets, and limited partnerships are all discussed in detail.
California Edition $15.95
National Edition $15.95

Plan Your Estate: Wills, Probate Avoidance, Trusts & Taxes

By attorney Clifford. Comprehensive information on making a will, alternatives to probate, planning to limit inheritance and estate taxes, living trusts, and providing for family and friends. An explanation of the new statutory will and usable, tear-out forms are included.
California Edition $15.95

Chapter 13: The Federal Plan To Repay Your Debts

By attorney Janice Kosel. This book allows an individual to develop and carry out a feasible plan to pay his or her debts in whole over a three-year period. Chapter 13 is an alternative to straight bankruptcy and yet it still means the end of creditor harassment, wage attachments and other collection efforts. Comes complete with all the forms and worksheets you need.
National Edition $12.95

Bankruptcy: Do-It-Yourself

By attorney Janice Kosel. Tells you exactly what bankruptcy is all about and how it affects your credit rating, your property and debts, with complete details on property you can keep under the state and federal exempt property rules. Shows you step-by-step how to do it yourself and comes with all forms and instructions necessary.
National Edition $12.95

225

Legal Care for Software

By Dan Remer. Here we show the software programmer how to protect his/her work through the use of trade secret, trade-work, copyright, patent and, most especially, contractual laws and agreements. This book is full of forms and instructions that give programmers the hands-on information to do it themselves.
National Edition $24.95

We Own It!

By C.P.A.s Kamoroff and Beatty and attorney Honigsberg. This book provides the legal, tax and management information you need to start and successfully operate all types of coops and collectives. $ 9.00

FAMILY & FRIENDS

How To Do Your Own Divorce

By attorney Charles Sherman. Now in its tenth edition, this is the original "do your own law" book. It contains tear-out copies of all the court forms required for an uncontested dissolution, as well as instructions for certain special forms--military waiver, pauper's oath, lost summons, and publications of summons.
California Edition $ 9.95
Texas Edition $ 9.95

California Marriage & Divorce Law

By attorneys Ihara and Warner. This book contains invaluable information for married couples and those considering marriage on community and separate property, names, debts, children, buying a house, etc. Includes sample marriage contracts, a simple will, probate avoidance information and an explanation of gift and inheritance taxes. Discusses "secret marriage" and "common law" marriage. California Edition $14.95

How To Adopt Your Stepchild

By Frank Zagone. Shows you how to prepare all the legal forms; includes information on how to get the consent of the natural parent and how to conduct an "abandonment" proceeding. Discusses appearing in court, making changes in birth certificates.
California Edition $14.95

Small-Time Operator

By Bernard Kamoroff, C.P.A. Shows you how to start and operate your small business, keep your books, pay your taxes and stay out of trouble. Comes complete with a year's supply of ledgers and worksheets designed especially for small businesses, and contains invaluable information on permits, licenses, financing, loans, insurance, bank accounts, etc. Published by Bell Springs Press. National Edition $ 8.95

SOURCEBOOK FOR OLDER AMERICANS

By attorney Joseph Matthews. The most comprehensive resource tool on the income rights & benefits of Americans over 55. Includes detailed information on social security, retirement rights, Medicare, Medicaid, supplemental security income, private pensions, age discrimination, as well as a thorough explanation of the new social security legislation.
National Edition $10.9

A Legal Guide for Lesbian/Gay Couples

By attorneys Hayden Curry and Denis Clifford. Here is a book that deals specifically with legal matters of lesbian and gay couples. Discusses areas such as raising children (custody, support, living with a lover), buying property together, wills, etc. and comes complete with sample contracts and agreements. National Edition $14.95

After The Divorce: How To Modify Alimony, Child Support and Child Custody

By attorney Joseph Matthews. Detailed information on how to increase alimony or child support, decrease what you pay, change custody and visitation, oppose modifications by your ex. Comes with all the forms and instructions you need. Sections on joint custody, mediation, and inflation.
California Edition $14.95

The Living Together Kit

By attorneys Ihara and Warner. A legal guide for unmarried couples with information about buying or sharing property, the Marvin decision, paternity statements, medical emergencies and tax consequences. Contains a sample will and Living Together Contract.
National Edition $14.9

The People's Law Review

Edited by Ralph Warner. This is the first compendium of people's law resources ever published. It celebrates the coming of age of the self-help law movement and contains a 50-state catalog of self-help law materials; articles on mediation and the new "non-adversary" mediation centers; information on self-help law programs and centers (programs for tenants, artists, battered women, the disabled, etc.); articles and interviews by the leaders of the self-help law movement, and articles dealing with many common legal problems which show people "how to do it themselves" without lawyers. National Edition $ 8.95

Author Law

By attorney Brad Bunnin and Peter Beren. A comprehensive explanation of the legal rights of authors. Covers contracts with publishers of books and periodicals, with sample contracts provided. Explains the legal responsibilities between co-authors and with agents, and how to do your own copyright. Discusses royalties negotiations, libel, and invasion of privacy. Includes a glossary of publishing terms. $14.95

The Criminal Records Book

By attorney Siegel. Takes you step-by-step through all the procedures available to get your records sealed, destroyed or changed. Detailed discussion on: your criminal record--what it is, how it can harm you, how to correct inaccuracies, marijuana possession records & juvenile court records. Complete with forms and instructions. $12.95

Legal Research: How To Find and Understand The Law

By attorney Steve Elias. A hands-on guide to unraveling the mysteries of the law library. For paralegals, law students, consumer activists, legal secretaries, business and media people. Shows exactly how to find laws relating to specific cases or legal questions, interpret statutes and regulations, find and research cases, understand case citations and Shepardize them.
National Edition $12.95

California Tenants' Handbook

By attorneys Moskovitz, Warner & Sherman. Discusses everything tenants need to know in order to protect themselves: getting deposits returned, breaking a lease, getting repairs made, using Small Claims Court, dealing with an unscrupulous landlord, forming a tenants' organization, etc. Completely updated to cover new rent control information and law changes for 1981. Sample Fair-to-Tenants lease and rental agreements.
California Edition $ 9.95

Everybody's Guide to Small Claims Court

By attorney Ralph Warner. Guides you step-by-step through the Small Claims procedure, providing practical information on how to evaluate your case, file and serve papers, prepare and present your case, and, most important, how to collect when you win. Separate chapters focus on common situations (landlord-tenant, automobile sales and repair, etc.). $ 9.95

Fight Your Ticket

By attorney David Brown. A comprehensive manual on how to fight your traffic ticket. Radar, drunk driving, preparing for court, arguing your case to a judge, cross-examining witnesses are all covered. California Edition $12.95

Homestead Your House

By attorney Warner. Under the California Homestead Act, you can file a Declaration of Homestead and thus protect your home from being sold to satisfy most debts. This book explains this simple and inexpensive procedure and includes all the forms and instructions. Contains information on exemptions for mobile homes and houseboats.
California Edition $ 8.95

How To Change Your Name

By David Loeb. Changing one's name is a very simple procedure. Using this book, people can file the necessary papers themselves, saving $200-300 in attorney's fees. Comes complete with all the forms and instructions necessary for the court petition method or the simpler usage method.
California Edition $14.95

Marijuana: Your Legal Rights

By attorney Richard Moller. Here is the legal information all marijuana users and growers need to guarantee their constitutional rights and protect their privacy and property. Discusses what the laws are, how they differ from state to state, and how legal loopholes can be used against smokers and growers.
National Edition $9.95

The Unemployment Benefits Handbook

By attorney Peter Jan Honigsberg. Comprehensive information on how to find out if you are eligible for benefits, how the amount of those benefits will be determined. It shows how to file and handle an appeal if benefits are denied and gives important advice on how to deal with the bureaucracy and the people at the unemployment office.
National Edition $ 5.95

How To Become A United States Citizen

By Sally Abel. Detailed explanation of the naturalization process. Includes step-by-step instructions from filing for naturalization to the final oath of allegiance. Includes study guide on U.S. history & government. Text is written in both English & Spanish. $9.95

Media Law: A Legal Handbook for the Working Journalist

By attorney Kathy Galvin. This is a practical legal guide for the working journalist (TV, radio and print) and those who desire a better understanding of how the law and journalism intersect. It informs you about: censorship, libel and invasion of privacy; how to gain access to public records including using the Freedom of Information Act; entry to public meetings and court rooms, and what to do about gag orders.
                                          $14.95

Murder On The Air

By Ralph Warner & Toni Ihara. An unconventional murder mystery set in Berkeley, California. When a noted environmentalist and anti-nuclear activist is killed at a local radio station, the Berkeley violent crime squad swings into action. James Rivers, an unplugged lawyer, and Sara Tamura, Berkeley's first murder squad detective, lead the chase. The action is fast, furious and fun. $5.95

Landlording

By Leigh Robinson. Written for the conscientious landlord or landlady, this comprehensive guide discusses maintenance and repairs, getting good tenants, how to avoid evictions, recordkeeping, and taxes. Published by Express Press.
National Edition $15.00

Write, Edit & Print

By Donald McCunn. Word processing with personal computers. A complete how-to manual including: evaluation of equipment, 4 fully annotated programs, operating instructions, sample application.
525 pages. $24.95

Computer Programming for The Complete Idiot

By Donald McCunn. An excellent introduction to computers. Hardware and software are explained in everyday language and the last chapter gives information on creating original programs.
                                          $6.95

Your Family Records: How to Prese Personal, Financial and Legal His

By Carol Pladsen & attorney Denis Clifford. Helps you organize and record all sorts of items that will affect you and your family when death or disability occur, e.g., where to find your will and the deed to your house. This practical yet charming book includes information about probate avoidance, joint ownership of property, genealogical research, and space is provided for financial and legal records. $12.95

29 Reasons Not To Go To Law School

A humorous and irreverent look at the dubious pleasures of going to law school. By attorneys Ihara and Warner with contributions by fellow lawyers and illustrations by Mari Stein. $ 6.95

Order Form

QUANTITY	TITLE	UNIT PRICE	TOTAL

Prices subject to change

☐ Please send me a
catalogue of your books

Tax: (California only) 6½% for Bart,
Los Angeles, San Mateo & Santa
Clara counties; 6% for all others

Name_____

Address_____

_____

☐ I am not on Nolo's mailing list and would like to be.
(If you receive the NOLO NEWS you are on the list and
need not check the box.)

SUBTOTAL _____

Tax _____

Postage & Handling $1.00

TOTAL _____

Send to:

NOLO PRESS
950 Parker St.
Berkeley, CA 94710
        or

NOLO DISTRIBUTING
Box 544
Occidental, CA 95465